Champions

The Story of the

First Two Oakland A's

Dynasties—and the

Building of the Third

Champions

The Story of the

First Two Oakland A's

Dynasties—and the

Building of the Third

Glenn Dickey

TRIUMPH
BOOKS
CHICAGO

Library of Congress Cataloging-in-Publication Data

Dickey, Glenn.
  Champions : the story of the first two Oakland A's dynasties and the building of the third / Glenn Dickey.
      p. cm.
  Includes index.
  ISBN 1-57243-421-X
  1. Oakland Athletics (Baseball team) I. Title.

GV875.O24 D53 2001
796.357'64'0979466—dc21

2001037806

This book is available in quantity at special discounts for your group or organization. For further information, contact:

Triumph Books
601 South LaSalle Street
Suite 500
Chicago, Illinois 60605
(312) 939-3330
Fax (312) 663-3557

Printed in the United States of America

ISBN 1-57243-421-X

Interior design by Patricia Frey
First insert photos by Jonathan Perry
Second and third insert photos by Michael Zagaris

*To my wife, Nancy, and son, Scott,
my joy and inspiration*

Contents

Foreword

Playing for those great Oakland A's teams of the seventies was something I'll always remember. I don't think people realize just how good those teams were, though we were the first team to "three-peat" until the Yankees did it with their 2000 championship. I'm not a jewelry guy, but I've always worn the ring I got for the 1972 championship. That meant a little more because the Cincinnati Reds were big favorites to beat us. They had great players, but we had better pitching, and we had some pretty good players, too.

The start of my career was special, too. I came up in September 1970 and pitched against the Minnesota Twins, who needed only one win to clinch the division, and I was lucky enough to throw a no-hitter. You have to be lucky to throw a no-hitter, unless you strike out 27 hitters. So, with that behind me, I had a leg up on getting a spot on the pitching staff the next year.

Because I went to basic training the next winter to fulfill my military commitment, I was in the best shape of my life when I went to spring training in 1971. That was just a magical year: to be the opening game pitcher and then go on to pitch in the All-Star Game. I was on all the magazine covers: *Life*, *Look*, *Sports Illustrated*. That was pretty big stuff for a country boy from Mansfield, Louisiana.

There were some rocky times after that because we always had to deal with Charlie Finley, but we had some big accomplishments despite Charlie. I'll always think of my time with the A's as something very special.

—Vida Blue
January 2002

Foreword

The Oakland A's have always been a fascinating team with great and colorful players. I've seen them from different perspectives as an athlete and a broadcaster, and this book reminds me of many of my memories of the team.

My first view of the A's was from the opposing dugout during the 1972 World Series, when I was playing second base for the Cincinnati Reds, and it was a shocker. I still believe the better team lost in that Series, but the team that won played better baseball. We were the better team on paper, but the games were played on grass.

That A's team had some of the best pitchers in pressure situations that I've ever seen, both their starters and their bullpen. They never seemed to make a mistake when it would hurt them. They put the ball right where they wanted to.

But, having said that, I thought the big difference in that Series was Gene Tenace. Here was a guy we didn't pay much attention to, but he beat us in the first two games with home runs.

Before that, everybody expected us to win the Series easily. To be truthful, I don't think the A's were too confident when the Series started, either. But after they won those two games, they thought, "Hey, we've got a chance to win this thing," and that attitude carried them through, not just in that Series but in the other two they won.

It wasn't a fluke, even though it was a shock to us that first year.

Those A's teams played very good baseball, with good pitching, good fielding, and timely hitting. But they still wouldn't have beaten us without Gene Tenace.

The next time I saw the A's up close I was playing for them, in 1984. It wasn't supposed to happen that way, because I had planned to retire after the 1983 season. In the last game of the World Series that year, I'd hit a triple and asked for the ball. Everybody wondered what that was all about because I hadn't made any public announcement about my plans, but I thought that would be my last hit, so I wanted the memento.

But Roy Eisenhardt, the A's president, was a very good friend and still is. We've played tennis together for years because I had kept my home in Oakland, where I grew up, even while I was playing for teams in other cities. When we played in the off-season, he kept asking me to play with the A's and I kept saying no. He asked me at least three times. Finally, he said, "Why don't you talk it over with your family?" I'd made the decision to retire without asking any of my family, so I talked to my wife and she thought it would be a great idea, because my family and friends could see me play.

So, I decided to play that last year with the A's, and I enjoyed it very much. That was before the great players like Jose Canseco, Mark McGwire, Dave Stewart, and Dennis Eckersley started arriving, but you could see that they were building a great foundation. Roy is such a smart man that I knew he'd find a way to build a winner.

Now they've put together another good team in a much different way. I've always said that the difference between a big-market team and a small-market team is that big-market teams have much more flexibility. They can just throw stuff against the wall and hope something sticks. If they make a mistake, they can pay for it and just bring in another player.

Small-market teams can't afford to make mistakes. They have to hit on everybody. I think these A's, with Billy Beane, have done a great job with that. I was really impressed with their attitude last year when they went into New York and played the Yankees in the divisional series. They really should have won both of those games. That game

Tim Hudson lost was a joke. Balls were taking crazy bounces and little squibblers hit off the end of the bat were falling in. The A's should have won that game and they'd have closed out the series in New York.

The one problem with operating with a small budget is that you can't keep many veterans around. I wasn't surprised that the A's struggled at the start of this season because they didn't have players like Randy Velarde and Matt Stairs, who had been there the year before. If you're a veteran and you have a bad streak, you realize it's a long season and you can make it back. Young players who get in a slump think they have to get it all back in a hurry. I know from experience. One year when I was just starting out, I had an early slump and I kept thinking, "I'll get five hits the next day and get it back." You can't do that. You have to look at it as a long season.

But I'm impressed with the young talent the A's keep bringing in, and I think they have a bright future. As a longtime Oakland resident, I know how important they are to the community and what a colorful history they've had. It's all here in this book.

—Joe Morgan
Baseball Hall of Fame inductee and ESPN broadcaster
May 2001

Acknowledgments

Because I have written about the A's every year since they first arrived in Oakland, I've relied on my own observations in writing this book; however, I've tried to frame it in the words and observations of the participants as much as possible. In most cases I interviewed the participants in the year 2001, but I've also relied on interviews done at the time the games were played.

Those I've interviewed, past and present, in alphabetical order: Sandy Alderson, Sal Bando, Billy Beane, Vida Blue, Jose Canseco, Alvin Dark, Andy Dolich, Dave Duncan, Dennis Eckersley, Roy Eisenhardt, Rollie Fingers, Charlie Finley, Ray Fosse, Jason Giambi, Ben Grieve, Wally Haas, Dave Henderson, Rickey Henderson, Ken Holtzman, Art Howe, Catfish Hunter, Reggie Jackson, Bill King, Tony La Russa, Billy Martin, Mark McGwire, Joe Morgan, Bill North, Rick Peterson, Joe Rudi, Steve Schott, Dave Stewart, and Dick Williams.

Introduction

Billy Beane was doing what he does best: working the phones. Shortly after the New Year broke with 2001, the A's general manager was talking to his counterparts with Tampa Bay and Kansas City about a three-way trade. While speculation mounted in the newspapers and on talk radio and TV that the Royals center fielder, Johnny Damon, was heading for either the New York Mets or the Los Angeles Dodgers, Beane was trying to get him to Oakland, which nobody thought was a possibility. "This is what I love most about the job," Beane said later, "surprising everybody."

Beane knew Kansas City wanted a stopper in the bullpen, but he wasn't going to trade his own, Jason Isringhausen. He also knew that Tampa Bay had the kind of pitcher the Royals wanted, Roberto Hernandez, and he had a player the Devil Rays wanted, outfielder Ben Grieve.

Less than three years before, when his sweet left-handed swing had earned him American League Rookie of the Year honors, Grieve had been considered the cornerstone of the A's rebuilding. Only 22, it seemed that he would get even better, and Beane had said many times that he thought Grieve would be a 40-homer, 100-RBI hitter when he reached his physical prime, between 27 and 32 years old.

Grieve's hitting had improved in his subsequent two seasons, though he had also fallen into a disturbing pattern of grounding into double plays in critical situations, but his fielding had deteriorated. In a candid talk after the 2000 season, Beane said he was bothered by the path of Grieve's career:

> I still believe he'll be a 40-homer guy, and you don't give up on a guy lightly. But he's a young player with old player's skills. I don't want to DH him, because that limits us too much, but there's no question he hurts us defensively. What really bothers me is that he's gotten worse defensively. In one way that's our fault, because he'd always played right field until we moved him to left, but I think he could work harder at it.

Despite Grieve's shortcomings and a steady rain of criticism from fans and media, Beane wasn't going to dump Grieve. But he made it plain that if he got the right offer, he was willing to trade the left fielder. He was, in fact, talking to Cincinnati about young right-handed pitcher Scott Williamson.

The Cincinnati trade didn't work, so Beane looked in another direction and started discussing the three-way trade with Tampa Bay and Kansas City. "Everything was going through me," he said. "Tampa Bay would call me and then I'd call Kansas City. Then I'd call back to Tampa Bay. Finally, we worked it all out."

When it all came together, the A's had grabbed Damon, the prize of the trading season. "We'll have to put in a steal sign," said Beane, whose notoriously slow-footed players had not had a combined total of steals as high as the 46 that Damon had compiled in the previous season. "He gives us a dimension we haven't had here since Rickey Henderson was in his prime. He can play all three outfield positions and he has some pop, too. He actually had a higher slugging average than Ben [Grieve] last year."

Trading for Damon involved a risk: the A's might just be renting him for a year. He was arbitration-eligible (the A's quickly signed him to a one-year contract to avoid that) and he'd be eligible for free agency the next season. "We'll worry about that when it comes," said Beane. "It's always easier to sign a free agent if he's already in your clubhouse. But we're most concerned about this year because Damon makes us a better club. He gives us a great chance to win."

Unspoken was the fact that the A's great farm system has given them a constant supply of good young players. One such prospect, 23-year-old outfielder Mario Encarnacion, was at Triple-A Sacramento, and Beane had expected that he would be ready for the major league level by 2002, if not sooner.

Most important was the imagination shown by Beane in making this trade, as well as in putting together the rest of the team. The A's have had three periods of success in their relatively brief (since 1968) history in Oakland. The three teams have been quite different, but there has been a thread running through all three periods: imagination.

The teams that won three straight American League pennants in 1988–1990, with one World Series sweep in the middle, were known primarily for their great offensive mixture, with the base running of Henderson and the majestic home runs of the "Bash Brothers," Jose Canseco and Mark McGwire. But they'd never have been in position to win anything without the imagination of manager Tony La Russa.

La Russa and his pitching coach, Dave Duncan, reversed the career paths of pitchers Dennis Eckersley and Dave Stewart. Eckersley had been a 20-game winner as a starter early in his career but had slipped badly, partly because of age and partly because of a drinking problem that had cost him his first marriage. Eckersley had put his drinking behind him, but he was considered washed-up after going 6–11 for the Chicago Cubs in 1986. When he was obtained by the A's in exchange for three minor leaguers in April, 1987, it was regarded as one of those "body shuffles" teams sometimes do just to try to prove to their fans that they're doing something.

A year earlier, in May of 1986, the A's had picked up Stewart as a free agent, and that aroused even less interest than the Eckersley deal. Once a promising young pitcher, Stewart had lost his confidence when he was shifted to the bullpen. He had made 54 appearances for Texas and Philadelphia in the 1985 season and the first month of 1986, and hadn't won a game, losing all six of his decisions.

But La Russa and Duncan saw something. Eckersley was switched to the bullpen, the reasoning being that he still had a potent fastball and curve for a limited stretch, though he lacked the stamina to be a starter. In a short time, Eckersley became the most dominant closer in the game and won both the Cy Young and Most Valuable Player awards in 1992.

Stewart went in the opposite direction, from the bullpen to a starter's role. Duncan worked on his mechanics and his confidence, and Stewart blossomed into a four-time 20-game winner who was especially good in the big-game situations, where his menacing stare and overpowering fastball intimidated hitters.

La Russa also virtually invented the idea of a "closer." In the past, relief pitchers had been brought in when trouble developed, but La Russa's idea was that his best reliever would not be brought in before the ninth inning, would usually go only one inning and never more than two, and would be brought in always at the start of the inning and only if his team was ahead. Tony also had his relievers slotted, with a setup man for the eighth inning and the closer for the ninth. He first used Eckersley as a setup man and Jay Howell as a closer, then moved Eckersley to the closer role and used Gene Nelson and Rick Honeycutt as setup men.

Honeycutt was another pitcher rescued from the discard file. La Russa regarded him as almost as important as Eckersley to the A's success because of his versatility. Honeycutt could virtually handcuff a tough left-handed hitter in the late innings, and he was also effective against right-handed hitters. In fact, defying convention, La Russa would sometimes bring him in against a right-handed hitter if there was a runner on first who was a base-stealing threat, because Honeycutt had such a great move to first. "If Rickey Henderson is on first and I bring in a right-handed pitcher," said La Russa in an interview for this book, "Rickey steals second and third. If I bring in Honeycutt, he stays on first—and Rick is likely to get a ground ball for a double play."

What Beane is to the current team and La Russa was to the late eighties teams, Charlie Finley was to the great champions of the seventies. There was never any doubt, because Finley was totally in charge. There was practically nobody else in the front office beyond his cousin, Carl, and secretaries, all of whom faithfully did Finley's bidding. Behind his bluster, Finley was a very smart man. He wouldn't have admitted it publicly, but he learned from others who knew the game better than he did. The manager of his first two World Series champions, Dick Williams, said that Finley frequently visited a baseball library at San Jose State to get ideas about how others had been successful in baseball.

Finley originally had a very good group of scouts who came up with excellent players, from Reggie Jackson to Catfish Hunter, and he also listened to other baseball executives to get ideas. He was constantly on the phone with general managers of other teams, and if he heard the name of a player repeatedly, he sought ways to get that player. Implying that he might want to hire them, he also picked the brains of scouts to get free information. Until free agency forced him into trades he didn't want to make, Finley's trades always helped the A's, playing a significant role in their championships.

These were three very different eras with the common thread of imagination running through them all. Inevitably, the story starts with Charlie Finley.

CHAPTER 1

The One and Only Charlie Finley

Charlie Finley stood at the rostrum in a conference room at the Oakland–Alameda County Coliseum. It was October 1967. Sports in Oakland and the entire San Francisco Bay Area would never be the same again.

Until the late sixties, the professional sports scene in the area had been almost entirely located in San Francisco. The 49ers had begun in 1946 and joined the National Football League in 1950. The Giants had moved to San Francisco (paired with the Dodgers moving to Los Angeles) in 1958; though they had won only one pennant, they had one of the most exciting teams in baseball history, with future Hall of Famers Willie Mays, Willie McCovey, Juan Marichal, Gaylord Perry, and Orlando Cepeda. San Francisco also had a franchise in the National Basketball Association; the Warriors had moved from Philadelphia in 1962.

Oakland had had the Raiders since 1960, but neither the team nor the league—the American Football League—had been taken seriously. Their home games were being played at a junior college field named after an undertaker, for heaven's sake. But in 1966 they moved into the newly built Coliseum, and in 1967 they were on their way to the Super Bowl.

Now Finley was telling listeners that he would move his team, the Kansas City Athletics, to Oakland to play in the Coliseum. Nobody was quite sure whether he could be believed, because Finley had gone to other cities, seeming to promise each time that he'd take the A's there. He had even signed a contract with Louisville, but could not get permission from the American League's owners. But Finley was serious about Oakland, and this time he got the permission he needed from the owners and moved his team.

Nobody knew quite what to expect from the team either. The A's had been bottom feeders in Kansas City, never finishing higher than sixth in a 10-team league in 13 seasons. Finley had gone through managers like Kleenex, seven in the seven years since buying the team in December of 1960, but his final season in Kansas City was more dismal than most, a 62–99 record and a last-place finish.

That record disguised the fact that Finley's scouts, among the best in the business, had signed a number of good young players, including two future Hall of Famers, Reggie Jackson and Catfish Hunter. But few baseball fans in Oakland knew of these players, because Finley was such an overpowering figure. When people thought of the A's, they thought of Charlie Finley, not his players. That was exactly the way Finley wanted it.

Charlie Finley was a man of many despicable qualities. His wife testified in divorce proceedings that he beat her regularly, and she had the sheriff's office bar Finley from visiting after they had separated for fear he would continue his beatings. Living most of his life in an era where sexual harassment was not yet an issue, he made obscene remarks to waitresses in restaurants and would often pinch or pat them on the rear. He browbeat employees and players, using the power baseball owners had in the era before free agency to keep salaries artificially low. "Even after we started winning, he wouldn't pay," said star reliever Rollie Fingers. "After we won our first World Series, he sent me a contract for a $1,000 raise. I thought, 'Thanks a lot, Charlie,' and I hired an agent. I never talked to him after that."

In 1973 baseball enacted arbitration, primarily because of Finley; there were more A's in arbitration than players from the rest of the teams combined. "I went to arbitration twice and won both times," said Fingers. When free agency came "It was bye-bye, Charlie," said Fingers. "Can you imagine Charlie paying these salaries today? He must be rolling over in his grave." Because the reserve clause had been interpreted to mean players were bound to a team as long as that team wanted them, owners had complete power before free agency. But Finley wasn't content with simply holding down a player's salary. If a player challenged him, he ordered him benched, as he did with Reggie Jackson, or ordered his manager to keep him in the bullpen, as he did with Vida Blue. He also threatened critical journalists with lawsuits (more than once with this writer), or banned them from the A's plane, as he did with *Oakland Tribune* beat writer Ron Bergman. Once he even raked his fingernails across the cheek of Jim Street, then a beat writer with the *San Jose Mercury*. He routinely withheld payment to those doing business with him, often forcing others to settle for 25 cents on the dollar. On one memorable occasion he tried to do that with the company printing the World Series programs in 1973. But the company refused to deliver the programs until Finley paid. Grudgingly, he did so, but his payment came so late that the programs were not even available by the time the first game had started.

Yet even with all this, he could also be charming when he chose to be. He had a salesman's ability to convince people that he was the most important person in the world. Knowing all the brutal facts about Finley's character, it was still impossible to resist the man when he turned on the charm.

The best example of that was probably Frank Lane, the legendary general manager who had had the misfortune of working for Finley in Kansas City. It was oil and water from the start. They disagreed on trades, they disagreed on managers, they even disagreed on spring-training sites. Finley fired Lane and refused to honor the rest of his contract. He had given Lane a Mercedes but had not transferred the title, and the car sat in Lane's garage. Lane sued for the money left on his contract and finally settled out of court for $113,000.

Shortly after the A's had moved to Oakland, however, Lane said that he and Finley had become friends again. "Maybe I'm as crazy as he is," said Lane, by then a scout for the Baltimore Orioles, "but it's hard to hate Charlie. He's quite a salesman. He can sell himself to his own worst enemy. He can talk himself out of any tangle." That night, Lane sat with a telephone for several hours relaying a pitch-by-pitch account of the game to Finley.

For sportswriters, Finley was an ongoing contradiction. He was always available and he spoke in short bursts, 3–4 words at a time, to make it easy for writers to take down every word. But he had no tolerance for criticism. In Kansas City he had had a ceremony in which he "honored" well-respected sports editor Ernest Mehl with a "poison pen." In Oakland, those of us who criticized him were in a constant battle. After one of my critical columns, Finley told me, "I don't want to ever talk to you again." When Reggie Jackson heard of that he said, "I hope you got that in writing."

Not surprisingly, it was his ability as a salesman that originally made Finley's fortune. Growing up poor in Indiana, he had gone to work in the steel mills in Gary. Then during World War II, he worked for the Kingsbury Ordnance Plant in La Porte, Indiana, after being declared 4-F because of a perforated eardrum. While still working at the ordnance plant he started selling insurance for first Equitable and then Travelers. Though he was working only part-time, he led Travelers in the sale of accident and health insurance for three years.

In December 1946 he contracted tuberculosis, which almost killed him. While recovering, he realized that doctors needed health insurance but seldom had it, so he concentrated in that area, eventually interesting the Continental Casualty Company of Chicago in underwriting a national plan for the American College of Surgeons. According to the U.S. Tax Court records, he earned $441,563 in commissions on that plan in 1952, the rough equivalent of $3 million today.

With the money pouring in, Finley turned to baseball, which had been an abiding interest since he had been a batboy as a child. He was rebuffed four times, first trying for the A's when they were still in Philadelphia, then the Detroit Tigers, the Chicago White Sox, and the expansion Los Angeles Angels. Finally, in December 1960, after owner Arnold Johnson had died, he made a deal to buy 52 percent of the Kansas City A's.

Finley's years in Kansas City were an unmitigated disaster, with very bad teams and low attendance. His years in Oakland would be much more successful on the field. But the attendance problems continued, partly because he was never able to stop promoting *himself* rather than the team.

There was never any shortage of ideas from Finley, many of them borrowed. Good and bad, he had a considerable influence on baseball because of his ideas. Here's a sampling of those he proposed, most of them during his Oakland years:

- Playoff and World Series games at night during the week, an idea that was also pushed by the television networks for the obvious reason that the ratings would be higher. Finley's reasoning was that having the games at night would give many more people a chance to watch. Despite the nostalgia of old-timers for the day games, it's hard to argue with that. However, there have been some obvious disadvantages to night games. To be on prime time in the east, games on the west coast have to start shortly after 5:00, when the setting sun can cause problems for hitters. Even then, because the pace of baseball seems to be continually slowing, the games go too late for children in the eastern and even central time zones to watch the end.
- Colored uniforms. The green-and-gold uniforms Finley had his team wearing were derided for making the A's look like a softball team. In truth, they were awful. They were in colors that should have been used only as an accent, as they were in the uniforms termed "wedding gown white." But the emergence of those gaudy uniforms pushed baseball away from its old baggy wool flannels to more contemporary, better-fitting uniforms with a splash of color.
- The designated hitter. This one was adopted by the American League in 1973. The AL was falling behind the National League in attendance, perhaps because scoring had dropped. The change accomplished its main purpose, increasing offense and attendance, but it has been controversial since its adoption. National League fans insist that the DH has ruined the purity of the game, though minor leagues and colleges have adopted

11

the rule, leaving the National League alone in its insistence on making the pitcher bat.

Finley also campaigned for orange baseballs similar to the "optic yellow" tennis balls that have been adopted because they're easier to follow than the white balls. He advocated a three-ball, two-strike count to hurry up the game—but when it was used in spring-training games, there were more walks and a slower game. He pushed the idea of a designated runner; when it wasn't adopted, he tried to use sprinter Herb Washington in that role, with generally bad results.

"We had to work with all of Charlie's experiments in spring training," remembered Dick Williams, who lasted three years as an A's manager, a record for a Finley-owned team:

One time I remember we were playing Cleveland and those orange balls were just jumping out of our little park in Mesa. We had traded George Hendrick to the Indians in the off-season and the first time he came up against Cat [Catfish Hunter] he hit one out to left. The next time, he hit one out to center. I don't remember who was pitching when Hendrick came up the third time, but he hit it out again, this time to right field.

[Commissioner] Bowie Kuhn was at the game and after it was over, he asked Hendrick what he thought of the orange ball. "I didn't like it," Hendrick told him. "I couldn't pick up the spin."

With Finley, there was never a dull moment. There was the mechanized rabbit popping up behind home plate to give the umpire fresh baseballs. There was Charlie O the mule, which Finley paraded through the media lunchroom at playoff time. There were the constant weird promotions, the most notable being the one that promoted the growth of facial hair; so many A's sprouted moustaches that they became known as "The Moustache Gang." There was Finley dancing with his wife on the dugout roof after the 1972 World Series win, and Finley sitting with Miss California when his wife was not there. One time, Finley spotted a 12-year-old boy and, noticing a resemblance to "Hammerin'" Hank Aaron, nicknamed the boy "Hammer." Though he was only a gofer for Finley, he was listed as a vice-president in the media guide. That 12-year-old boy later became rap star MC Hammer.

Though Finley's promotions and antics always drew tremendous attention, there was never a stampede at the box office. Even as the A's were winning three straight World Series, they could draw more than 1 million fans only in the middle year of that stretch. Though baseball people liked to picture Oakland as a bad baseball city, the problem lay much more with Finley. When Walter Haas bought the team, the A's drew 200,000 more in the first year of the Haas ownership during their best attendance season under Finley, even though the first Haas season was cut by a third because of a strike. More evidence: Finley owned two other teams, the Seals hockey team in Oakland and the Memphis team in the American Basketball Association, and both those teams also had dreadful attendance. Watching the A's firsthand in those days, I identified three main problems:

1) Lack of staff. Finley had no marketing director, nor any marketing staff. Since there was nobody out in the community marketing season tickets, very few were being sold. That meant that the A's depended on walk-up sales. But when they had big games this caused a problem, because Finley never had enough ticket sellers. Fans would wait in long lines to buy tickets and then not get into the games until the third or fourth inning. Few of them returned for other games.

2) Despite his reputation as a promotional genius, Finley actually knew very little about what it took to build attendance. In the highly urbanized Bay Area, he had promotions like "Farmer's Night," which drew more ridicule than fans. He instituted half-priced "Family Nights" for one game in a three-game series, which was a fundamental marketing error. The crowds for those games were relatively high, but they came at the expense of the other two nights, as could have been predicted. Since the opponent was the same, why come for a game that was at full price? So, the A's would draw about as much for the series as

they would have without the half-price night, but the bulk of the tickets would be discounted.

3) He always put himself above his players. That just doesn't work, anywhere at any time. Fans come out to see the players. They don't come out to see a coach or manager, and they especially don't come out to see an owner. Finley had great players the fans really wanted to watch, but as soon as a player poked his way up from the crowd and threatened to take the publicity spotlight away from Finley, he suffered.

The first three young players who reached the heights in Oakland would soon learn that harsh lesson.

CHAPTER 2

Players Grab
the Spotlight
. . . Temporarily

The first sign that the Oakland A's might be something special came on the night of May 8, 1968, when Jim "Catfish" Hunter threw a perfect game against the Minnesota Twins. However, this was not the first sign that Hunter might be something special.

Hunter had been one of the top prospects signed by Charlie Finley when the club was still in Kansas City, getting a $75,000 signing bonus in 1964—very big money for the time. Hunter had been 23–2 in his final two high school seasons, throwing five no-hitters, one of them a seven-inning perfect game.

Finley loved to give nicknames to players. The one he came up with for Hunter was "Catfish." Though nobody had ever called him that before, it seemed to fit Hunter, who would head back to his native North Carolina to hunt and fish at the end of each baseball season. In the clubhouse, his teammates shortened it to "Cat."

Hunter never pitched an inning in the minor leagues. A hunting accident that cost him part of his foot kept him on the disabled list in 1964.

But he was 8–8, 9–11, and 13–17 (with a 2.81 earned run average) during the next three seasons, pitching for very bad teams in Kansas City.

Hunter's perfect game came with a caveat. Because the game started in twilight, at 6:00 P.M., hitters had trouble picking up the ball in the early innings. For the first six innings, neither team scored.

Still, Hunter was in complete control that night. After the game he said that he had thrown only one bad pitch the whole night, a hanging curve that Harmon Killebrew swung at mightily but missed. A's catcher Jim Pagliaroni stood up and started out to the mound, but stopped when Catfish signalled that he'd got the message: no more like that. In fact, it was the only curve he threw in the entire game. There were only four hard-hit balls off Hunter: liners to left by Cesar Tovar and Rod Carew; a fly deep to right by Ted Uhlaender; and a one-hop grounder to third base by Bob Allison that Sal Bando gloved, throwing Allison out.

Perhaps nothing showcased Hunter's mastery more than the final out of the game. Pinch-hitter Rich Reese had fouled off four straight pitches before Catfish threw a fastball on the inside corner for what he and Pagliaroni thought was the third strike. Pagliaroni had even started toward the mound to congratulate Hunter. But plate umpire Jerry Neudecker called the pitch a ball. Catfish just shrugged. He put another pitch in virtually the same spot, and this time Reese swung and missed. Hunter had his perfect game.

To make it even better, he also had three hits and three RBIs in the 4–0 win. In those pre-DH days, Hunter was a pitcher who could hit well too, averaging as high as .350 in the 1971 season.

But that game was not a typical Hunter outing. Catfish's style was very economical. His control was very good, and he preferred to make the hitter hit his pitch early in the count—letting his fielders do the work—rather than going for strikeouts. He gave up home runs but seldom with men on base, and he worked very fast. I covered successive games by Catfish in that year that lasted only 1:56 and 1:58. In this game, relying on his fastball, he struck out 11 batters, and the game lasted 2:28. Nobody complained.

Dave Duncan, who caught all the A's great pitchers during the championship years of the 1970s, thinks Hunter was clearly the best:

Catfish was the consummate pitcher. He could change speeds, his control was very good. He was like Greg Maddux; he kept hitters from getting the barrel of the bat on the ball. Guys used to want to hit against Cat because they thought he would give them something they could really drive, but he never did. Hell, when I was traded to Cleveland, I could hardly wait to hit against him because I was sure I could hit him. But I couldn't.

Understandably, his perfect game was quite a thrill for Hunter. In 1975, by which time he was with the Yankees, he talked about what the game meant to him:

It has to be one of my biggest thrills in baseball, right up there with winning a World Series game. At the time, it was my biggest thrill, because I hadn't pitched in a World Series yet.

Everything has to be going for you when you pitch a no-hitter. You have to have your best stuff and you have to be lucky, too, because sometimes balls are hit hard but right at a fielder.

The night I pitched my perfect game, I just felt great. I'm not a fastball pitcher, but I felt like I could throw the ball past anyone that night—Tony Oliva, Harmon Killebrew, anybody.

Nothing bothered me. I remember once I was 3–0 on Oliva, and then I threw three straight strikes.

I've had some other games I thought I had the stuff and control to pitch a no-hitter, but I wound up giving up two or three hits. I remember one game in particular just before the end of the 1973 season. We had clinched the divisional title and I was just supposed to pitch part of the game and then come out. But I hadn't given up a hit until the seventh, and so [manager] Dick Williams left me in. In the seventh, there was a ball hit just wide of first base. [Second baseman] Dick Green was waiting for it but [first baseman] Gene Tenace tried for it and the ball went off his glove. Well, you couldn't give Gino an error, so the batter got a hit and I came out of the game.

I had another game against Kansas City, I think it was in 1972, when I really felt sharp, as sharp as I had since I pitched my perfect game. But we had a 7–0 lead, and it's hard to concentrate on a no-hitter when you've got that kind of lead. I think I wound up giving up three hits that night.

But I've never worried about those games. Not when I'd pitched a perfect game before that.

After that famous perfect game, Finley called Catfish and told him that he'd get a $5,000 bonus. But the relationship between Finley and Hunter soon soured, as it always did with Finley and his players. In this case, it was over a loan Finley gave Hunter in 1970.

As Hunter told the story to Ron Bergman, then the A's beat writer for the *Oakland Tribune*, Finley had loaned him $150,000 in 1970 so Catfish could buy a 500-acre farm near his home in Hertford, North Carolina. They had a verbal agreement that Hunter would pay back at least $20,000 each year, with 6 percent interest, until the money was repaid.

Then, during the season, a curious pattern began: Finley would call Hunter on days he was supposed to pitch and ask about repayment of the loan. As with so many of Finley's actions, it was counterproductive for the team. Hunter remembered that he didn't win a single game in August of 1970 because he was so upset by Finley's calls.

Why did Finley do it? Probably for the same reason he later messed with the minds of Reggie Jackson and Vida Blue: he always wanted to show the players who was really boss, no matter how much it hurt the team.

Hunter finally sold off 400 acres of his farm and repaid the total loan to Finley so that he could concentrate on baseball again. The incident turned out to be foreshadowing for another Hunter-Finley struggle a few years later. When Finley defaulted on a provision of Hunter's contract in 1975, Catfish stuck it to the A's owner big time by taking his case to an arbitrator who ruled him a free agent. This decision effectively ended the A's dynasty. What goes around, comes around.

The A's came to Oakland with a nucleus of good, young players, but there was no doubt that Reggie Jackson was the brightest prospect.

Jackson, who had signed a $90,000 bonus contract in 1966 after starring at Arizona State, had it all. Those who only saw him later in his career would remark on his great power, but at the start of his career Jackson invited comparisons with Mickey Mantle because of his combination of speed and power. Jackson would steal at least 22 bases in a season four times in his early career, with a high of 26 in 1976, his one season with the Baltimore Orioles. He was an erratic out-fielder, but he also made great plays at times because of his speed and powerful arm.

Like Mantle, Jackson was so muscular that he suffered frequent muscle tears. A hamstring tear would keep him out of the 1972 World Series, and his injuries eventually robbed him of his speed. But in those early years, he was an exciting base runner as well as a powerful hitter.

It was his power that truly made Jackson a legend in baseball history. From his towering home run during the 1971 All-Star Game in Detroit, which set a power standard, reaching the top of the right-field stands only inches away from leaving the stadium, to the three consecutive home runs he hit in the last game of the 1977 World Series, Jackson's power left fans and press alike awestruck. As early as 1968, when Jackson hit 29 homers in his first full season, Finley was urging sports-writers to do stories on Reggie; the A's owner knew that Jackson's home runs would bring him more attention than the other players.

So, it was fitting that it was his power that first brought Jackson to national prominence in 1969, when he smashed 37 home runs before the All-Star Game in July. Inevitably, the sports pages were full of charts showing Jackson ahead of Roger Maris, who had hit 61 homers just eight years before, and of Babe Ruth when he hit 60 homers in 1927.

Jackson has the reputation of having a huge ego, which is true enough; but he's actually a curious mixture of bravado and insecurity. The second part of his personality suffered in the second half of the 1969 season. The pitchers, of course, were pitching him differently, giving him fewer pitches he could power out, but he continued to hit homers at a near-record pace until September. On September 1 he had 45 homers, 2 more than Ruth had had at that pace.

But then the pressure got to him. Microphones were being shoved in his face everywhere: before games, after games, even when he was eating in a restaurant. It not only affected him but also his marriage, which was breaking up. He even developed a case of shingles at one point. "He didn't have much left by then," remembered Bergman. "He was washed out. He seemed more testy. There was no way he could hit 15 or 16 homers in September."

Oddly, in light of what happened later, Finley was supportive of Jackson at this time; Reggie remembered him calling and encouraging him to resist the pressure, usually offering one of his corny little sayings like, "Keep driving; don't dim the headlights," whatever that might mean. But Jackson hit only two homers in September, and the comparisons to Ruth and Maris had disappeared by midmonth. In fact, he did not even win the American League home-run championship; Harmon Killebrew closed fast to finish with 49.

Still, 47 homers was remarkable for a player in his second full season. Jackson was the hottest player in the league, a fresh face who was a big attendance draw around the league. His box office appeal was especially important to the A's, who had drawn only 778,000 in 1969.

And then, once again, Finley stepped up to the plate to show a star player who was boss. First, there was a protracted salary negotiation. Jackson received $20,000 in 1969 after his friend and agent, Gary Walker, moved Finley up from his original offer of $16,000. This time, Walker wanted to ask for $75,000; but Reggie told him to ask for $60,000. That was considerably more than Finley had in mind. The A's owner offered $35,000 and then came up to $40,000, which he said was his final offer. He said the A's two biggest stars were Jackson and Hunter, and since he was paying Catfish $40,000, he couldn't give Jackson more. Of course, he probably used the same argument to convince Hunter to sign for $40,000.

"Every argument we ever had really stemmed from money," Jackson recalled many years later. "The man could squeeze a nickel out of you, and when he did that, he'd go for a dime."

Jackson held out past the start of spring training in 1970, but he got itchy to play again. So when Finley came up to $45,000, he signed. Finley was not happy about having to pay that much, and he was determined to teach Jackson a lesson.

Finley told manager John McNamara to bench Jackson against left-handed pitchers, though Jackson had hit all kinds of pitchers during the previous years. He also ordered McNamara to put in a pinch-hitter for Jackson—the ultimate humiliation—and even threatened to send Jackson down to the minors, though he didn't follow through on that threat.

Jackson tried to make a joke of his treatment, carrying Sal Bando's bags in the airport on one road trip. Getting in the spirit, Bando tipped him. "I have to do something to earn my money," Jackson said; but his bitterness showed through. When the A's went to Chicago to play the White Sox in midseason, Finley was at the game (he rarely came to games in Oakland), and he invited the team to a postgame barbecue at his farm in LaPorte, Indiana, just across the state border from Chicago. Jackson hit a home run in the game and, as he crossed home plate, flipped a one-finger salute at Finley. He didn't go to the postgame party, either.

Jackson's season was wasted: he hit only .237 with 23 homers, slightly under half his total from the previous year. Once again, Finley had humbled his big star at the expense of the team. It wasn't until Jackson went to the Yankees that he again became the big gate attraction he had been in 1969.

The experience was a harsh lesson for Jackson. "I learned that the owner always has the hammer," he said four years later, "and when it's Finley, it's really a hammer. He was determined to break me. He wanted the spotlight and I took it away from him, so he had to teach me a lesson." Jackson, who is half Black and half Mexican, also thought that Finley was a racist. The A's owner certainly was insensitive about racial matters. But he also mistreated Hunter, who was white. He was an equal opportunity tyrant.

Jackson rebounded from that disappointing year to hit 32 homers the next season, and he went on to have a great career, eventually hitting 563 homers and easily making the Baseball Hall of Fame. Could he have been even better? Perhaps. "After that year," he said later, "I decided to have good years, not great ones, and just try to help my team win." The full-time Reggie swagger didn't return until he joined the Yankees in 1977 and declared that he was "the straw that stirs the drink." Though he was a consistent power hitter, it wasn't until 1980 that he again got in the 40-homer range, with 41 for the Yankees. That was the closest he ever came to his career high, set in 1969, at a time when he seemed easily capable of surpassing 50.

Despite Jackson's later success, the 1970 season proved conclusively how vicious Finley could be when a player threatened to take the spotlight from him.

$$\ominus \quad \ominus \quad \ominus$$

The third young player to find out what it was like in Charlie Finley's world was Vida Blue, and his lesson may have been the hardest of all.

Looking back 30 years later at his 1971 season, Blue called it "a magical season," and indeed it was. Vida was as dominant as any pitcher has been in the "lively ball" era. It seemed too good to last, and it was. Though Blue went on to have an excellent career, he never again reached the heights of his rookie year. Said Blue:

> I remember something I read years later that Al Kaline [a Hall of Fame outfielder with Detroit] said, to the effect that if you have a career year when you're a rookie, where do you go from there? I wasn't thinking that at the time, but I know now that that year didn't give me anything to build on. I was already there. I didn't know how much I had to learn yet. I really didn't learn to pitch for years, not until I went to the National League [in a trade to the Giants in 1978]. I learned a little something about getting movement on my pitches, but I was still basically living off my fastball.

Blue had given notice of what kind of pitcher he could be when he was brought up in September of 1970. Facing the Minnesota Twins, who needed only one more win to clinch the American League Western

Division title, he threw a no-hitter, which he later ascribed to luck. "You have to be lucky to throw a no-hitter, unless you strike out 27 hitters."

Still, playing for Des Moines in the Triple-A American Association that year had truly prepared Blue for the big leagues. Sherm Lollar, who had been a catcher in the big leagues, warmed him up on the sidelines and gave him advice. "My fastball was really popping his glove, but he wasn't impressed," said Blue. "He told me, 'You've got to get that high fastball down to be a winner,' and he was right."

Juan Pizarro, a left-hander who had pitched in the majors, tutored Blue. The A's roving minor league pitching instructor, Bill Posedel, was named the A's pitching coach in 1971, so Blue was comfortable with him as well. "Then, I had to go to basic training at Fort Bragg, North Carolina, to fulfill my military commitment," he remembered. "After that, I was in the best shape of my life when I reported to spring training, and I was just so happy to get away from Fayetteville, North Carolina."

New A's manager Dick Williams was already thinking that Blue would be his second starter, behind Catfish Hunter. But Blue was so impressive in spring training that he vaulted over Hunter and was chosen to pitch the season opener, in Washington, D.C. "Cat always had a terrible time in the spring," remembered Williams years later. "The next couple of years, when I knew him better, I ignored that, but that year, I decided to start Vida because I wasn't sure about Cat."

That was too much for Blue, who had a very bad case of the nerves. Third baseman and team captain Sal Bando noted that "Whatever you said to him, he just said 'Yes.' If you'd said he was full of bull——, he'd have said 'Yes.'" In the first three innings, Blue gave up four runs, and the bullpen was only marginally better when he was taken out. The A's lost, 8–0.

After that disastrous start, however, it was smooth sailing for Blue, who cruised to a 17–3 record by the All-Star Game, in which he was naturally the starter. "To be the opening-game pitcher in Washington, D.C., and then go on to pitch in the All-Star Game, well, it was all pretty unbelievable," remembered Blue. "I was on all the magazine covers: *Life, Look, Sports Illustrated*. That was pretty big stuff for a country boy from Mansfield, Louisiana."

Naturally, there were girls, too. Blue remembered one trip to Chicago when he brought a woman up to his room. "Dick Williams found out about it," said Blue. "He told me, 'You rookies bringing girls up to your rooms . . . The next time you do that, it's going to cost you $500.'" That didn't stop Blue from bringing girls up to his room, but it certainly taught him to be more discreet.

Even the president, Richard Nixon, was impressed with this rookie sensation. Meeting Blue and being told he was making only $13,000, he said, "You must be the lowest-paid superstar in America." He would remain so, of course, as long as he was pitching for Finley.

"Vida in 1971 just overpowered hitters," remembered Duncan:

> He basically just threw the fastball. He didn't have much of a curve and he didn't throw it very often, and he had no off-speed pitch. Hitters knew what was coming and they still couldn't hit him. He'd throw that fastball right in on their fists, and they couldn't do a damn thing with it.

It wasn't just that Blue was winning games. He was dominating. Even the best hitters couldn't catch up to his fastball; in consecutive games against a star-studded Baltimore Orioles team, he struck out 18 batters in 18 innings.

Sportswriters started calling Blue a "black Koufax," comparing him to Sandy Koufax, that dominating pitcher from the previous decade. It wasn't just sportswriters who made the comparison. Koufax himself was doing work for NBC-TV; before one game, he talked to Williams. "Who does he remind you of?" asked Koufax. "I'm looking at him," said Williams, who had briefly been a teammate of Koufax's with the Brooklyn Dodgers in the fifties.

The league was buzzing, and huge crowds were showing up whenever Blue pitched. Finley ordered Williams to shift the rotation in order to give Blue the maximum number of starts at home. Once he ordered Williams to exchange the two star pitchers so Blue wouldn't be starting on Bat Day in Oakland; he didn't want Blue's drawing power wasted on a game that would already draw a big crowd because of the promotion.

"I knew there were some big crowds when I was pitching, but it was you newspaper guys who told me what it really meant," said Blue. At the end of the season, adding up the crowds on the days he pitched, nearly ½th of the total attendance in the American League that season came at games pitched by Blue.

Of course, Finley could not let Blue get all the attention. He had to do something. His first stunt was to try to get the rookie to adopt "True" as his nickname, even offering him a $2,000 bonus. Blue resisted, but Finley didn't stop. He had his game announcers use the nickname and put "True Blue" up on the message board at the Oakland Coliseum. Said Blue:

I was even hearing my teammates call me "True." I decided this had to stop, so I went to the equipment manager and asked him to sew my first name onto the back of my uniform [uniforms usually have the player's last name]. That finally put an end to it.

Vida is a family name, and I wanted to keep it to honor my father, who died while I was still in high school; I'm Vida Jr. It means "life" in Spanish. I don't really know the origin of the name as far as my family goes. But I was determined to keep it.

Even with Finley's penchant for nicknames, it seemed strange that he would want to tinker with a name as distinctive as Vida Blue. Blue felt the same way. "I always tell people that my family knew I was going to be a star, so they gave me a star's name," he laughed.

There was yet another Finley episode to come: the A's owner gave Blue a Cadillac in midseason. There was a lot of confusion about the car. Blue originally thought he did not have title to the car because it was addressed to the Oakland A's. Even when he learned that he did indeed have the title, he wasn't happy about the gift:

Finley was a world traveler, so I know he must have known what the image was for a black man and a Cadillac. Some of my friends wondered if he'd put a watermelon in the trunk.

25

He never asked me what I wanted. Like any young kid at the time, I might have said something like a Corvette. Or I might have just told him to buy a car for my mother and forget about me.

Dealing with Finley, as well as everyone's high expectations, wore on Blue as the season progressed. During spring training and early in the season, he had been a delight. He was so happy to be there that he answered all the questions from writers and broadcasters, joking along as he did. But the media attention became much more intense as he became the most important story of the season, and he started snapping at reporters, talking about the questions he hated most, and blaming "pressure" when he didn't pitch well.

And his pitching was suffering. Whether it was because he tired in the second half and lost a little off his fastball, or whether he was worn down by all the media attention, he did not pitch as well in the last two months as he had in the first four, with a 7–5 record in his last 12 decisions. But even with that drop-off, he finished with one of the most remarkable seasons ever: 24–8, a 1.82 earned run average, 24 complete games, 8 shutouts, and 301 strikeouts in 312 innings.

In the American League Championship Series, Blue got bombed by the Orioles, yielding seven hits and five runs in the first game of what became a three-game sweep by Baltimore. In the dressing room after the game, Blue sat on his stool in front of his locker with a dazed look. He seemed exhausted, physically and mentally.

It would get worse. During the off-season Blue hired an agent—Bob Gerst—who asked for $115,000 for his client. He then retreated to $92,000. Finley offered $50,000, which he said was his one and only offer.

Gerst cited the salaries of other top pitchers—Bob Gibson was the highest at $150,000—and Blue's economic importance to the team. Finley countered that Blue was only coming into his second full season. In baseball, star players traditionally didn't get top salaries until they were well into their careers.

Finley had the leverage because there was no free agency at that time. The reserve clause in baseball contracts, which gave the club authority to renew the player's contract for the next season if no agreement could be reached, had always been interpreted to mean that a player was bound to that team for as long as the team wanted him. If Finley didn't want to make another offer, there was nothing Blue or his agent could do about it.

Although Finley did eventually relent, it wasn't until Commissioner Bowie Kuhn intervened, demanding that Finley and Blue work out a contract. Finally, Blue signed for $63,000: a $50,000 salary, a $5,000 bonus for his great year, and another $8,000 to be used by Blue to continue his college education. But, as was always the case with Finley, there was more there than met the eye. Said Blue years later:

> Finley always had to break his stars. He did it with Catfish, he did it with Reggie, he did it with me. I did get a good raise finally, but then he put me on the disabled list for awhile, saying I wasn't in condition to play, so I lost a lot of that money. He won that round.
>
> That's always the way it was with Finley. He could be charming when he wanted to be, but that was only when he wanted something from you.
>
> I don't know what would have happened with my career if I hadn't gone through that, if my mental outlook would have been a lot better. I know I was very bitter that next year.

It wasn't until he was traded to the Giants in 1978 that Blue regained the enthusiasm he'd had in 1971. Playing for Charlie Finley always took its toll.

CHAPTER 3

The Championship Run Begins

Vida Blue's great year was the biggest story in 1971, but there was another change that made a bigger difference for the A's: Dick Williams' arrival as manager.

Tony La Russa, who later became a fine manager for the A's, was a reserve infielder in 1971, and he later had a vivid memory of the first day Williams talked to the team, during spring training:

> We were all standing out in center field. Everybody knew in those days that there were players who would go behind the manager's back and run to Charlie Finley if they didn't like what the manager was doing. So, Dick started off by saying, "I know it's been a heckuva problem to the manager when you guys run off to Charlie. So, here are his numbers," and he held up a list. "If any of you guys want to leave right now and call him, go ahead. If you want to wait until after practice to call him, that's your business. But that's the last time any of you are going to call Charlie. I'm the manager. If you have a problem, come to me and I'll take care of it."

In La Russa's mind and in the minds of the other players, that established Williams' authority in a way that the previous A's managers in Oakland—John McNamara, Hank Bauer, and Bob Kennedy—never had. "I loved Dick Williams," said La Russa. "He was tough, but he was fair, and he really taught us how to play the game. He really emphasized the little things."

Blue remembered one of the little things, as it applied to pitching: "It would just drive him crazy if a pitcher had two strikes on the hitter and then gave up a base hit. He just didn't think that should ever happen."

Williams understood physical errors, which happen to the best of players. What he wouldn't tolerate were the mental errors: an outfielder throwing to the wrong base, a base runner taking an unreasonable gamble and running into an out. Williams didn't fly into a rage; even fans sitting near the dugout wouldn't know when he was chewing out a player. But his cold fury cut through a player's psyche. "If you make a mental mistake," Reggie Jackson once said, "he makes it so uncomfortable for you that you make sure it doesn't happen again."

It was hardly unusual for Finley to change managers. As usual, angry words had preceded this change from McNamara to Williams.

Catcher Dave Duncan had seen his playing time dwindle in the last half of the 1970 season, and he knew why. After the season, he had gone public with his comments. "There's only one man who manages this club—Charlie Finley—and we'll never win as long as he manages it," Duncan told reporters. "We had the team to win it [the American League West]. But because of the atmosphere he creates, there's no spirit, no feeling of harmony."

Finley seized on Duncan's comments as an excuse to fire McNamara, claiming that he didn't have the respect of his players. Finley always thought that if he were forceful enough in his comments, people would believe him without looking behind his words. Sometimes that worked. This time it didn't. There had been newspaper speculation for at least a month that McNamara would be fired. Billy Martin, fired as the manager of the Minnesota Twins, claimed that Finley had offered him McNamara's job in July. McNamara himself said that when the club had started out below .500 in the first six weeks of the 1970 season, he knew that he would be fired, perhaps even before the end of the season.

Talking about that time more than 30 years later, Williams said he'd been contacted two days before the end of the season, when McNamara was still under contract. "I had played briefly for Charlie in 1960 [it was actually spring training of 1961]," Williams remembered, "but Frank Lane traded me two days into the season. Anyway, I wanted to get back into managing, so we worked out a deal right away. I knew Charlie's reputation, but that didn't bother me." Fortunately for Finley, he had hired a manager who had the mental toughness to deal with a challenge, as he had already proved in Boston.

Williams had once been a promising outfield prospect in the Brooklyn Dodgers system but had injured his shoulder making a diving catch and was never the same player again, though he wound up playing 13 years in the majors for five different teams, always as a reserve. One of those teams, the Baltimore Orioles, was managed by Paul Richards, who admired Williams' mind and encouraged him to become a manager. Before the 1967 season, he was hired by the Boston Red Sox, the last team for which he had played.

Few people envied him. The Red Sox had long had a "country club" reputation because owner Tom Yawkey spoiled them, undermining the authority of his manager. Indeed, many years later Williams said that it was more difficult to manage for Yawkey than for Finley.

The team Williams took over in Boston had finished ninth in the 10-team American League in 1966, but Williams pulled together this group of disorganized underachievers and won the pennant in 1967, a victory known as "the Impossible Dream."

There would be no happy ending in Boston, though. Even though the Red Sox won the pennant, Yawkey didn't like Williams' hard-driving style, and players who shared his dislike found the owner sympathetic to their complaints. Yawkey didn't hide his dislike for Williams, either, telling a newspaper reporter that, on a scale of 1–4, with 4 the highest, he would rate Williams no more than 2 as a manager.

Yawkey fired Williams during the 1969 season, and Williams took a job as a coach in Montreal under manager Gene Mauch, whom he later credited with teaching him what it took to be a successful

31

manager. Coaching under Mauch was like attending a baseball seminar, said Williams. He also learned from Mauch about how to deal with an owner who caused problems. That lesson would be especially valuable to Williams with the A's.

Though Finley's treatment of McNamara was harsh, he had made the right move by hiring Williams. McNamara was well liked by the players, many of whom had played for him in the minor leagues, but he did not have their respect. They knew that Finley was dictating lineup changes, and they knew that if they were unhappy about their playing time, they had a good chance of changing it by complaining to Finley. No manager can be successful under those conditions.

Finley also knew that the A's were a much better team than their record indicated (89–73, a scant single game improvement from the previous season). More by accident than design, the A's had been built into an ideal team for their Oakland surroundings, with potentially outstanding pitching and defense and good power. The Oakland Coliseum was a pitcher's park. Because it was a multi-purpose stadium, it had very large foul areas; foul balls that would have gone in the stands in other parks were often caught. That meant batting averages would suffer. The A's of the seventies were often underrated offensively because of that, but it also meant that good pitching and defense gave a team a big advantage playing in the Coliseum. The A's had that kind of team. But McNamara, whose concept of managing seldom got much beyond making out the lineup card, was not the kind of manager who would make the most of that advantage.

Team captain Sal Bando, who couldn't be blamed for McNamara's problems—Bando was always a player who gave his best, no matter the circumstances—said he would keep McNamara as a friend, but he also felt that the A's needed the kind of demanding manager Williams would be:

> We need a guy to kick us in the rear now and then. Mac said he just wasn't the type to jump all over guys, and we liked that. We knew that if we made a mistake, it wouldn't be too bad. But we didn't learn from our mistakes. We didn't take them seriously. I think that hurt us as the season wore on.

The A's players wouldn't have the luxury of repeated mistakes under Williams, as they learned very early in the 1971 season. Said Williams:

> I thought that was a great club when I first saw them in spring training. We had some great young arms: Vida, Cat, Blue Moon Odom, Chuck Dobson. I thought this was a young team that just didn't know how to win yet. They were weak on fundamentals, so I really stressed that in spring training.
>
> The players responded in the spring, but then, when we got into the season, we started off poorly. Charlie called us up to his penthouse apartment in Oakland, the coaches and me, and he just ripped the s__t out of us, especially me and Bill Posedel. Well, after that, we really put the hammer to the team, and we got rolling and never looked back.

In fact, the A's were 11 games up at the All-Star break.

Blue's great season obscured the fact that 1971 was the year when Catfish Hunter became a polished pitcher, winning 21 games and starting a run of five straight seasons in which he won more than 20 games. Rollie Fingers had also found his niche as a reliever. Jackson and Bando were the primary power hitters, with 32 and 24 homers, respectively. The great defense that was the trademark of the championship teams began to assert itself, anchored by shortstop Campy Campaneris and second baseman Dick Green.

And the A's had Dick Williams. His importance in developing an attitude that would carry the A's to a division win in his first year and World Series championships the next two cannot be overestimated. Williams was the complete package as a manager. He had an excellent strategic sense, and his moves in the 1972 World Series would be critically important. He had a good sense of how to use bench players. When a player who would not be starting came to the A's, Williams would carefully explain his role; he did not want unhappy players on the bench.

Most of all, though, he was the burr under the saddle, driving players to their best performances. He did not wear well; Williams eventually managed six teams and never lasted more than five years with any of them. But Finley could not have made a better choice to drive this talented but underachieving group to almost unprecedented success.

Finley would prove to be more of a challenge for Williams than the players were. He had his fingers in everything. Said Williams:

> He even decided which color uniforms he wanted us to wear [either the gaudy green and gold or the much more subdued white with splashes of green and gold] for home games. There were many times we'd be waiting in the dressing room for Charlie's call before we knew which uniforms we'd be wearing out to the field. We actually had six variations. One year for the All-Star game, I had to pack all six uniforms because Charlie hadn't decided which one he wanted me to wear.

There were also the constant phone calls. Blue has joked that it was a good thing that cell phones hadn't been around in the seventies. "Can you imagine the manager going to the mound and getting a call from Charlie on his cell phone, and then having to turn his back on the pitcher to get the best reception?"

In fact, Williams says, Finley never called him in the dugout:

> Hank Bauer told me he'd done that once, and Hank had ripped out the phone. But Charlie talked to me after every game, either in his office upstairs or on the phone. He'd always critique the game. We might have won, 4–2, and he'd say, "You should have won, 6–2." Well, we knew where he was getting his information: from Monte Moore's broadcasts. We used to call him Charlie's "spy in the sky." Monte was a nice enough guy, but he didn't know enough to manage a meat market. I wasn't going to worry about what he said, no matter how much Finley listened to him.

The players, who were united in their dislike of Finley, also thought that Moore reported what he'd heard in the dressing room. That couldn't have been much, however, because they were quite wary of the broadcaster.

In retirement, Williams could be philosophical about his years with Finley, and he claimed there was more good than bad in the man:

> Charlie was smart, and as he spent more time in baseball, he really learned a lot about the game. Where he really helped me was in bringing in guys when we got somebody injured. He always knew where he could get players, either bringing them up from the minor leagues or getting them off the waiver wire. If we got a player injured, Charlie would tell me, "Don't worry. I know where we can get a guy," and the next day, the player would be there in our dressing room.

But when Williams was managing, he wasn't always so sanguine about what was happening:

> Charlie never told me who to play, but there were times when players would arrive without me knowing. He'd bring in his favorite—"the Panamanian Express," Allen Lewis—when our rosters expanded in September. He was strictly a runner. I don't know if Lewis even owned a glove.

But Williams did short-circuit the connection between Finley and the players, which had been such a big factor when McNamara was the manager. He put up with constant pressure from Finley without letting the players know. All he asked of them was that they play their best and let him deal with Finley. The players responded with a great season, winning 101 games, which would stand as an Oakland record for 17 years, and finishing 16 games ahead of the Royals, who had replaced them in Kansas City.

To get to the World Series, though, the A's would have to beat the Baltimore Orioles, who had also won 101 games during the season. That represented a decline for the Orioles, who had won 109 and 108 games the previous two seasons, and who had won the Series in 1970. The Orioles were a true dynasty team, having also won the World

Series in 1966. They had even better pitching than the A's, with four pitchers who had won at least 20 games: Dave McNally with 21, and Jim Palmer, Mike Cuellar, and Pat Dobson all with 20. They had a great defense anchored by third baseman Brooks Robinson and center fielder Paul Blair. They had one of the all-time greats in right field, Frank Robinson, who had started the Orioles' championship run when he was traded from Cincinnati before the 1966 season.

That American League Championship Series was an interesting matchup in between a team that had been great (and still was), and a team that was just starting to understand how good it could be. As usual, there was also a great contrast between the two organizations. The Orioles were a traditional club, with a full complement of front office staff. The A's were . . . well, the A's were Charlie Finley. If anybody had any doubts about the difference, they had only to look at the official program. On one page, the Orioles had small pictures of every member of their front office staff, perhaps 50 people. On the opposing page was the A's contribution: a full-page photo of Finley on the telephone.

The A's got off to a fast start against the Orioles, taking a 3–1 lead into the seventh behind Blue, but Vida gave up four runs during that inning, and that was the ball game.

After the game, Williams was second-guessed for leaving Blue in when he had already thrown 120 pitches coming into the seventh. Orioles manager Earl Weaver guessed that Vida might have been tired. But high pitch counts were common for Blue, who struck out 301 and walked 88 that year but still threw 24 complete games. Blue was the A's best, and Williams had elected to stick with him. A year later, Williams would no doubt have pulled him because he had Fingers available as a dominating reliever; but in 1971 Fingers had not yet evolved into that kind of a pitcher. (Fingers did pitch the eighth inning for the A's, but by that time the game was lost.)

As it turned out, that fateful seventh inning was the last time the A's would lead in the ALCS. Behind Cuellar, the Orioles won easily in the second game, 5–1. Hunter gave up only five hits, but four of them were homers, two by Boog Powell.

There was little doubt at that point about who was going to win the ALCS. The A's put up a good fight in the third game, in Oakland, but the Orioles won, 5–3, as Palmer pitched the second straight complete game for Baltimore.

In retrospect, the outcome wasn't surprising. As well as the A's had played during the season, it was unrealistic to expect them to win a short series against a team that could use Jim Palmer as its third starter, and that had had a great deal of postseason experience.

For the A's, it was only the beginning. For the next three years, they would be baseball's best, though the question as they went into the 1972 season was not whether they'd get to the World Series but whether they could even repeat as Western Division champions.

The A's, who had relief on pitching and defense, suddenly had visions of their starting rotation in shambles. Both Odom and Dobson had arm problems. So Finley—with the approval of Williams—made a gambling trade, sending center fielder Rick Monday to the Chicago Cubs for left-handed starter Ken Holtzman.

Both Monday and Holtzman had been disappointments to the clubs that had just traded them. Monday had been the first pick in the first-ever amateur draft in 1965, and Finley had given him a signing bonus of $104,000, very big money at the time. Monday, a star out-fielder at Arizona State, was an excellent defensive center fielder with speed and power. He seemed destined for stardom in the big leagues, too, but a steady string of injuries had kept him well below that level with the A's. (Though he would play 19 seasons in the majors, Monday never really fulfilled his potential.)

Holtzman had had flashes of brilliance with the Cubs, twice throwing a no-hitter—the last time against the power-packed Cincinnati lineup in 1971—and contributing back-to-back seasons with 17 wins in 1969–1970. In 1971, though, he had had several confrontations with manager Leo Durocher because of Durocher's habit of publicly criticizing his players. "I wasn't happy when I read in the papers that Leo Durocher thought I wasn't trying," Holtzman said after he'd been traded to the A's.

Durocher felt that Holtzman should use his fastball more, instead of the slow curve that he liked. In this case, the manager was right, even if he was wrong in the way he made his criticism. Against the Reds, Holtzman had been unable to get his curve over, so he threw primarily fastballs and shut down a lineup that featured such power-ful right-handed hitters as Johnny Bench, Tony Perez, George Foster, Lee May, and Hal McRae. When he came to the A's, he was throwing probably 80 to 90 percent fastballs in most games. By that time, he had learned to make his fastball sink or rise, depending on his grip.

Holtzman was a thorough professional who studied his craft. Though he liked to say he was only in baseball for the money (he was with the wrong team in Oakland!), his behavior seemed to indicate otherwise. He came to the park four hours before the game, well before any other player, so he could get himself in the proper frame of mind.

Because he read books with hard covers, he got a reputation within baseball as an intellectual, which probably wasn't deserved. But he certainly was intelligent, and he had street smarts too, as anybody who played cards with him quickly learned. "He changed Rollie Fingers," laughed Williams when he remembered the A's clubhouse of the early seventies:

> Rollie just kind of wandered around in those days. He never seemed to be very aware of what was going on. Holtzie would take his money in card games, and he taught Rollie some street smarts, which made Rollie a better pitcher.

Holtzman also made himself a better pitcher, mainly by improving his control. In the team's three championship years, he walked fewer than two men per nine innings, and his ERA averaged under three runs a game as he won 19, 21, 19 in successive years. He was only a shade less effective than Hunter during that span.

He came along just in time, because Finley's contract battle with Blue took a big bite out of the pitcher's season. Blue pitched only 151 innings, roughly half what he had done the year before, and saw his victory total sliced from 24 to 6, though his 2.80 ERA, four shutouts, and just 117 hits allowed in those 151 innings are better indicators of how he pitched than his 6–10 won-lost record.

Odom recovered from his arm problems to post 15 wins and Fingers stepped up big-time in the bullpen with 21 saves. He was aided by Darold Knowles, Bob Locker, and Joel Horlen in the 'pen. That enabled the A's to keep control of the Western Division, though it wasn't the cakewalk of the year before.

The key game came in the next-to-the-last week of the season. The Chicago White Sox had come to Oakland for a crucial two-game series, trailing by five games. They won the first one, a 15-inning struggle, 8–7. A win the next day would have put the White Sox within three games, but Bando and Jackson got the A's off winging and Fingers pitched 3⅔ innings of scoreless ball in relief of Holtzman. The A's won, 6–3. Their five game lead was back, and they eventually won by five and a half, with 93 victories. They would be back in the American League Championship Series.

CHAPTER 4

The Big Red Machine Stalled

There was no dynasty team to block the A's path to the World Series in 1972. Their opposition within the American League was the Detroit Tigers, who had won their division with just an 86–70 record. The Tigers were a team seemingly held together by trainer's tape, with a starting lineup that averaged 32 years of age. The A's were younger, faster, and had better pitching and defense. Yet the A's barely survived the five-game playoff series, and it cost them the services of their best player, Reggie Jackson.

It didn't start that way. The A's won the first game in Oakland and were on their way to a second win the next day, leading 5–0, when Detroit reliever Lerrin LaGrow hit A's leadoff hitter Campy Campaneris in the ankle with his first pitch. Campaneris hesitated for a moment, then threw his bat at the pitcher's mound. LaGrow ducked, and the bat landed a few feet behind him.

Campaneris's action, though extreme, could almost have been predicted; the animosity between these two teams was palpable, mostly because of fiery Detroit manager Billy Martin, who would manage the A's later in the decade.

Martin and A's owner Charlie Finley had exchanged insults over a contract supposedly offered Martin in 1970; Martin claimed he had agreed and Finley had reneged, while Finley claimed that Martin had backed out. There had also been a bench-clearing fight between the teams in a game during the regular season, after Tigers reliever Bill Slayback had thrown at Campaneris and Angel Mangual in consecutive at-bats, hitting both.

Martin, who went careening through life from brawl to brawl, was a throwback to earlier days in baseball, when it was routine for managers to shout, "Put it in his ear," from the dugout. Tigers pitchers had been throwing at Campaneris's legs throughout the series, obviously trying to injure him. "There's no question in anybody's mind," said A's first baseman Mike Hegan, who had been watching from the bench. "Those orders to Lerrin LaGrow came directly from Billy Martin."

But it didn't seem that way to American League President Joe Cronin, who suspended Campaneris for the rest of the series but did not discipline either LaGrow or Martin. Now the A's were without a player who was critical to them, both offensively and defensively. Campaneris never got the acclaim he deserved, probably because he never learned to speak English beyond the very basics, so he was seldom interviewed. But he was the A's best base stealer and the defensive glue for the infield.

Campaneris was even more important defensively in 1972 because that was the year Finley decided to rotate his second basemen. Dick Green, a superior defensive second baseman, was a weak hitter (Green was injured and played only 26 games during the season), as were the A's reserve infielders. So Finley came up with a plan to pinch-hit every time the second baseman was supposed to come up to bat and then to put a defensive replacement in for the next inning.

Amazingly, manager Dick Williams went along with the strategy. Even more amazingly, the A's did not lose a game in the regular season because of this strange plan. But when Campaneris was suspended, Dal Maxvill replaced him at shortstop, with Tim Cullen in reserve; both had been part of the second base rotation. That left only Ted Kubiak as a backup at second. When Williams, under orders from

Finley, put in pinch-hitters for both Green and Kubiak, he was forced to use Gene Tenace, a catcher and reserve first baseman, at second.

That move cost the A's their chance to sweep the playoff series. They were leading by two runs in the bottom of the tenth during the third game when the Tigers started a rally. With the bases loaded, Bill Freehan grounded to third baseman Sal Bando, who threw to second to start what should have been a double play. But Tenace dropped the ball. "I think he heard my footsteps," said runner Gates Brown, a sturdy 230-pounder, "because he got out of there before he got the ball."

Given that reprieve, the Tigers scored three runs in the inning to win the game. Williams resolved that he'd never use the rotating second basemen routine again, no matter how many phone calls he got from Finley:

> I never liked it, but I went along with it because Charlie was the owner. I had to keep Dick Green on the bench so I'd have him for late-inning defense, and he was my best second baseman, the best defensive second baseman in the league. But after that play against Detroit, I balked at doing it any more. I should have balked at doing it before.

The Tigers tied the series in the fourth game, leading to a dramatic finish in the fifth game, which was played in Detroit. In the second inning, on the front end of a delayed double steal, Jackson pulled a hamstring muscle but courageously continued to run hard down the line, overrunning the Detroit catcher, Freehan, to score the tying run. Jackson watched the rest of the game from the clubhouse.

Tenace singled in George Hendrick with the go-ahead run in the fourth, and that was all the A's needed. John "Blue Moon" Odom pitched five innings and gave up just one unearned run, but he complained of breathing problems, so Blue took the ball in the sixth and shut out the Tigers on three hits the rest of the way. The A's were in the World Series for the first time since they'd been in Oakland—and for the first time since 1931, when they were in Philadelphia.

They would get Campaneris back; commissioner Bowie Kuhn ruled that although the A's shortstop would be suspended for another seven games for his bat throwing, those seven games would be at the start of the next season. However, there would be no World Series for Jackson. By running so hard after pulling his hamstring muscle, he had done great damage to his leg and would be on crutches for months. But if he hadn't run so hard, the A's might not have made the Series.

The 1972 World Series would turn out to be one of the best ever, with many dramatic plays and turnarounds; but that didn't seem likely at the start. The A's were a collection of unknowns to the baseball world; their best-known players were Jackson, who was out, and Blue, who had been consigned to the bullpen. By contrast, the Reds were a collection of All-Stars: Joe Morgan, Johnny Bench, Pete Rose, Tony Perez. Most neutral observers agreed with the always-cocky Rose, who said before the first game that the National League playoffs between the Reds and the Pittsburgh Pirates had matched the two best teams in baseball, and that the Reds had already proven they were the best in baseball by winning that matchup.

Williams understood why the Reds were favored:

> We had lost our best power hitter, and we had also lost Darold Knowles—who was a key left-handed reliever for us—when he tripped and broke his thumb after hitting a fly ball in a game in the last week of the season. So it figured we might have a little trouble in the Series.
>
> Plus, nobody really knew us. We only had two writers, Ron Bergman and Jim Street, traveling with us. The Reds weren't in a big media town, but they had a lot of guys with them, and they were from the Midwest/East, where there's more media concentration. Everybody knew the Reds.

Still, the A's were loose and confident going into the Series. "The Reds were a great team," said Fingers later, "but I felt the pressure was all on them. They were expected to win. Nobody expected anything from us, but we knew we were good."

Thinking there was little point in writing about the competitive aspect of the Series—since the Reds would probably sweep—the national media concentrated on the different physical appearances of the teams. Though they might grow sidebars or mustaches in the off-season (Rose said he started a mustache as soon as the season ended), the Reds had to be clean-shaven as soon as they hit spring training, an edict from general manager Bob Howsam. Hair lengths also had to be conservative, stopping short of the top of their uniforms.

The A's were quite different. Finley had had one of his bizarre promotions: free admission for one game for men who had beards or mustaches. As a corollary, he had promised bonuses to players who grew mustaches. Like so many of Finley's promotions, this one had no positive impact on attendance; however, many of the players liked the mustaches and kept them. "It became my trademark," said Fingers, who had one of the best, which he twirled up at each end. "Hardly anybody even remembers what I looked like before."

In truth, the A's were much closer to the mainstream than the Reds. Pictures from the seventies make it obvious that men's hairstyles were drastically changing at that time. Long hair and sideburns were becoming common, sometimes joined by mustaches, or beards, or both. But not in the Reds clubhouse.

Despite their victory in the playoffs, the A's were still angry at their owner and sometimes at each other. Blue, still seething because of his treatment by Finley, even quarreled briefly with Odom, who was otherwise his closest friend on the team. After he had saved Odom's win in the final game of the American League Championship Series, he asked Odom why he couldn't finish what he started and gave the "choke" sign, his hands around his neck. That's the type of rough kidding that goes on in any baseball clubhouse; but this time, Odom got very angry and had to be restrained by teammates when he started to go after Blue.

Odom and Blue quickly patched up their differences, but Blue remained angry at Williams when he learned that he'd be pitching out of the bullpen. "He never says anything to me," Blue complained. "The only way I find out what I'm going to do is by reading the newspapers." He was convinced, with some justification, that

Finley had ordered Williams to keep him in the bullpen, to further punish him.

With all the stars in the Cincinnati lineup, it was natural to expect that one of them would be the dominant player in the Series. But Knowles had a bizarre thought: he expected Tenace to have a big Series. "I like the way he's swinging the bat," said the injured A's reliever. So did the A's manager. "I just had a hunch," said Williams, who put Tenace in as the catcher, replacing Dave Duncan. "Tenace hadn't had a good series against Detroit. He only got one hit. But that hit knocked in the winning run in the fifth game, so I thought he might be a good guy to have in the lineup."

Tenace made that prediction look good when, with a runner on base, he hit a Gary Nolan fastball into the left-field seats on his first at-bat, giving the A's a 2–0 lead. The Reds tied it with single runs in the second and fourth, but Tenace came up again in the fifth, with nobody on. This time, Nolan threw him a curve. "It hung like a feather," the Cincinnati pitcher said after the game. Tenace, who had never before hit two homers in a game, had become the first player to hit home runs in his first two at-bats in a World Series.

"I'm not impressed by the A's," said Rose after the game. "Outside of Tenace, they didn't do much. They only got four hits. They had a couple of shots at double plays and didn't make them, so I'm not impressed with their defense."

Rose might have changed his mind about the Oakland defense in the ninth inning of the second game. Behind their ace, Catfish Hunter, who had not been able to pitch the opener because he'd pitched the fourth game of the championship series, the A's had taken a 2–0 lead into the bottom of the ninth. Perez led off with a single, only the fifth hit allowed by Hunter, and then Denis Menke crashed a long drive to left that seemed destined for the seats, a home run that would tie the game.

A's left fielder Joe Rudi gave chase. When Rudi had first come to the A's, he had been a good hitter but was weak defensively. Joe DiMaggio, then a coach for the A's, worked with him on his fielding. "He taught me how to turn and go balls hit over my head," remembered Rudi, "but I really didn't think I was going to learn how. In practice, they'd have that machine which would spit out balls and I'd turn and run for where I thought the ball was going to land, but when I'd look for it, the ball would be 50 feet away." Eventually he learned. Rudi, though not a fleet man, became a very reliable outfielder who got a good jump on the ball and caught everything he reached.

Rudi didn't think he'd catch this one. "I thought it was out of the park when he hit it," he recalled. "But it was just like DiMaggio had taught me. I turned and ran for the wall and then jumped up. I was lucky because the sun was just inches away from where it would have been right in my eyes." Rudi caught the ball and reacted very quickly when he hit the wall, pulling his glove away. "If I hadn't, the ball probably would have popped out," he said.

Perez was so certain the ball could not be caught that he had already rounded second and had to scurry back to first to avoid being doubled off. The catch later inspired hyperbolic comment from Williams, who said it was better than Willie Mays's catch of Vic Wertz's drive in the 1954 Series. But it was only one out. The A's needed two more.

They got one of them on another superb defensive play, with Hegan diving full out to his right to cut off Cesar Geronimo's drive toward right and then crawling to first for the out. Perez went to second on the play and scored when Hal McRae singled, but then Williams brought in Fingers, who was sure death in these situations. Fingers was quite possibly the best late-inning relief pitcher in baseball history.

Fingers hadn't started as a reliever; in his early career, he shuttled back and forth between starting and relieving. "I became a reliever because I couldn't make it as a starter," he said. "I was starting 15–18 games a year and getting shelled, so Dick Williams put me in the 'pen in '71. Then, the next year he made me the short man."

It wasn't actually Williams's idea but that of pitching coach Bill Posedel. Remembered Williams:

> Rollie would get so nervous when he was starting. By the time
> his turn in the rotation came up, he'd be a basket case. Bill
> Posedel came up with the idea of putting him in the bullpen

and bringing him in during the middle innings, when there wasn't much pressure. That way, he wouldn't have time to worry about his pitching. That worked fine, and then we started trying him in situations with a little more pressure. Finally, we decided he could be the late man.

That was fine with Rollie:

I liked to come to the park knowing I had a good chance to get in the game that day, instead of sitting around four days between starts and then getting knocked out in the second inning. I liked to come into the game in pressure situations, knowing it was up to me to save the game. We went longer in those days than the closers do today—I remember in the '74 Series, Alvin Dark brought me in with two outs in the fifth inning in one game—but usually I figured I wasn't going to throw more than 2–3 innings, so I could throw as hard as I could, instead of trying to pace myself for nine innings.

This time, he only had to get one out, which was automatic. He got pinch-hitter Julian Javier to foul out and the A's had won, 2–1. They were going back to Oakland with an improbable 2–0 lead in the Series.

The A's being the A's, though, they weren't going back happy. Hegan had been in the game because starting first baseman Mike Epstein had been removed for a pinch-runner, Allen Lewis, who was on the roster because he was a Finley favorite. Because of his speed, Finley had nicknamed Lewis "The Panamanian Express." But Lewis was a very poor base runner despite his speed, and writer Herb Michelson renamed him, "The Panamanian Local," because, Michelson explained, "He always stops at second."

On the plane home, Epstein yelled at Williams, "You don't appreciate me. I've been busting my ass and I don't want this to happen again." "I'm the manager," Williams said. "I'll do whatever I want."

Meanwhile, Finley was walking up and down the aisle. He paused and put a hand on the shoulder of Duncan, who would later become the A's pitching coach. "I know you, Dave Duncan."

"Bullshit!" snapped Duncan. "You don't know me because you've never taken the trouble to know me."

Just one big happy family.

Blue, who was doing more talking than pitching at the time, told a reporter, "We're handling Cincinnati easier than the Texas Rangers." When that comment was relayed to Reds manager Sparky Anderson, he snapped, "Before the Series is over, we'll thank Vida Blue. I've always heard that when you've got an athlete down, let him sleep. Don't wake him up."

It didn't matter immediately whether the Reds were awake or sleeping because the Series was delayed a day in Oakland by a freak storm, with a cloud that hung over the Coliseum and dumped substantial rain while areas all around were cloudless and dry. When the Series did resume, the next game was just as strange. The Reds won, 1–0, to get back into the Series; but after the game, everybody was talking about how Bench had fallen for an A's ruse.

In the eighth inning, with Bobby Tolan on second and one out, Fingers went to a 3–2 count on Bench. Williams rushed to the mound to talk to Fingers, and as he walked back to the dugout, he pointed to first as if he wanted the pitcher to throw a fourth ball in order to intentionally walk Bench. But with Bench relaxed at the plate, Fingers threw a low slider on the outside corner for strike three. Said Fingers:

> We had never practiced that. Hell, I had never even thought of it. Maybe I might have done it in Little League, but that was the last time. I couldn't figure what Dick Williams was doing when he came out to the mound, but I said OK. If I had been out there with a bucket of balls just throwing pitches without a batter, I couldn't have thrown a better pitch than that. Bench has always said that was the most embarrassing thing that ever happened to him, so I don't mention it when I see him.

The A's came back to win the fourth game, 3–2, to take a 3–1 lead in the Series. Once again, Tenace was the hero, first hitting his third home run in the fifth and then taking part in the A's comeback rally in the bottom of the ninth. Williams punched all the right buttons in the ninth too, using three pinch-hitters. The first, Gonzalo Marquez, singled with one out to start the rally. The third, Mangual, knocked in Tenace with the winning run.

Special circumstances played a role in Mangual's hit. With only one out and runners on first and third, the Reds infield was playing in to try to keep Tenace from scoring on an infield grounder; but Mangual's grounder, which would probably have been a double-play ball if the Reds were playing in normal position, squirted just to the left of second baseman Morgan.

After coming into the Series as huge underdogs, the A's were suddenly in a position to wrap it up at home the next day. When Tenace hit a three-run homer in the second, it seemed that might happen. Tenace's home run was his fourth of the Series, a feat previously accomplished only by Babe Ruth, Lou Gehrig, Duke Snider, and Hank Bauer.

With Hunter—the A's ace—and a 3–1 lead, the A's seemed to be in control. But Catfish didn't have much that day. With two outs in the fifth, Williams brought in Fingers, who struck out Bench to end a Cincinnati rally that had closed the gap to 4–3. Unfortunately, on that day even Fingers was mortal. Pitching in his fifth straight game, he went 3⅔ innings, which was too much for his already tired arm. He yielded the tying run in the eighth and the winning run in the ninth for a 5–4 Reds win. The Series was going back to Cincinnati.

Before the sixth game, a woman standing in line outside the stadium in Cincinnati heard a man say, "If Tenace hits another homer, he won't walk out of this ballpark." The woman told the police, and the man, who had a loaded gun, was arrested. (Ten years later, Tenace got a letter from the man, who apologized and said he was glad the police had caught him.)

Tenace, who admitted he had been frightened by the threat, didn't hit any home runs in that game, and neither did any of his teammates. The A's went down meekly, 8–1, in a game that tied the Series and confirmed the Reds fans' belief that the first five games had been just a bad dream. The loss didn't bother the A's, who kidded Tenace about his "death threat" after the game. "If you got to go, Gino," said Jackson, "at least it will be on national television."

The A's had lost the battle but they were prepared to win the war in the seventh game because of a decision Williams had made about his pitching, one that was virtually forced on him. Because the third game had been delayed by rain, the teams had played on Friday, which was supposed to be a travel day. Saturday was a prime day for television, so the travel day was eliminated. The A's pitching staff was exhausted. Williams decided to start Blue in game six and rest his top starters—Odom, Hunter, and Holtzman—as well as Fingers, his ace reliever. He would use all four in the final game. For the seventh game, Williams made a defensive change, putting Duncan behind the plate. "I had to go for defense," he said. "The Reds were running wild on the bases. Tenace couldn't throw anybody out." He kept Tenace in the lineup, though, at first base; he also moved Tenace from seventh to fourth in the batting order, a move that quickly paid off. Tenace ripped a ground ball past Reds third baseman Menke in the first inning to knock in Mangual with the first run of the game. Duncan threw out Morgan, who was trying to steal second, in the fourth. "The Reds didn't try to run after that," noted Williams.

Odom started for the A's, but Williams quickly went to Hunter at the first sign of trouble in the fifth, bringing in Catfish with one out, two men on, and a 2–1 count on Dave Concepcion. Hunter completed the walk and then gave up a deep sacrifice fly by pinch-hitter McRae, which scored Perez with the run that tied the score at 1–1.

In the sixth, Campaneris singled and was sacrificed to second by Mangual. It would have been prudent to pitch around the red-hot Tenace, but Reds reliever Pedro Borbon challenged him with a fastball. Tenace laced it into the left-field corner for a double, scoring Campaneris. Williams lifted Tenace for a pinch-runner, Lewis, who also scored on a double by Sal Bando.

Before the game, Williams had said he wouldn't hesitate to use all his best pitchers. "They can rest in the off-season," he said. So when Rose led off the eighth with a single, Williams brought in the left-handed Holtzman to face Morgan, a left-handed hitter. That strategy failed—Morgan laced a line drive down the first-base line— but when first baseman Hegan dived for the ball, Rose had to jump over him and was delayed in running. That delay forced third-base coach Alex Grammas to hold Rose at third.

Now Williams brought in Fingers, who got pinch-hitter Joe Hague on an infield fly. Williams ordered Bench intentionally walked, and this time he wasn't kidding. There would be no attempts to slip a third strike past the Reds' catcher. Bench represented the winning run, and Williams didn't want to give him a chance to win the game with one swing; Bench had hit 40 homers in the regular season. The strategy worked. Perez hit a sacrifice fly to score Rose but Fingers then got Menke on a fly ball to left, and the A's still had a 3–2 lead going into the ninth.

Those of us who watched A's baseball in those days called the ninth inning "Hold 'em, Rollie" time. And hold them he did. There was only one anxious moment when, with two outs, he hit pinch-hitter Darrel Chaney. Williams came to the mound, wondering whether Fingers was tiring and thinking he might bring in Blue to face Rose. But Duncan told him Fingers was still sharp, so he left Rollie in, and Rose hit his first pitch to left field where it was caught by Joe Rudi.

Improbable as it seemed, the A's were World Champions. Even more improbably, Tenace had tied a Series record with his four home runs, had hit .348, and led all the hitters with nine RBIs and a remarkable .913 slugging average.

For the A's as a team, it was only the beginning.

Chapter 5

Changes—and Another Title

Even though they were coming off a championship, the A's were embroiled in a controversy the next spring. Charlie Finley wouldn't have it any other way. This one involved the trading of first baseman Mike Epstein—who had led the A's in homers with 26 in their first World Series season—to the Texas Rangers for reliever Horacio Piña.

Though Piña would pitch in 47 games for the A's that season (his only one in an Oakland uniform), this was clearly a matter of addition by subtraction. Both Finley and his manager, Dick Williams, wanted to get rid of Epstein, who had had verbal battles with both of them. Epstein wanted to play every day and every inning, though he didn't hit well against left-handers and was such a defensive liability that Williams often benched him in late innings to bring in Mike Hegan.

But Finley insisted that the real reason the trade was made was so Gene Tenace could be moved to first base—because he had injured his shoulder during the World Series and couldn't throw. Finley "forgot" to brief anyone else about this injury. Tenace insisted there was nothing wrong with his shoulder, and when *San Francisco Examiner* beat writer Glenn Schwarz talked to the team's orthopedist, Dr. Harry Walker, the doctor said he knew nothing of a shoulder injury. Tenace did have bursitis in his elbow, but it didn't affect his throwing.

There was no question that Dave Duncan was a better defensive catcher than Tenace, which is why Williams had played him in the seventh game of the 1972 Series against Cincinnati. And Tenace had proved that he could be a potent hitter, so it made sense to move him to first to keep both his bat and Duncan's glove in the lineup. There was no need for Finley to pretend that Tenace was injured. Finley just never went from point A to point B without first going to C, D, E—or maybe even Z.

The situation became more complicated when Duncan refused to sign a new contract, hinted that he might not play on Opening Day without one, and criticized Williams, saying the manager had been closer to the players before he got a new contract, which Duncan did not regard as coincidental. Suddenly, Finley announced that Tenace's shoulder had healed, and he was moved back to catcher, with Joe Rudi coming in from left field to play first base. But that was clearly nothing more than a stopgap gesture; Duncan and George Hendrick were soon traded to Cleveland for catcher Ray Fosse. "I feel like I've been released from prison," said Duncan. Hendrick later became a star outfielder for the Indians. Fosse pokes fun at himself now by saying, "Some people call that one of the worst trades of all time."

At one time Fosse had looked like a sure shot for stardom; he was a young catcher who was excellent defensively and a strong hitter, too. But in the twelfth inning of the 1970 All-Star Game, Pete Rose slammed into him so hard while scoring the winning run for the National League that Fosse's shoulder was severely injured—much more seriously, it turned out, than was originally thought. However, because it was his left shoulder, the injury did not affect Fosse's ability to catch and throw. So he continued playing through August, until the increasing pain finally caused him to quit for the season. Fosse was tough, obviously, and the times were different. "There was always talk of players 'jaking,' faking an injury so they didn't have to play," he said 30 years later. "I didn't want to be accused of that."

The available medical equipment wasn't as sophisticated then either. It wasn't until the next April that the swelling had subsided enough for X rays to show that Fosse's shoulder had been both separated and broken. The break had healed by the time of the 1971 X ray, but Fosse's hitting was permanently affected. Said Fosse:

> Every hitter likes to get in a groove. I didn't have any strength in my left shoulder after that collision, so I changed my swing and developed some bad habits. I never really did get my good swing back. If I'd injured my right shoulder, I wouldn't have been able to throw, so I'd have had to sit down. Maybe then I'd have healed the way I should have, but I was still able to play another nine years, so I can't complain.

Fosse was shocked and disappointed by the trade to Oakland; he and his wife had just bought a home in Cleveland, and he had hoped to play his entire career for the Indians. However, after making the short drive north from Cleveland's spring base in Tucson to Mesa, where the A's trained, it didn't take him long to become emotionally attached to his new club. He soon bought a home in the San Francisco Bay Area and, after his retirement, became a broadcaster for the A's. Remembered Fosse:

> That was really a close-knit club. I'm not denying that we had our share of fights. We even had one just before the start of the World Series in '74. But I always thought the image of the "Fighting A's" was blown out of proportion. We were together all the time it seemed, and guys would get on each other more than they do today. So, there would be blowups, but you have that on any team, whether or not it gets reported. Every clubhouse has a lot of big egos, because these guys have been stars most of their lives. But generally, we got along very well, and we certainly played well together.

One of the pitchers who threw to Fosse, Ken Holtzman, had an interesting opinion on the A's chemistry. "Finley kept us all hungry and at each other's throats—and at his, too," said Holtzman. "That gave us the edge we needed to win."

Fosse quickly learned that the A's attitude was different in other ways from what he had been used to in Cleveland. "I thought the players were pretty lackadaisical," he said. "They didn't seem very intense to me. They were so relaxed, I thought, 'How are they getting ready for the season?'" Standing at the batting cage that day with Dick Green, Fosse voiced his concerns. Green just looked at him for a moment and then said, "We know we're going to win the Western Division, and then the American League pennant, and then the World Series. That's just the way it is." As Fosse recalled:

> That's the kind of confidence that team had. They didn't try to overwhelm anybody. It seemed we won most of our games by one run. There were no blowouts. Nobody was interested in that. We just wanted to win, and a one-run win counted just as much as if we'd won by ten runs.

It wasn't just the players who counted on winning the World Series. When Fosse went to negotiate a contract with Finley, he heard the same argument. Finley's figure, which was the one that prevailed, wasn't as high as Fosse's. But the A's owner told him, "You'll make it up with your World Series share." When Fosse asked if Finley could guarantee the World Series, Charlie said, "You'll see."

The Fosse-for-Duncan trade was pretty much a wash. Both were excellent defensive catchers. Fosse had a slightly stronger arm, Duncan had more power. Neither catcher hit for average.

Another trade—right-handed reliever Bob Locker for young outfielder Billy North—would prove to have much more immediate impact on the team. That trade showed both Finley's tenacity and his understanding of the game. He had been trying to get North for two years before he succeeded; his ultimate success was due only to a chance remark by North that resulted in a total falling out with Chicago Cubs manager Leo Durocher.

North had hit more than .400 for the Cubs during the spring of 1972 and was scheduled to be the starting right fielder. Then the Cubs played a game in New Orleans on a diamond placed within the football field at Tulane University. The field had a track with a concrete wall around it, and as the Cubs came out of the dressing room, several players reacted in dismay as they saw the field. North was one of them, and his comments were relayed to Durocher by a coach, Hank Aguirre.

"Durocher was told I'd said I wouldn't play that night, which wasn't true," said North. "After that, I was on the bench." North was even sent down to the minors for about three weeks—when he first said he wouldn't go, he was told he'd be suspended if he didn't—and got little chance to play until Durocher was fired late in the season. He wound up hitting just .181.

But the A's had had ample opportunity to see North because the Cubs and the A's both trained in the Phoenix area (the Cubs trained in Scottsdale). Both Finley and Williams liked what they saw. If the Cubs didn't realize North's potential, that was their loss and the A's gain.

Clearly, the A's needed help in center field. With Rick Monday gone, Reggie Jackson had played there for most of the 1972 season, but after the injury that kept him out of the 1972 World Series, he didn't want to risk any further injury that might occur due to the demands of center field. So he was returned to right field.

Angel Mangual had replaced Jackson for the Series, but nobody close to the A's thought Mangual was the answer. He looked like Roberto Clemente but didn't play like him. He had only fair power—five homers in 91 games in 1972. He had hit only .246 and lacked the speed to cover much ground in center. Hendrick might have been able to do the job (as he did later in Cleveland), but of course he'd left in the trade for Fosse.

North was a perfect fit for the position. "He covers more ground than anybody we've got," said Jackson, presumably including himself in that assessment.

But because of the usual Finley maneuvering, it still took some time for North to be put where he belonged. "Right after he got me, Charlie had traded for Billy Conigliaro, who was supposed to be a big player," remembered North, "so he had to get his shot." Williams didn't want Conigliaro, but he played him, biding his time; he knew he couldn't immediately buck Finley on this one. The manager wanted North's bat and feet in the lineup that first week because Campy Campaneris, the A's leadoff hitter and best base stealer, was serving his one-week suspension for throwing his bat at Detroit pitcher Lerrin LaGrow during the American League Championship Series the previous fall. So Williams used North as the A's first designated hitter during that initial week of the season.

Conigliaro played reasonably well in center field until he injured a knee ligament sliding into second on April 21. He continued playing for two weeks but finally had to consent to surgery, which knocked him out for two months.

But there was still another obstacle for North. Williams called him aside and said, "I've got to give a shot to Mangual after what he did for us in the Series last fall." North didn't dispute that. "That's what a manager is supposed to do," he said, "reward the players who win for him." Inevitably, Mangual played his way out of the lineup, too; North remembers a Mangual overthrow to the cutoff man as the last straw for Williams. The A's manager called North into his office and told him, "You're my center fielder unless you fall flat on your face."

North was an excellent defensive center fielder; this was important because defense was always the first priority for Williams. As North remembered:

> We had great pitching and very good defense, and Dick Williams taught us how to play sound fundamental baseball. He was on us constantly not to make mental mistakes. "Don't throw to the wrong base. Don't run into an out. Keep your head in the game." We didn't have a great offensive team, but we had Reggie. He loved to hit with the spotlight on, which was fine with me. That made me a lot of money.

The comment about Jackson was a sarcastic one, but it highlighted an important fact: Reggie was unique among the A's in his desire for the spotlight. "He ached to be the leader on that team," said Catfish Hunter after he had left the A's. "We let him be the guy who talked to the press. We didn't take anything he said seriously."

Jackson loved to talk to the press. Ron Bergman, the *Oakland Tribune*'s beat writer, christened him the "MVQ"—Most Valuable Quote. Reggie was always willing to talk about anything, especially himself. Every conversation with Jackson, no matter how it started, quickly veered to the subject of Reggie. At the very end of his playing career, he was brought back to the A's, less for what he could contribute than as a mentor to teach Jose Canseco how to deal with fame. When asked about that, Jackson's first words were, "Jose is like me," and the conversation then went to the way Jackson had handled his own fame.

That personality soon caused a chasm to develop between Jackson and the rest of the A's. When he first came to the club, he and Sal Bando were close, largely because they'd been teammates at Arizona State. But by 1973, Jackson wasn't close to any of the A's. He has continued to go his own way in retirement. The players from those seventies teams often get together, but Reggie is never part of those gatherings.

Still, his personality helped the A's because he took pressure off other players, both in dealing with the press and on the field. Though his home-run production never approached that of his great year in 1969, his homers often came during clutch situations.

When Jackson wasn't homering, the A's often had to scratch out runs. North was important there because he was an excellent base runner. He stole 53 bases in his first season. Though he later led the league in 1974 and 1976 with 54 and 75 steals respectively, it is that first year he remembers most because he lost the stolen-base title by just one base:

> I was leading all the way until I got injured the last month. I'd read the papers and see Tommy Harper creeping up on me until he finally caught and passed me. That still burns me.

North was also part of the fighting A's, becoming involved in one of the more celebrated clubhouse brawls, in Detroit during midseason. He and Jackson had adjoining stalls in the clubhouse, and they'd been going back and forth verbally since the first game of the season, when Jackson got on North for failing to run out a ground ball. They were both dating the same girl, too, which was a further irritant. Who won the fight? "I played that night, and Reggie didn't," said North mischievously. Fosse broke up the fight and was injured himself in the process. "I learned my lesson," he said. "When Blue Moon and Rollie went at it later, I moved to the other side of the clubhouse."

$$\ominus \quad \ominus \quad \ominus$$

In the fall of 1972, the American League owners changed their rules to permit the use of a designated hitter. This was one of the changes Finley had campaigned for; but when it came, the A's were caught short with nobody to fill the role. North was just a stopgap for the first month, and even if he had not won the center-field position, he was not what the A's needed. Most American League clubs had decided that it made more sense to use a power hitter in the DH slot, and that was especially true for the A's. Since the trading of Epstein, their only consistent power hitter was Jackson. Sal Bando had hit as many as 31 homers in a season (1969), but his power was up and down; he had hit only 15 homers in 1972, though he would hit 29 in 1973.

To add to the irony, the A's had had Orlando Cepeda on their roster at the time the DH rule was adopted, and Cepeda would have been an ideal choice for them. But Finley had traded Cepeda to the Boston Red Sox. There were reasons for the trade: 90,000 of them. Cepeda's $90,000 salary was far too much for Finley's budget. At the time he was obtained, in a trade with the Atlanta Braves for Denny McLain, Cepeda was thought of as a candidate for the A's first-base job. But his bad knees prevented that. He had been an outstanding player for the San Francisco Giants early in his career and had won the National League's Most Valuable Player award in 1967 with the St. Louis Cardinals. But he was no longer a full-time player.

Nor was he happy to be with the A's. Perhaps because he had started his career across the bay, Cepeda didn't like the Oakland fans or the ballpark. But mostly, he didn't like Finley:

> He was a crazy man. We argued about everything. Money, of course. He said he didn't want to pay me because I couldn't play every day. My knees hurt so bad. I was ready to quit baseball.

Finley traded Cepeda to the Boston Red Sox. He hit 20 homers for them, and was named as the outstanding designated hitter. He eventually made it to the Baseball Hall of Fame.

Without Cepeda, the A's still needed a power hitter. Said Williams: "Charlie always knew where the players were when we needed help." Finley traded minor league infielder Jack Bastable and cash to the Phillies for 34-year-old first baseman Deron Johnson. The Phillies were on a youth movement, but Bastable would never have a single at-bat in the major leagues. Meanwhile, Johnson hit 19 home runs in 131 games for the A's, 107 of them as the DH.

Meanwhile, Williams was still doing some juggling in the second-base slot to get better performance. On the road, he would sometimes start Gonzalo Marquez, a left-handed thrower, at second and bat him second in the order. But Marquez was never allowed to do more than bat; Dick Green would take his place as soon as the A's took the field in the bottom of the first. Often, Williams also substituted a pinch-hitter for the weak-hitting Green, who had only 332 at-bats during the year. But when Green came out of the lineup, he was replaced in the field by Ted Kubiak, who was excellent defensively. Williams would never again be caught with a misfit like Tenace at second base, as he had been in the previous year's American League Championship Series. Williams's juggling at second helped the A's to a solid offensive year; they led the American League in runs scored with 758, a significant jump from the 604 runs of the previous season.

They needed all those runs because of a sudden void in their starting pitching, which started with the decline of Blue Moon Odom, who would win only five games all season, and deepened with an injury to Hunter. At the All-Star break, Hunter was 15–3, which earned him a start in the All-Star Game. In the second inning, Billy Williams lined a ball to the right of the mound and Hunter stabbed at it instinctively. The ball caromed off his hand, but not before he had suffered a hairline fracture to his right thumb, which would keep him on the bench for a month.

Williams had to dip into his bullpen for starters. Fortunately for the A's, Vida Blue had regained his top form, winning 20 games that season, and Holtzman had his first 20-win season, actually finishing with 21. "I don't think I pitched any better that year than in '72 or '74," said Holtzman nearly 30 years later:

I had a couple of years with the Cubs when I probably pitched just as well, too. Pitching statistics can be deceptive because a lot depends on your run support and the defense behind you. I always thought it helped me pitching those cool nights at the Oakland Coliseum, too, as opposed to the hot days in Chicago that just drained me.

In 1973 pitching coach Wes Stock marveled at Holtzman's control:

I've never seen a pitcher who throws as fast as he does who has his control. He gets the ball exactly where he wants it time after time. You keep waiting for him to miss, but he almost never does.

Williams wanted Holtzman to use his curve more, but the strong-willed pitcher knew what worked for him. "My fastball is my best pitch," he said. "I have much better control with it than with the curve. If I get in a tight spot, 99 percent of the time I'm going to throw my fastball." In one game, he said, 91 of his 97 pitches had been fastballs. Looking back, Holtzman hasn't changed his mind:

I believed in throwing my fastball to the right spot. Keep it simple. I've always thought that the simpler the better. That's the way Catfish operated. He never tried to overpower hitters. He just changed speeds, moved the ball around. Hitters might feel comfortable, but they never got good wood on his pitch.

During Hunter's absence, the A's had virtually treaded water, leading by two when he went down and still leading by two when he returned. But everybody relaxed when Catfish returned, even though he did not get a decision in a 6–4 Oakland win over the

Milwaukee Brewers. Hunter would go on to have his best season statistically, 21–5.

With Hunter back in the rotation, the final result was a foregone conclusion. The A's clinched their third straight Western Division title with a 10–5 win over the Chicago White Sox, Blue's 20th victory, on September 23. The postseason beckoned again.

CHAPTER 6

Exit Dick Williams

The 1973 playoffs were vintage Oakland A's: great pitching, controversy swirling around owner Charlie Finley, a fight in the clubhouse, and, finally, a dramatic victory.

The team's win in the World Series the previous year hadn't convinced the skeptics about the A's; the Baltimore Orioles were 11–10 favorites in the American League Championship Series. There certainly were reasons to like the Orioles. Like the A's, they had great pitching—with Jim Palmer, Mike Cuellar, and Dave McNally—and they had the edge in postseason experience, having played in three World Series in the four previous years.

With Vida Blue, Catfish Hunter, and Ken Holtzman, the A's had three 20-game winners; but they had also lost center fielder Billy North because of a sprained ankle suffered near the end of the season. From his spot at the top of the batting order, North was often the catalyst for the A's offense. Of course, the absence of Reggie Jackson in the 1972 Series hadn't stopped them.

Because the A's had clinched with a week to go in the season, manager Dick Williams had all three of his 20-game winners ready to go. Hunter, who had been the staff's ace for five years, appeared to be the logical choice for the first game, but Williams went with Blue, who had the best record down the stretch of any of the starters. Palmer, in fact, thought that Blue might be pitching even better than he had in 1971, at least in the last part of that season. "He seemed tired in the '71 play-offs," said Palmer, who thought Blue looked fresh now. "He had pitched an awful lot of innings." But Blue didn't survive the first inning; the Orioles scored four times and then coasted to a 6–0 win behind Palmer, who struck out 12.

The A's bounced back with a 6–3 win over McNally in the second game. The A's hit four home runs off McNally, two by Sal Bando; he just missed a third when Baltimore left fielder Al Bumbry reached over the left-field fence to grab a drive. That game's events were significant beyond that day; though he didn't say it until later, Baltimore manager Earl Weaver had decided that that would be McNally's last start of the series.

The predictable Finley controversy came a couple of days later, with the series having switched to Oakland for what was scheduled as an afternoon game. Rain had started the day before and continued into Monday. After looking at a weather forecast that predicted still more rain, American League President Joe Cronin postponed the game for a day.

Finley cornered Cronin in the tunnel leading to the dressing room and started screaming at him. Cronin tried to tell him that that wasn't the place to "discuss" his decision, but Finley continued screaming as several members of the media, a few A's players, and Williams all watched, with emotions varying from amusement to embarrassment.

Finley was angry because the postponement would allow Palmer, who had won 22 games and led the league with an ERA of 2.40, to come back for the fourth game on three days rest, which was the norm for starters at that time. Cronin's decision stood, and the matter became academic when the rain continued well into the evening. If Cronin had waited to make his decision, it would have been the same.

The next day, Holtzman and Cuellar hooked up in a classic pitching duel. Going into the bottom of the eleventh, the two had given up only three hits each and had struck out 18 between them in a 1–1 game. Then, Campy Campaneris led off the bottom of the inning with a home run, which shocked the A's as much as it did the Orioles. Campaneris had hit 22 home runs in 1970, but that was an aberration. He never again reached double digits in a year, and he had hit only four home runs in 1973. His fifth was a lulu.

The next day, after knocking out Palmer in the second, the A's seemed to be on their way to clinching the ALCS as they took a 4–0 lead into the seventh behind Blue. But then Blue lost it, giving up four runs to tie the game and getting only one out before he was relieved by Rollie Fingers. In the next inning Fingers had one of his few failures, giving up the game-winning homer to Bobby Grich.

Almost 30 years later, Blue still could not explain what happened in that game, or in other postseason appearances; he won only one game out of six decisions in the postseason. "I was 0–3 in the World Series," he said, "but I've got three World Series rings, and I'm not giving them back."

That day, Blue was in the middle of a typical A's upheaval in the clubhouse. Fingers talked disgustedly of how the A's had the Orioles by the throat but let them get away. Blue Moon Odom thought he was putting the blame on Blue, Odom's friend, and he started yelling at Fingers. "If you don't give up the home run to Grich, we don't lose the game." Soon, Fingers and Odom were brawling, though other players quickly separated them.

The next day, Weaver surprised everybody by starting Doyle Alexander instead of McNally. Alexander had won 12 games that year, his third season. Asked about it, Weaver said, "I hadn't thought about it until I saw Bando's last shot sailing over the wall in the second game."

Weaver's decision probably made no difference because Catfish Hunter pitched superbly for the A's, scattering five hits, never allowing a Baltimore base runner to get as far as third base, and never allowing more than one base runner an inning. The A's won, 3–0. They were in the World Series once again.

The 1973 World Series would be an exciting one, as dramatic in its own way as the 1972 Series, again extending to the full seven games. But as so often happened in the Finley years, the action on the field was overshadowed by the off-field antics of the A's bombastic owner.

The rules of professional baseball specify that only players on a major league roster on August 31 are eligible for postseason play. Because Finley had sold reserve catcher Jose Morales to the Montreal Expos on September 18, the A's had only 24 players who qualified. The number was reduced to 23 when North sprained his ankle. His injury would keep him out of the World Series, and he quickly became a non-person to Finley. Said North, now a stockbroker in Seattle:

> I have a picture in my office of me sitting between Charlie Finley and Dick Williams as Finley told me I wouldn't even be able to sit on the bench for the Series. Teams do that all the time for injured players, and I'd had a pretty good season. I'd led the league in stolen bases and runs scored until I was hurt.

North would sit in the third deck at Shea Stadium for the third game, but no more. "I thought, 'I don't need this,' so I went home."

The A's had petitioned to add designated runner Allen Lewis and reserve infielder Manny Trillo to their roster for the ALCS games, and Baltimore had agreed, so the A's had a full 25-player team. The Mets, the National League champions, were not as agreeable as the Orioles had been. They OK'd the addition of Lewis to the roster (since nobody other than Finley ever thought he did the A's any good), but refused to allow Trillo to be added. The A's would play the Series with only 24 men.

Before the first game in Oakland, Finley ordered his public address announcer to tell the fans that the Mets had refused to allow Trillo to be added to the roster. The announcement was obviously intended to be a public embarrassment to the Mets, and commissioner Bowie Kuhn issued a statement reprimanding Finley.

The first game was a pitching duel between left-handers Holtzman and Jon Matlack, but it was Holtzman's hitting that was the big story. Designated hitters weren't used in any of the Series games, which seemed to be a disadvantage for the A's because their pitchers were not accustomed to batting. But in the third, Holtzman hit a two-out double down the left-field line. Then, when Mets second baseman Felix Millan allowed a Campaneris grounder to go through his legs, Holtzman scored. Campaneris stole second and scored on a single by Joe Rudi. That run was the difference in the eventual 2–1 A's win. Holtzman got another double in his next Series start. Many years later, he said:

That's what I remember most about the '73 Series. I don't really remember much about the pitching part of it. We hadn't hit that year, of course, but about two weeks before the playoffs, we started taking batting practice. And, of course, I had come from the National League, so it wasn't like this was the first time I had hit. We took pride in our hitting. Catfish was always a good hitter, and Vida was pretty good, and Blue Moon, too. I didn't hit for average, but I felt I could hit when it really counted, as I did.

The next game, which is still remembered while the other games from that Series have faded out of memory, came to be known as the Mike Andrews game. It started a classic Finley controversy.

It was a sloppy game, with the A's committing five of the six errors and the teams combining for a record 11 pitchers in a game that lasted a then-record four hours and 13 minutes. It was also a sad reminder of how far Willie Mays, usually considered the best baseball player of the second half of the 20th century, had slipped. Mays let two balls drop in front of him, balls he would have caught easily in his prime.

Mays partially atoned for his fielding lapses in the top of the twelfth. With Bud Harrelson at third and Tug McGraw at first, Rollie Fingers tried to throw a fastball past Mays; word was that Mays couldn't get around on fastballs any more. He barely did this time, but was able to bounce a ball just over Fingers's reach and into center field to score Harrelson with the go-ahead run.

After Cleon Jones singled to load the bases, Williams brought in left-hander Paul Lindblad to face John Milner. In the eighth, Williams put in pinch-hitter Andrews for the good-fielding, poor-hitting Ted Kubiak; Andrews remained in the game at second base. Andrews, in the final year of his eight-year major league career, had been injured during most of the season and had started only 15 games at second, being used mostly as a designated hitter. He was not prepared to play in the field, but he was there when Milner grounded to second for what should have been the third out. The ball went through Andrews's legs, and two runs scored. Jerry Grote then grounded a ball to Andrews's right; this time, he handled the grounder but threw wide of first base, allowing the Mets to score the fourth run of the inning. The A's finally got the third out, with Bando throwing out Don Hahn on a grounder to third base.

In his box along the third-base line, Finley called team physician Dr. Charles Hudson as the inning finally ended. When Andrews entered the dressing room, he was told to report to orthopedist Dr. Harry Walker, who had been summoned by Dr. Hudson after Finley's phone call. After the examination, Finley had a long talk with Andrews and then showed the press a statement from Dr. Walker that read: "Mike Andrews is unable to play his position because of a bicep groove tencosynotitis of the right shoulder. It is my opinion that he is disabled for the rest of the year." The doctor had signed the report and so had Andrews, under the words "I agree to the above."

Finley would later claim that Andrews had signed the statement in exchange for a guaranteed 1974 contract. Andrews told UPI that Finley "had threatened to destroy me in baseball" if he didn't sign the statement.

Andrews's version of events had much more credibility, because Finley's motive was obvious: he wanted to be able to put Trillo on the roster. Even though they should have been accustomed to Finley's bizarre behavior, Andrews's teammates were shocked when they learned of his "suspension" just before boarding their flight to New York for the third game of the Series. At practice the next day, at Bando's suggestion, they wore black patches with the number 17, Andrews's number, on their sleeves. Jackson hinted at stronger action, saying there might be a player boycott. Holtzman later recalled:

We had voted on the plane to boycott if Andrews wasn't rein-stated. And you know that bunch, they would have done it.

Remembered Joe Rudi:

> Finley was really being unfair to Andrews. He [Andrews] hadn't been playing and it's really hard to come in like that in such a pressure situation. The first ball, you could see that he really had trouble judging the bounce, which can happen when you're rusty.
>
> We were going to go to Finley and tell him that if he didn't reinstate Andrews, there'd be no more World Series. The good thing about that team, despite all the talk about the fights, was that we stuck together. We weren't going to let Finley get away with making Andrews the scapegoat.

Fortunately, the players didn't have to follow through on their threat. After meeting with Andrews, commissioner Kuhn reinstated him, ending Finley's attempt to activate Trillo. Kuhn told the media that baseball rules only allow for a substitution if a player is injured during the Series, and he saw no evidence that Andrews had suffered a new injury. Said Kuhn:

> I might add that the handling of this matter by the Oakland club [read: Finley] has had the unfortunate effect of unfairly embarrassing a player who has given many years of able service to professional baseball.

Finley accused Kuhn of making his statement to the media before even sending a copy to the A's owner:

> It is my ballclub, my money, and I don't appreciate anybody telling me how to spend my money to run my business. I don't think the commissioner treated us fairly in turning down our request. He's talking about embarrassing Andrews. We're not out to embarrass Andrews. But I sure as hell was embarrassed by what the commissioner did.

When the rhetoric finally died down, baseball once again took center stage. The third game was probably the best of the Series. Both teams started their aces—Hunter for the A's, Tom Seaver for the Mets—but neither was around for the finish in the twelfth inning.

The Mets earned two runs in the bottom of the first before Hunter settled down and pitched shutout ball; he left after the sixth inning. Seaver lasted eight innings and struck out 12, but he lost a 2–1 Mets lead in the eighth, primarily because of Campaneris, who singled, stole second, and scored on a single by Rudi. It was classic A's baseball.

Campaneris struck again in the eleventh with his third hit of the game, this one a single that drove in the winning run. Fingers closed down the Mets in the bottom of the inning to get the save.

The fourth game was an easy 6–1 Mets triumph, noteworthy primarily because Williams used Andrews as a pinch-hitter in the eighth. The New York fans showed their opinion about the controversy by giving Andrews a standing ovation. Williams had the satisfaction of embarrassing Finley, who had to stand with the crowd and weakly applaud.

In the fifth game, Jerry Koosman and McGraw combined to hold the A's to three hits in a 2–0 victory; the Mets now had a 3–2 lead in the series. As the teams went back to Oakland, New York writers were predicting that the Mets would wrap it up behind Seaver in the sixth game. Matlack, who was scheduled to pitch the seventh game, said he didn't think a seventh game would be necessary.

Mets manager Yogi Berra was later second-guessed for using Seaver on three days rest instead of saving him for the seventh game. After the sixth game, some A's hitters said that Seaver didn't seem to have the snap in his fastball that he'd had in the third game. But Seaver was accustomed to pitching on three days rest during the season, and the Mets had the momentum, with two straight wins. It made sense for Berra to go with his ace in hopes of closing out the Series in six games.

Meanwhile, Williams had no choice: with the A's one loss away from the end, he had to go with his ace, Catfish Hunter. This time, Hunter was sharper than Seaver, pitching scoreless ball for the first seven innings before yielding the Mets one run in the eighth. Jackson had run-scoring doubles in the first and third off Seaver, and scored the A's final run in the eighth in a 3–1 A's victory. Fingers got his second save.

The Mets still seemed to have the edge for the seventh game because Matlack had not yielded an earned run in 23 innings of post-season pitching. He extended his streak to 25 as he and Holtzman put up zeroes for the first two innings; but the A's ended Matlack's streak in the third. Holtzman started the rally with his second double of the Series and Campaneris followed with another uncharacteristic home run. Rudi singled and then Jackson hit the A's second homer of the inning, giving the A's a 4–0 lead. One step away from home plate, Jackson gathered himself and jumped on with both feet to lend an exclamation point to his home run. The rest of the game was a formality. The A's won, 5–2, for their second straight World Series triumph.

Their victory was quickly forgotten after the game, however, when Williams announced on national television that he was quitting as the A's manager. It was no surprise to his players; Williams had told them before the third game of the Series that he would be quitting.

Because of the timing, even his players assumed that the Andrews incident had led to Williams's decision; but in truth, his decision had been made earlier in the season. If there was one incident that precipitated it, it was probably one that involved Jackson. In September, Jackson had pulled a muscle and Williams wanted to use him as a designated hitter. Finley, probably trying to keep Jackson's statistics down for salary-negotiation purposes, instead ordered Williams to put Jackson on the bench. Williams had secretly been talking to the New York Yankees, who were about to make a managing change. "The Andrews case was the final straw," he said, "but I was ready to quit before then. I wanted to go to New York."

But Williams was still under contract, and Finley wouldn't release him unless the Yankees compensated the A's with either pitcher Scott McGregor or outfielder Otto Velez. New York wouldn't part with their best minor league talent, so the Yankees made their managerial change—from Ralph Houk to Bill Virdon—and Williams went home to Florida. Finley finally released Williams from his contract so he could take over the California Angels in midseason, but the Angels, who went 36–48 under Williams that year, were not the Yankees. "I guess Charlie won, after all," said Williams.

CHAPTER 7

Alvin Dark in Charge . . . Almost

The Oakland A's were once again in turmoil. Dick Williams insisted he was through with the team, while Charlie Finley insisted that he was going to hold Williams to his contract. But that was just a ploy; Finley just wanted to keep Williams twisting in the wind. Charlie had a manager in waiting: Alvin Dark.

Dark had a history with Finley, and he also owed him a debt: Finley had rescued him from baseball purgatory when he hired him as the Kansas City A's manager in 1966. Finley fired Dark the next year, but that was to be expected; Charlie never had any patience with his managers.

A great athlete in his youth—he was a tailback for Louisiana State University during his college career and went on to become a top shortstop with the Boston Braves and the New York Giants—Dark had a brilliant baseball mind. He first revealed this talent as manager of the San Francisco Giants, with whom he won a National League pennant in 1962.

He also had some less-admirable qualities, as he would later admit. Though he professed to be a devout Christian, Dark was having an extramarital affair with an airline stewardess; he later divorced his first wife and married the stewardess, to whom he was still married when this book when to print. Apparently that bothered Giants owner Horace Stoneham. But what damaged Dark's reputation almost beyond repair in baseball circles was a 1964 interview in which he seemed to be suggesting that black and Latino players weren't as smart as whites. He was labeled a racist and became a pariah when Stoneham fired him after that season. Despite his unquestioned managerial ability, he remained unemployed during the 1965 season because nobody would touch him. But Finley brought him back into baseball in 1966, and after he was fired in 1967, Cleveland hired him for four seasons. He was fired by the Indians during the 1971 season, and was unemployed when Finley called again.

Said Dark:

I always got along fine with Charlie. I know that wasn't the experience of some other people, but he was always honest with me, never tried to deceive me. I had been out of baseball for a couple of years and I wanted to get back in, so when he called me just before spring training that year and said he might want me to manage for him again, I said sure.

Dick Williams was still under contract. Charlie had told me that if Dick showed up for spring training, he'd have to honor his contract. So, I went to spring training not knowing whether I'd have a job. But when I got there, Dick wasn't there, so I was the manager.

I had to learn about the team. I knew they'd won two straight World Series, of course, so they were a good team, but I didn't know much about the players. When you take over a team, you have to find out who your fourth and fifth starters are going to be, for instance, and your long relievers. You have to know who's on your bench, who can pinch hit for you, that type of thing. You don't know that until you actually see the team.

While talking to Dark, Finley discussed reviving the idea of the designated runner (although the Allen Lewis experiment had run its course). Whatever his faults, Finley had done a good job of educating himself about baseball. Because he had built up the A's into a solid team, he knew that he could afford to fill the 25th spot on the roster with a specialist.

Dark had just seen Herb Washington win a 60-yard sprint in a televised indoor track meet, so he suggested that Washington might be a good choice. Finley started working on the deal immediately, and Washington was signed shortly after the A's opened spring training. In typical Finley fashion, he put out a news release saying he and Dark felt Washington would make a 10-game difference for the A's. That was news to Dark, though he thought then and now that the signing was a good idea, despite the fact that Washington totally lacked baseball instincts:

> When Washington got to camp he didn't know the first thing about base running or stealing a base. But we worked with him. I spent a lot of time myself with him because earlier in my career, with the Giants, I had worked with players on running the bases.

Dark said he had kept track of Washington's contributions at the time and remembered that he had won 7–8 games with his base running. Those of us who watched that team don't remember it that way, but there are no statistics to prove either argument. "You have to figure," said Dark, "that he was the 25th player on the roster. How many times does your 25th player win a game for you?"

The players had to learn as much about Dark as he had to learn about them. It was a learning experience for writers, too, because those of us who had worked with Dark when he managed the Giants couldn't believe the sea change in his personality. He was a fiery, intense man when he managed the Giants, often critical of his players, and curt with writers. He was totally different by the time he came to the A's: he had become soft-spoken, was never critical of players (at least in public), and was seemingly subservient to Finley.

The players didn't like it at first. After one memorable early-season loss in extra innings in which Dark made some questionable decisions, an angry Bando walked into the dressing room and threw his glove

77

against the wall, screaming, "He couldn't manage a meat market." The headline in the *Chronicle* the next day read, "BANDO SAYS DARK CAN'T MANAGE A MEAT MARKET." Dark defused the matter in a quiet meeting with Bando. (And the third baseman got a telegram from the meat packers union saying, "If you think managing a meat market is easy, you don't know what you're talking about."

At about the same time, Blue was saying, "Dark worships the wrong god: COF [Charles Oscar Finley]." Vida had been permanently embittered by his contract problems with Finley in 1972, and he distrusted Dark because of his reputation for racial bias when he had managed the Giants. The pitcher/manager relationship suffered further when Dark yanked Blue early in a couple of early-season starts.

Writers were bemused because Dark talked about his religion constantly; he once gave Ron Bergman a booklet entitled "Jews for Jesus." Some players were bothered by Dark's overt Christianity. Others were not. "It helped some of us who wanted to have somebody to talk to about religion," said Joe Rudi.

Dark compounded his early problems with both players and writers by sometimes answering questions about who would be in the starting lineup by saying, "I don't know. Charlie hasn't called yet." He was having a little fun with his reputation for being a yes-man for Finley, but that point was lost.

Said Billy North:

I thought it was just a tough situation for any manager, to take over for a manager who had just won two World Series. I think when a strong manager leaves, the spirit he put in the club stays for a year, like with Earl Weaver and Joe Altobelli in Baltimore. That's the way it was with us; we just carried on the next year.

The players felt that Dick Williams had stood up for them with Finley, whether he really did or not. They didn't think Dark would. But Finley could wear down any manager.

Probably the best example of the players' wariness of Dark came in a humorous incident in an early-season game, with Ken Holtzman on the mound and Ray Fosse behind the plate. Fosse had gotten tickets for his father- and mother-in-law, right behind the A's dugout. Just before settling into his position, he looked over to make sure his in-laws were in their seats. Remembered Fosse:

> When I turned back, Holtzman was shaking his head vigorously. What was that all about? I went out to the mound and Ken said, "He's not calling pitches for me." He had thought I was looking in the dugout for signs from Alvin. I had played for Alvin in Cleveland and he did call pitches then, but he never did it with the A's.

In time, the players accepted that Dark understood strategy as well as Williams had and that, despite his comments to reporters, Dark, not Finley, was making the playing decisions. "Some of the players didn't like Dick Williams because he could be sarcastic and a pain in the rear," said Joe Rudi, who had actually been managed by Dark back in Kansas City in 1967. "But with the veterans, Dick had reached a point where he left us alone as long as we were doing the job. When Alvin came in, he carried on the same way."

Writers never really did understand where Dark was coming from, but it was the players Dark needed, not the writers. Said Dark:

> My managing style was different than when I was with the Giants because I was a different person. I was always able to manage the game but I wasn't very good at managing myself my last couple of years with the Giants. I had turned myself over to the Lord before I came to Oakland. I know a lot of people out there didn't want to hear about that, but that's the truth. It was a lot different working for Charlie Finley. Usually, an owner doesn't talk directly to the manager. When I was with the Giants, Horace Stoneham had a lot of ideas, but he'd never come to me directly. I'd hear from somebody else that this was the way Horace wanted it. But there was never anybody in between with Charlie. When he had an idea, he came right to me with it.

We had a good relationship. We'd discuss what he wanted and what I wanted. I remember one time in '74, when Ray Fosse was coming back from an injury. He wasn't the same player he'd been before he got hurt but he was still our best defensive catcher. Charlie wanted Gene Tenace to catch. Well, I wanted Tenace in the lineup, but at first base. I told Charlie I wanted Fosse handling our pitchers. He argued with me for awhile, but then he said all right.

In mid-July, the turning point came for Dark and his players. As Bergman reported in *The Sporting News*, Dark was upset with pitchers who flipped the ball to him when he came to the mound to take them out. He called a meeting with his players and told them: "When I come out to the mound, I don't want to play catch out there. Just hand me the ball." For all players, he added, "I'm the manager of this ballclub. If you want to be the manager, phone Charlie and ask for the job. But don't be second-guessing me." That was a message his players wanted to hear: Alvin Dark was in charge. From then on, the manager and his players were on the same page.

Months before that, with arbitration, there was a foreshadowing of the enormous change coming to baseball that would break up the great champions in just three years: free agency. The arbitration process had been established primarily because Finley refused to pay his stars what other teams were paying theirs. In the winter of 1974, nine A's had gone to arbitration, more than the number for any other team.

The baseball arbitration system is unlike others because there is no compromise: the team submits one figure, the player another, and the arbitrator picks the number he thinks most reasonable. Reggie Jackson won his case, getting $135,000 instead of the $100,000 Finley proposed. Bando also won, getting $100,000; Finley had proposed $75,000. The A's now had three players (Catfish Hunter was the third) making at least $100,000.

Jackson had also signed an endorsement contract with Puma for $30,000 for three years. That angered Finley because he had a contract with Adidas that promised that all the A's would wear Adidas shoes.

Jackson refused to wear Adidas. Finley threatened to suspend him if he didn't. Reggie backed down. Same old A's.

Fortunately, it was the same old A's on the field too, playing through all the controversies, such as one in September when the A's beat the California Angels, now managed by Williams. Finley ordered the message board operator to put up "GOOD NIGHT, DICK." Dark and his players reacted angrily to this lack of class, but it was simply typical Finley.

By now, the A's knew exactly what it took to win. Different players stepped up in individual games or during the season. This was Hunter's best year, as he won 25; Holtzman had 19, Blue 17. The A's had their lowest win total of the championship years, 90, but the race was never in doubt. They won by five games over the Texas Rangers, clinching with a week to go. That enabled Dark to pull Holtzman from his last start, costing the left-hander his chance to win 20 games again, which angered him.

Winning the division was not enough for this team. Only another World Series would do.

⊖ ⊖ ⊖

To get to the Series, the A's would once again have to get past the Baltimore Orioles, the third time in four years that this matchup would decide the American League pennant.

Hunter naturally drew the starting assignment for the first game, but had one of his very rare off days, not lasting even five innings as the Orioles won, 6–3, behind Mike Cuellar, who was supported by home runs from Bobby Grich, Brooks Robinson, and Paul Blair.

But that was it for the Orioles; the A's pitchers gave up only one run in the next three games as the A's wrapped up the ALCS. First, it was a fresh Holtzman, pitching nine innings of five-hit ball in a 5–0 A's win. Then it was Blue, pitching by far the best game he ever had in the postseason, outdueling Jim Palmer, 1–0. Vida gave up only two hits and didn't walk a batter, striking out seven. Finally, Hunter got his revenge in the fourth game, pitching seven shutout innings in a 2–1 win. The A's got only one hit—a seventh-inning double by Jackson that

81

drove in the winning run—but that was all they needed. The Baltimore pitchers gave up 11 walks, 9 by the starter and loser, Cuellar, in just 4⅔ innings.

The ALCS also showed that Dark now had firm control of his team. His decision to rest Holtzman in the last week of the season was a good one; his top three starters were all rested for the playoffs. Early in the season, Dark had angered his starters with a quick hook; but he allowed Holtzman and Blue to pitch complete games in this series. Said Hunter, who had been openly critical of Dark early in the season:

> Everyone was against him, including me. But he proved him-self by winning. Believe me, it's tough to take over a champi-onship team and win again.

All this harmony was unsettling for the A's, who always seemed to play their best when they were battling among themselves. But any worries about complacency disappeared after a workout at Dodger Stadium before the first game of the Series.

When baseball players have personal problems, they know better than to expect sympathy. Instead, teammates will often make rough jokes. Rollie Fingers's marriage was coming apart, and he had heard plenty from his teammates. Finally, several weeks before the end of the season, he had had it. The next player to mention his problems was going to get his rear kicked.

John "Blue Moon" Odom was that next player. When the A's came into the clubhouse after practice, Odom came up to Fingers and made a remark. Fingers immediately punched him, sending Odom sprawl-ing. Odom retaliated by butting his head against Fingers's chest, knock-ing him against his stall. Fingers suffered a scalp cut that would later require five stitches. Odom sprained his ankle. The A's were ready.

The next day, the A's got off to a fast start with a second-inning home run by Jackson. Holtzman, the starter, couldn't get out of the fifth, but in the top of that inning he contributed with his bat, doubling and later scoring on a squeeze bunt by Campy Campaneris.

But the big story was that Hunter saved the game, coming on in relief of the tiring Fingers with two outs in the ninth to strike out Joe

Ferguson, a dangerous right-handed hitter. Hunter rarely pitched in relief—having done so only once in the previous five seasons and never in 1974, when he started 41 games—but Dark felt this was the ideal spot for Catfish because he wasn't scheduled to start until the third game. Once again, Dark was making all the right strategic moves.

The second game was noteworthy mainly because it effectively ended the Herb Washington experiment. Down 3–0 going into the ninth, the A's had rallied, starting when Bando was hit by a Don Sutton pitch. Jackson followed with a checked-swing double down the left-field line; Bando stopped at third because his run was meaningless and there was no sense in taking a chance on getting thrown out at home. Rudi singled sharply to center, scoring both runners and bringing the A's within one run.

This was the spot Washington had been brought in to fill. Dark put him in as a pinch-runner for Rudi, hoping Washington could steal second. But Mike Marshall, relieving Sutton, played with Washington. Three times he stepped off the rubber, working on Washington's nerves. He threw over to first, and Washington barely beat the throw. Washington had just taken his lead again when Marshall quickly turned and threw, this time nailing the pinch-runner. The Dodgers won, 3–2, to tie the Series.

Washington would return in 1975, but not for long; on May 5, the A's cut him. He only lasted that long because Finley was reluctant to admit a mistake. Washington's embarrassing gaffe in the national spotlight during the World Series had sealed his fate.

The Series returned to normal in the next game as Hunter started and won, with Fingers closing out the 3–2 win. Second baseman Dick Green played a vital role as he twice turned line drives into double plays, blunting potential Dodger rallies. The plays were typical of the underrated Green, who was a big part of the A's success despite his weak bat.

Despite their previous World Series wins, the A's were underdogs going into the championship; they still hadn't impressed the Dodgers, who were convinced they were better. First baseman Bill Buckner was the most vocal, claiming that Jackson, Bando, and Rudi were the only position players who could make the Dodgers. "If we played them 162 times, we'd win 100," Buckner told a reporter. The A's said nothing. As always, they did their talking on the field.

Holtzman continued his improbable hitting with a home run in the fourth game and also pitched into the eighth inning before turning the ball over to Fingers. Green ended the game with a spectacular diving stop of a drive up the middle by Von Joshua, starting a 4–6–3 double play. The A's won, 5–2, in what would be the only game in the Series not decided by one run.

Rudi broke a 2–2 tie by turning on a Marshall fastball and driving it into the left-field bleachers in the seventh inning of the fifth game. Then the loquacious Buckner became the goat of the game. Leading off the eighth, he lined a single to right center that was misplayed by North. Buckner went to second and then decided he could make third, but Jackson picked up the ball in right center and fired a perfect throw to Green, who relayed it to Bando at third to get Buckner. Fingers then got Steve Garvey and Joe Ferguson to fly out to end that potential threat, and he retired the Dodgers in order in the ninth.

Fingers had figured in all four of the A's wins, with one win and two saves, and was named the Series' Most Valuable Player by *Sport* magazine. Though Green had not gotten a hit in the Series, the New York Baseball Writers gave him the Babe Ruth Award, their MVP, because of his spectacular fielding.

Most importantly, the A's had won their third straight World Series. In baseball history, only the New York Yankees, with streaks of four and five straight world championships, had done better. Nobody else—including the storied teams of the St. Louis Cardinals, the New York Giants, and the Philadelphia Athletics—had done as well.

But this great success story was about to end because of a problem that had first surfaced a month before the A's third world championship.

CHAPTER 8

Free Agency Destroys the A's

In early September 1974, Catfish Hunter approached teammate Billy North in the clubhouse. "Because I had gone to college and liked to read, the other players thought I was smart," laughed North in recalling the incident.

Hunter told him that Charlie Finley had not made a payment he was supposed to make on Hunter's life insurance policy. "Is that in your contract?" asked North. Told that it was, North said it was simple: "He's breached your contract." Hunter then called his agent, Jerry Kapstein.

Baseball would never be the same again.

The two-year contract Hunter had signed before the 1974 season provided that $50,000 (half of the pitcher's salary) was to be paid by Finley to the Jefferson Standard Life Insurance Company. Finley had not made the payment so, in mid-September, Hunter's lawyer sent a letter to Finley demanding that he do so. The A's owner still did not pay.

At that time, the standard player's contract clearly gave players the right to terminate a contract if the owner: 1) failed to live up to a provision of it; and 2) did not remedy that failure within 10 days of getting a written complaint from the player or his representatives. On September 26, when those 10 days had elapsed, Marvin Miller, executive director of the Players Association, said that Hunter could declare himself a free agent. Hunter did not want to do anything until the season was over, and the A's season would not end until October 17, the date of the final World Series game. On October 4, Finley finally offered to make the $50,000 payment, but Hunter refused to accept the money.

The story finally broke on October 11 in the *Chicago Sun-Times*. The next day, the *Sun-Times* published an interview with American League President Lee MacPhail, who said that the fact that Finley had finally offered to make the payment and Hunter had refused it weakened Hunter's case. "I seriously doubt that Hunter will win his free agency," said MacPhail.

Dick Moss, an attorney for the Players Association, quoted from the standard players' contract in contradicting MacPhail's opinion. In fact, Moss had sent Finley a telegram on October 4 saying that Hunter's contract would elapse as soon as the A's season ended. That telegram had no doubt precipitated Finley's offer to Hunter that same day, but it was too late. Hunter would become a free agent.

It didn't happen immediately. First, the Players Association filed a grievance with the arbitration committee. Though this was a three-member group, one member was from the Players Association and always voted for its position, and another was from Major League Baseball and automatically took the owners' position. That meant that Peter Seitz, the only independent member, was always the decision maker.

On December 13, Seitz announced his decision: Hunter would become an unrestricted free agent. Finley would have to pay him the $50,000 he was owed, plus 6 percent interest, and the A's would not have the right to match offers to Hunter from other clubs. Of the 24 major league clubs, 22 would eventually make an offer to Hunter. Only the San Francisco Giants and the A's did not.

Finley made one more attempt to keep Hunter. Alvin Dark lived in South Carolina, relatively close to Hunter's home. Finley asked his manager to try to talk Hunter out of his decision. Maybe he felt that one Southerner could reason with another. Though he tried, that was asking too much of Dark. "Catfish told me he'd decided to go out on the free market, so I had to call Charlie and tell him we were going to lose him," said Dark.

Hunter had come to like Oakland and he was close to his team-mates, so he briefly considered coming back to the A's when he heard a rumor that the club was for sale. But Finley announced that he had no intention of selling, and Catfish was determined not to play for Finley again.

Because of the reserve clause in each contract, it had always been believed that players belonged to a team as long as that team wanted them. There was no free-market standard for players. When Hunter, who would be named the 1974 Cy Young Award winner for the American League, was free to negotiate, players quickly learned how valuable they could be on the free market. Eventually, Hunter signed with the New York Yankees for $3.75 million for five years. That contract now seems insignificant, compared to the 10-year, $252-million contract signed by Alex Rodriguez before the 2001 season; but at the time it was a bombshell. Salaries were much lower in those days. Hunter's had been $100,000, less than 14 percent of his average salary for the next five years.

The loss of Hunter forced Finley to do some frantic trading, bringing in veterans Dick Bosman, Sonny Siebert, and Stan Bahnsen to strengthen the pitching staff. But only Bosman, with 11 victories, was much of a factor. In fact, the Bahnsen trade actually cost the A's a top prospect, outfielder Chet Lemon, who went on to have a solid, 15-year major league career. Now the A's had to rely even more on Vida Blue (22 wins), Ken Holtzman (18 wins), and Rollie Fingers, who led the league with 75 appearances while winning 10 games and saving another 24.

Amazingly, the A's won 98 games, eight more than the season before and more than in any season since 1971. Said Dark:

> That was the hardest year, and I thought it was the best job of managing I'd done. When you lose a pitcher who had been

winning 20 games and pitching a lot of innings, you have to piecemeal it with other pitchers.

However, the A's weaknesses showed up in the American League Championship Series; the Boston Red Sox swept them in three games. Even the A's great pitchers failed them this time. Holtzman was knocked out during a five-run seventh as the Red Sox won the opener in Boston, 7–1. Blue was gone even sooner, in the fourth inning, as Boston won the second game, 6–3. In their championship years, the A's had always been three-deep in great starters, but there were only two left now; back in Oakland for the third game, Dark had no choice but to go back to Holtzman on just two days rest. The left-hander couldn't get out of the fifth inning as the Red Sox won, 5–3.

The championship run had ended, and it would be another 14 years before the A's won another.

To make things worse, another Finley controversy was right around the corner. Just before the playoffs, Dark spoke at his church, giving testimony. As Dark remembered:

I always ended by inviting youngsters to come up and accept Christ. I don't know why I used Charlie's name, but I said, 'If you don't accept Jesus Christ as your personal Savior, you'll go to Hell. Even Charlie Finley, with all that he's done, if he doesn't accept Jesus Christ, will go to Hell.'

Dark didn't realize it, but there was a reporter sitting in the congregation. The next day, the Hayward *Daily Review* headline read: "Dark: Finley Going to Hell."

"Charlie didn't call me then," said Dark, "but after the playoffs, he called me and said, 'I've decided not to renew your contract.' Technically, I wasn't fired, because I had fulfilled my contract. I told him I understood."

Years later, Dark and Finley were at a baseball banquet, and Finley told his former manager, "I shouldn't have let you go. You always did the best job of handling my pitchers." Dark assured him that if their positions had been reversed, he would have acted just as Finley had.

"I made a terrible mistake of judgment," said Dark years later. "I should never have said that. I said exactly what a lot of writers hoped I'd say. It made a great story."

$$\ominus \quad \ominus \quad \ominus$$

Finley had always bragged that he was making money in Oakland, even though attendance was consistently much lower than it should have been for those great teams. He did it by operating with a bare-bones business structure and holding player salaries down. But despite his efforts, salaries were moving up because of the arbitration process. To compensate, Finley was cutting corners elsewhere, mainly in his scouting staff. What had once been perhaps the best scouting staff in the majors had been sharply reduced. It was like cutting away the roots of a tree. Eventually, that would have brought the A's down even without the departure of Hunter.

The process would soon be accelerated. Between the 1975 and 1976 seasons, Seitz made an even more historic ruling than the one concerning Hunter when he decided that Andy Messersmith and Dave McNally were free agents. Seitz ruled that the reserve clause in players' contracts bound them to their teams for only one year beyond the contract. After that, they could become free agents. The two pitchers had lodged their grievance largely because of the principle involved; McNally, in fact, retired before the next season.

This decision totally changed the way major league baseball does business. Because the owners and the Players Association were negotiating a new basic operating agreement as the 1976 season began, nobody could be quite sure what would happen. It was certain, though, that Charlie Finley's method of operation would no longer work.

Finley certainly understood that, and he started to remake his club as a consequence. His first move was a bombshell: he traded Reggie Jackson and Holtzman to Baltimore for outfielder/first baseman Don Baylor and pitcher Mike Torrez. The exchange of Holtzman and Torrez was a wash—both were superb pitchers—but the loss of Jackson was a shocker. Baylor was a good player but he was not the dynamic leader or the pressure hitter that Jackson was, and he'd suffered a severe shoulder injury that hurt him defensively. But Jackson and Holtzman were both unsigned, while Torrez and minor league pitcher Paul Mitchell, included in the trade, were signed through the 1977 season. Finley was taking no chances on losing more players to free agency.

There was more to come. On June 15, the day of the trading deadline, Finley announced the sale of Fingers and Joe Rudi to the Boston Red Sox for $1 million each. Shortly after that, he announced the sale of Blue to the New York Yankees for even more: $1.5 million. The Yankees would not make the deal unless Blue signed a new contract, so Finley convinced Blue to agree to a new deal that day. Remembered Vida:

> He sweet-talked me. I should have known better, because that's the way Charlie was. When he wanted something from you, he couldn't have been nicer. He told me he wanted me to stay with the A's for the rest of my career. I went to lunch with friends, and as I was driving home, I heard on the radio that I'd been sold!

As it happened, the Red Sox were in Oakland for a series at the time; so, Rudi and Fingers switched uniforms, but they stayed on the Boston bench and didn't play that night. "Nobody really knew what was happening," remembered Rudi. "It had all been so unexpected."

Three days later, commissioner Bowie Kuhn declared the sales null and void. Brushing aside Finley's claim that he was going to use the money to build up his minor league system, Kuhn said:

> Shorn of much of its finest talent in exchange for cash, the Oakland club, which has been a divisional champion for the last five years, has little chance to compete effectively in its division.

Kuhn cited the authority he had in his contract with owners. In truth, there was considerable precedent for cash-starved owners selling star players. Connie Mack had done it twice when the A's were in Philadelphia, breaking up the 1910–1914 team, which won four pennants and three World Series in five years, and the 1929–1931 team, which won three straight pennants and two World Series. But in this case, Kuhn knew he wouldn't have to answer questions from other owners, who disliked Finley almost as much as Kuhn did. Finley filed a $10-million lawsuit against Kuhn, but his claim was denied in U.S. District Court in 1977 and his attempt to appeal failed when the U. S. Supreme Court refused to hear it the following year.

In the meantime, Finley refused to play the players he had tried to sell. The A's were temporarily stuck with a 22-player squad. "He told us, 'You don't belong to me,'" remembered Rudi. "We didn't know what was going on. We couldn't even practice with the team." Finally, the other players told manager Chuck Tanner that they'd boycott if Finley didn't allow Rudi, Fingers, and Blue back in uniform. Tanner called upstairs and told Finley, and the players were back in uniform for the rest of the season. Remembered Rudi:

Chuck Tanner was just unbelievably positive through all this, and he helped us keep our focus. But it was really hard, with all that was going on that year. I don't think I could have gotten through it if we hadn't been so close as a team.

Given the chaos, it's remarkable that the A's played as well as they did that season, ending up only 2½ games out of first place in the Western Division. They might even have won if they hadn't lost Rudi, Fingers, and Blue for 11 games during the confusion over which team owned them. But that was the last gasp. Rudi, Fingers, and Sal Bando left as free agents after the season, as did Baylor. Blue was traded to the Giants after one more season. North left early in the 1978 season, traded to the Dodgers.

The next year, the once-proud A's lost 108 games. Said North:

I was the last one to leave. I got what I wanted from Charlie in 1976, but the others left and made millions, so I wasn't as smart as I thought I was. But I played on a team in Chicago that had Ernie Banks, Ron Santo, Billy Williams, and Ferguson Jenkins, and none of them made it to the World Series. I've got those World Series rings, and nobody can take them away.

CHAPTER 9

A New Owner

Charlie Finley had to sell. He had known that since free agency was declared but had held on, thinking he could survive by keeping costs low. But the results were showing on the field and in the many empty seats at the Oakland Coliseum. During 1979, the A's lost 108 games (an Oakland record) and attendance was 306,763, another record low for Oakland. There were minor league teams with better attendance that year.

For the next year, 1980, Finley signed Billy Martin to manage. It was a masterstroke. For a short period of time, before his inevitable self-destruction, Martin was the best manager in baseball, and he proved it by going 83–79 with the A's during 1980, a whopping 29-game improvement. Attendance rose to 842,259.

But there was another complication surfacing for Finley: his wife had sued for divorce, and she wouldn't accept part of a baseball club in the settlement. Finley had to find a buyer. At first that didn't seem to be a problem: Denver oil man Marvin Davis was eager to buy a team that he could move to his home city. He and Finley quickly struck a deal. Unfortunately for Finley, the Coliseum Board had an ironclad contract committing Finley to keep the A's in Oakland through the 1987 season. The deal with Davis was off. Finley had looked for an out-of-area buyer because he thought he could get a better price for his franchise that way; everyone assumed the team would draw better in a city that was hungry for major league baseball, as Denver clearly was. But when his deal with Davis fell through, Finley had no choice: he had to look for buyers who would keep the club in Oakland.

A group of Oakland businessmen, headed up by Kaiser CEO Cornell Maier, was formed to make Finley an offer; Maier also contacted Walter A. Haas Jr., CEO of Levi Strauss in San Francisco. Remembered Haas' son Wally:

> My dad told them he'd have to think about it. My dad was a San Franciscan. He had always lived in San Francisco and, except for Cal [the University of California], all his interests were in San Francisco.

Walter Haas was also a good friend of Bob Lurie, who owned the Giants. The two belonged to the prestigious Lake Merced Country Club, which was started because Jews had been barred from membership in other San Francisco country clubs during the early part of the century. Haas and Lurie lived only a mile away from one another in the Pacific Heights neighborhood in San Francisco.

When Finley heard that Haas was part of the group, he decided he would deal only with Haas, rather than with the group. He didn't give a reason, but he didn't have to. One of Finley's favorite remarks was a derisive one, "big talk but no cattle," referring to men who had big plans but lacked the money to back up their words. He obviously felt that the Oakland group would not come up with the price he wanted. Haas, however, was a different matter.

Walter Haas was a wealthy man who came from a family with a long tradition of philanthropy. He had continued that tradition, giving liberally to his alma mater, the University of California (both the business school and the basketball arena are named after the Haas family because of the massive contributions they have made to the two enterprises), and to many organizations in San Francisco and the Bay Area. Only a few of his charitable contributions became public, as the Cal ones were, but every charity in the Bay Area had his name on its speed dial.

Haas was an astute businessman, but was also very personable and surprisingly humble for a man of his accomplishment. Broadcaster Lon Simmons often tells the story of a visit Haas once made to the A's dressing room during his tenure as owner. Picking up a baseball, he asked Simmons if the team would let him keep it. "Hell, Walter," said Simmons, "I think they'd let you take the whole box."

Haas was ambivalent about buying the A's. Keeping the team in Oakland was appealing, but he was also aware that it would damage his friendship with Lurie. The owner of the Giants was convinced that two major league clubs could not survive in the Bay Area, which was the smallest of the two-team markets; New York, Los Angeles, and Chicago were the only other markets with two baseball teams. Lurie hoped that Finley would make a deal to get out of his lease so the A's could be moved out of the area. Finally, after considering all the aspects of the possible deal, Haas told Finley he wasn't interested.

Time was running out for Oakland. The city's mayor, Lionel Wilson, was toying with the idea of buying out Finley's lease and using the money for a new contract with the Raiders, who were negotiating a move to Los Angeles. That would have required the approval of both the Oakland City Council and the Alameda County Board of Supervisors, but that wouldn't have been difficult. There was little support for the A's among the area politicians, who were consumed with worry that the Raiders would leave (as they eventually did).

At that point, Haas hadn't even mentioned his conversations with Finley to his family. When he told Wally and son-in-law Roy Eisenhardt about turning down the offer, they both reacted very strongly, asking, "How could you do that?" Said Wally:

I think he was surprised at how strong our reaction was. So, he said, "At this stage of my life, I don't want to have to take over any new projects, so if I buy the team, you'll have to run it." Roy and I had both decided, independently, that we were at a stage of our lives where we wanted to try something new, so we said we'd do it.

Finley was notorious for getting an offer and then shopping it around. Haas told him that he would negotiate only if he were the only one Finley talked to, and only if the negotiations were entirely secret. If he heard a whisper about the negotiations anywhere, that would be the end.

Wally was the point man on the negotiations, traveling to Chicago to get more information from Finley in person:

That was an eye-opener. We'd go to dinner, then go barhopping. The man was in his sixties, but he had incredible energy. I'd be woozy from drinking when I finally got to bed and then, an hour later, the phone would ring. It would be Charlie with another idea. The man was just bubbling over with ideas and energy.

Wally and Roy had promised Finley that, if the deal went through, they'd buy him dinner at a San Francisco restaurant the night before the public announcement. Walter Haas and Finley finally reached an agreement, and then Wally started sweating:

All of a sudden, I started thinking, "Where can we take him?" Finley was a very recognizable figure, and we didn't want people seeing us together and maybe putting two and two together.

So, we decided to take him to a private club where we were members. When we got there, nobody else was there but the maître d' and wait staff. I thought, "Oh, no, we've taken him to a terrible place. Nobody wants to come here." But he looked around and said, "You guys have bought out the restaurant. That shows me a lot of class." Then I worried through the meal that somebody else would come in, but nobody ever did. It was just a very slow night.

Once the deal was done, Wally and Eisenhardt had to decide on a division of responsibility. Said Wally, who shares his father's humble nature:

Reggie Jackson and Charlie Finley talk before a 1974 game. The two weren't always this friendly.

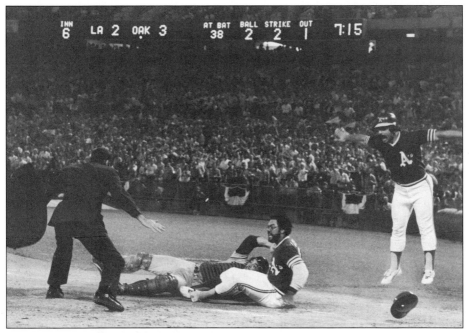

Reggie Jackson slides into home during one of the 1974 World Series games, knocking Dodger catcher Steve Yeager off his feet. Both the umpire and Sal Bando signal safe.

Gene Tenace, the surprise hero of the 1972 World Series, watching one of his long drives leave the bat.

Vida Blue, shown at the end of his follow-through, was the best pitcher in baseball in 1971 and an important part of the A's until he was traded in 1978.

Rollie Fingers, who became the best relief pitcher in baseball and a key to the A's success in the seventies, is shown releasing one of his pitches during a 1974 game.

Jim "Catfish" Hunter, the ace of the pitching staff for the championship run of the seventies, grimaces in concentration as he releases a pitch.

Ken Holtzman, the A's No. 2 pitcher during the championship run, reacts to a ball hit off his pitch, which was almost certainly a fastball.

Campy Campaneris, who was often the catalyst for the A's offense in the seventies, slides into third against the California Angels during a 1974 game.

A's manager Dick Williams loudly disputes a call with plate umpire Nestor Shylock during one of the 1973 World Series games.

Outfielder Joe Rudi, who worked very hard to convert from the infield, posing with his 1974 Gold Glove award.

Billy North, the A's top base stealer, is careful to keep his foot on third base after a steal, as the umpire and A's third-base coach Bobby Winkles watch.

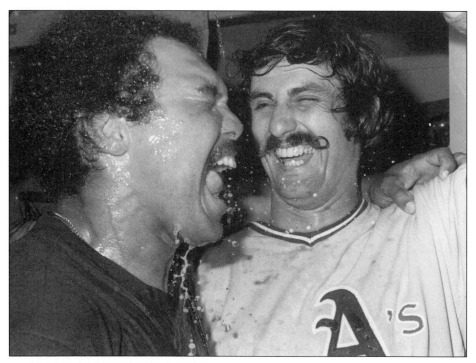

As champagne is poured over their heads, Reggie Jackson and Rollie Fingers gleefully celebrate the 1975 divisional title.

Roy was older and smarter than I was, so he became the president and ran the day-to-day operation. I became executive
vice president and in charge of the community outreach. That
was one of the main reasons Dad got involved in the first
place, to help the community by saving the team for Oakland, so it was a natural for me. Later, when Roy left, I
became the president and was in charge of the day-to-day
operation, which by that time was simpler because everything was in place.

Eisenhardt made one move almost immediately, hiring Bill King
and Simmons to be the A's broadcasters. Said Eisenhardt:

They were icons in the Bay Area. The only question in my mind
was whether they would be able to work together. As it happened, they got along famously.

I just thought they were a perfect match because of their
different styles. Lon was laid back, a natural storyteller. Bill
was, and is, so detail oriented. When a hitter knocks a drive
into the alley, he tells you where the ball is, where the fielders
are, where the runner is. You know everything about the play.

For Eisenhardt, it was also an exciting moment personally:

Other people wanted to meet the players. I wanted to meet the
announcers. That was such a thrill for me. I had listened to both
of them for so long. I was a huge Warriors fan, and there was
nothing like Bill King on pro basketball.

Eisenhardt also felt that radio broadcasts were a great selling tool for
the team:

Television wasn't as much of a factor then, but even now, radio
is probably still the most important. Your radio announcer is
really the club's representative. People talk of an announcer
being "The Voice of the A's," and it's really true.

That attitude was quite different from Finley's; Charlie had never paid much attention to the importance of radio broadcasts, another reason his team did so poorly at the gate. The A's even began one season without a radio contract; the first 10 games could be heard only on a student-run FM station broadcasting from the Berkeley campus of the University of California. The broadcaster was Larry Baer who, after working his way up the corporate ladder at CBS in New York, returned to the Bay Area as chief operating officer and limited partner of the San Francisco Giants.

The primary announcer for the A's under Finley had been Monte Moore, whose style didn't play well in the Bay Area. One year, Finley brought in Harry Caray, who was in between jobs in St. Louis and Chicago. Caray's style also fell flat in the Bay Area. Finley did employ one broadcaster who later became famous, Jon Miller, but he only did so because Miller was just 23 at the time and worked cheap.

King and Simmons were superstars in Bay Area broadcasting. King was best known for his Raiders and Warriors broadcasts, but he had a background of minor league announcing and had actually been on the Giants' first broadcasting team in 1958, with Russ Hodges and Simmons as the lead announcers. Simmons was dropped from the Giants' broadcasts when the station with which he was affiliated, KSFO, lost the rights to KNBR, but he was still fondly remembered by baseball fans in the area.

Hiring King and Simmons gave the A's credibility in the market and established immediately that the new owners knew what they were doing. As it happened, Simmons was between announcing jobs (though he was still doing daily sports reports for KSFO), because KCBS had won the 49ers broadcast rights away from KSFO and used its sports director, Don Klein, on game play-by-play. Having lost two play-by-play jobs through no fault of his own, Simmons was happy to get back into baseball broadcasting.

However King, who was already doing play-by-play for both the Warriors and the Raiders, had to be convinced—and he had to convince himself. "I wasn't sure, after all those years of being away from baseball, that I could still do it," he remembered. King met with Wally Haas and Roy Eisenhardt at a friend's house and talked for 4½ hours, covering a wide range of subjects away from baseball. Haas was only 31 and was a true sports fan. "Here I was, supposedly auditioning for the job, and Wally was bringing up specific broadcasts of mine," said King. "It was an ideal situation for me." He was, he said, "absolutely exhilarated at the idea of working for this new group." For the next three years, King broadcast games for three teams. Then in 1983 he dropped the Warriors, and later the Raiders, to concentrate on the A's.

$$\ominus \quad \ominus \quad \ominus$$

Walter Haas was true to his word. He left the operation entirely in the hands of Wally and Eisenhardt. Said Wally:

> Later on, he took more interest in it, but that first year, he was back in Minneapolis on business and, when he checked in at the hotel, the clerk made a reference to the A's playing there that week. He hadn't known.

There were some surprises ahead. Finley had eliminated almost the entire staff of the operation to save money. Said Wally:

> He had cut the scouting staff to the bone. There was nobody in the front office. When we came in that first day, there wasn't even a receptionist. Instead, there was a sign reading, "If you have a question, push the buzzer." It wasn't exactly a tough act to follow. Anything we did was going to look good.
>
> There probably hadn't been an operation like his in baseball for years. The switchboard was one of those old models where lines were plugged in. It literally blew up that season, just exploding, with smoke everywhere.

Under Finley, the ticket manager had left all the unsold tickets in drawers, 81 different ones for each individual game. Said Haas:

> For weeks before opening day that year, we had been told by what seemed like 17 different people that opening day was sold

out, but the week before the game, Roy and I were in the office and opened up that drawer. There were a stack of tickets left. We turned green.

The Haas/Eisenhardt team went to work immediately. Marketing director Andy Dolich was a very important early hire. Dolich had been running a soccer team for Sonny Werblin in Washington and at first turned the A's down because he had been given a chance to put together a group to buy the soccer team. When that failed, he called Eisenhardt back and asked him if the A's job was still open. It was. Dolich was and is an imaginative marketer, but he thinks, looking back, that he and the A's management team got more credit than they deserved:

Basically, you had a franchise that had been run at a minor league level for five to six years. After those championship years, Finley had shut everything down. People were hungry for something to happen, so anything we did looked good because of the comparison. And, with Walter Haas owning the team, in the Bay Area, we had the equivalent of the Good Housekeeping Seal of Approval.

Dolich immediately expanded the A's outreach:

Finley had sold tickets within about a 20-mile radius of the Coliseum. We aimed at a market that went from Sacramento in the north to Fresno in the south and to Novato in the west.

Meanwhile, because Finley had nearly eliminated the A's farm system, a new one had to be put into place. Eventually, that system would produce some great players, including the Bash Brothers—Mark McGwire and Jose Canseco.

In the meantime, Martin did an incredible job of managing that year. He put together a strong, four-man starting rotation made up by Rick Langford, Mike Norris, Steve McCatty, and Matt Keough, and backed them up with an offense sparked by Rickey Henderson, at the start of his brilliant career. Martin had turned Henderson loose the previous season, and he had stolen 100 bases.

The A's were a tremendously exciting team that year. With little real power, Martin decided to primarily use a running game. He used stolen bases, hit-and-run plays, and suicide squeezes. His trademark became the delayed steal of home. If the pitcher threw to first to hold the runner on with men on first and third, the runner on third would break for home. Martin had timed the play in practice so he knew that it would almost always work. Even a slow runner like Wayne Gross was able to pull it off.

It all added up to what Oakland sportswriter Ralph Wiley called, "Billy Ball." The A's won 17 of their first 18 games and were pictured on the cover of *Time* magazine; Dolich started marketing "Billy Ball" sweatshirts and jerseys immediately. They were at 37–23 when baseball came to a midseason halt because of a players' strike.

When the strike was settled, Commissioner Bowie Kuhn ruled that there would be split seasons, with a playoff between winners of the two halves, if necessary. The A's won the first half in the American League West and beat Kansas City, the second half winner, in a playoff. Though they lost to the New York Yankees in three straight in the American League Championship Series, everything was upbeat for the A's. In just two-thirds of a regular season, the A's had drawn 1,304,054 (200,000 more than the best attendance for a Finley World Series champion in a full season). Said Dolich:

> I've always regretted that strike because we would have set a record for the biggest attendance boost in one season in baseball history. We were on a pace to draw 2.2, 2.3 million, but we lost those prime summer dates.

If there was any doubt that the A's poor attendance was the result of Finley's business practices (and not a lack of interest from Oakland fans), that attendance showing dispelled it. Said Wally Haas:

> That first year was a magical time, even though the strike came in the middle of it. Everything seemed to go right. Billy Martin

did a fantastic job. When we got in the playoffs, my dad didn't even go to the road games. He thought, well, the team would be in the playoffs every year. I think we all did.

That first year masked a lot of problems. It took us years to build up our farm system, because we had to start almost from scratch, so we had to go through some lean years.

Dolich remembers those lean years, too:

When the farm system started producing and we started winning the championships, we got a lot of recognition for our organization, but everybody forgot that we went through some years where we were mediocre or downright bad. There were a lot of seasons where you heard things like, "The opening day pitcher will be Chris Codiroli [a very mediocre pitcher]."

The first bad season came the very next year, and the A's downfall started with the same man who had been responsible for their success the year before: Martin. It is impossible to describe Martin without using the term *self-destructive*. No amount of success was ever enough to erase the insecurity he had carried with him since childhood. Every time he came to a team, he went through the same cycle: initial success followed by tearing everything down.

Martin seemed to be in the perfect situation with the A's. His nominal boss, Eisenhardt, deferred to him on all baseball matters. Martin had total authority over personnel managers, and he was never second-guessed. He could have been the A's manager indefinitely. Said Eisenhardt:

In a sense, he educated me about baseball, because I'd pop into his office and ask him things like, "How does the second baseman know whether he should cover second or stay at his position on a hit-and-run?"

But that control was not enough for Martin. Nothing ever was. He started drinking even more heavily, and he flew into monumental rages. After one game, he destroyed his own office. Meanwhile, he was losing interest in the team, and the results were obvious on the field, where the A's fell to 68–94, 25 games out of first place in the division. The only reason to go to an A's game was to see Henderson run. Martin had given him a permanent green light, and Henderson stole a record 130 bases.

While this turmoil was taking place on the field and in the manager's office, the front office was also going through a learning curve. Eisenhardt was a brilliant man and a longtime devotee of sports. Everyone who talked with him was impressed by his intellect and imagination; in fact, *New Yorker* baseball writer Roger Angell wrote a piece in which he predicted Eisenhardt would one day be the baseball commissioner. But he had no practical experience in running a team. He devised a system that encouraged input from several sources, all the way from the minor league administrator to Martin. Said Eisenhardt:

> We got input from coaches, too, especially Clete Boyer, because Billy trusted him. When the strike came that first year, we sent all the coaches out to look at minor league players so they'd know about the players when they came up.

Originally, because they lacked practical baseball experience, Haas and Eisenhardt had planned to hire a general manager. "But it seemed all the good general managers already had jobs, and they didn't want to leave," said Eisenhardt. "We eventually decided to 'grow our own' with Sandy Alderson."

Alderson had first been hired by the A's to work on arbitration cases; he was working at a San Francisco law firm at the time. Said Eisenhardt:

> We were really impressed with his breadth of knowledge about the structure of baseball, so we decided it would be better to hire him to work in the organization as a lawyer/administrator. After our second season [1982], when we were still looking for a baseball man to be our general manager, I thought, would it be easier to teach finance to a baseball man

or baseball to Sandy? That seemed to be an easy choice, and Sandy certainly worked out well for us.

Eisenhardt and Alderson were very different people. In a capsule, Eisenhardt looked for the why, Alderson for the how. One-on-one interviews with Eisenhardt usually turned into thoroughly enjoyable philosophical discussions on everything from baseball to world politics. Alderson was much more specific. He identified a problem and sought a solution; philosophical considerations seldom entered into the equation. Perhaps because of his background with the marines, he could be a bulldog when it came to making a trade, a trait which would make possible the three-way trade that brought the A's starting pitcher Bob Welch before the 1988 season—a key move in putting together the championship team. Yet Alderson could also be flexible. He twice traded away superstars—Rickey Henderson and Mark McGwire—because it made no sense to keep them around. But when, in 1989, the team needed one more part to become great, he traded to get Henderson back.

After the 1982 season, Martin had to be fired. Said Eisenhardt:

I have nothing but good thoughts about Billy Martin because he really made a lot of things possible for us, and he really did an amazing job for us in '81, but things just went sour in '82. Tony Armas got hurt, a lot of our pitchers had arm problems. Billy lost interest, no question. He was used to winning, and we weren't winning. So, he went on to the Yankees, which is where he always wanted to go, anyway.

The A's struggled to find the right replacement. Steve Boros, a mild-mannered man who was a better teacher than a leader, was the first choice, but he lasted only 44 games into his second season. During his first season, an Oakland columnist wrote that Joe Morgan, then playing for the A's, was plotting with Eisenhardt to supplant Boros as manager. That idea occurred to the columnist when he learned that Eisenhardt was visiting Morgan at his home. In fact, they were only playing tennis, as they had before Morgan came to the A's and as they would for several years after. There was certainly no discussion about

Morgan becoming the A's manager. Morgan had no interest in managing, as he had said often. After he retired as a player, he went into a successful career in broadcasting.

Boros survived that nonsense but he sealed his fate during spring training of 1984 with a bizarre experiment that had Henderson batting third instead of leadoff. Though he said it was his idea, Boros had actually made the change because of a demand by Henderson's mother, who wanted him to get more RBIs. That episode cost him the respect of his players. Said Eisenhardt:

> In fairness to Boros, he was really important to us in the building-blocks stage. He was a very straightforward, very honest guy. He was a very good representative for us.

Unfortunately, it was too late to save Boros.

Meanwhile Henderson was traded after the 1984 season to the New York Yankees for major league pitcher Jay Howell, minor league pitching prospects Jose Rijo, Eric Plunk, and Tim Birtsas, and outfielder Stan Javier. It seemed to be a gutsy move by Alderson; actually, he had no choice. Henderson was an immensely talented player but he had lost interest when the A's started sliding. His play was often lackadaisical and he sometimes took himself out of the lineup due to minor ailments. Remembered Alderson:

> We had been to arbitration a couple of times with Rickey, winning one, losing one. He had been talking about wanting to go to another team. But mostly it was that we just felt our prospects for winning in the near future weren't good, so we were better off developing players than hanging on to one star. It basically came down to the Dodgers and the Yankees, and the Yankees offered more good players.

When teams are forced to trade a superstar, they seldom get good value because it's so difficult to evaluate minor league prospects. This trade turned out well, however, because the A's got players who could help them during their building era, and who would be valuable in later trades. Howell was an All-Star closer one year, and, of course, they eventually got Henderson back in time to win the World Championship in 1989.

Boros's replacement was Jackie Moore. "Jackie had been our third-base coach, and I thought he deserved a shot," said Eisenhardt. But Moore fared no better than Boros. The A's seemed to be mired in mediocrity, with consecutive seasons of 74–88, 77–85, and 77–85. When Moore's team went 29–44 in the first 73 games of the 1986 season, he was replaced by Tony La Russa. "That was the last piece of the puzzle," said Haas.

At the press conference announcing La Russa's appointment, one writer thought he had found a pattern: Eisenhardt was a lawyer, Alderson was a lawyer, and La Russa had a law degree, though he had never practiced. Had they hired La Russa because he was a lawyer? Remarking on La Russa's earlier success with the Chicago White Sox, Eisenhardt fired back, "How about the fact that he was American League Manager of the Year in '83? Is that a good enough reason?"

It was. By the 1988 season, La Russa would have the A's back in the World Series.

CHAPTER 10

La Russa Arrives

Tony La Russa had managed in the same division as the A's (with the Chicago White Sox), so he'd had a chance to evaluate his new team even before he came to Oakland:

> I thought there was a legitimate talent base to be competitive. They had traded for Carney Lansford and had made a couple of other moves that made sense. I think there were expectations that the club would be at least a winning team. That was the buzz around the league over the winter. But if the team gets off to a bad start, guys get discouraged, and they end up playing below their ability. My impression was that the A's were better than they were playing.

From a distance, La Russa had noticed some actions that he said were "not acceptable for professionals." The A's weren't hustling, they weren't paying attention to the "little things" that were so important, as he had learned from Dick Williams—not throwing to the right base, making base-running errors. Said La Russa:

> I pretty much said, hey, we're going to do the stuff that's easy to do, like run things out, try harder, don't miss signs, just

hustling. If you add that to decent talent, you've got something.

La Russa knew he had to find some veteran leaders quickly, because players can tune out what a manager is saying. "But if you've got senior leaders who buy into what you're saying," he said, "they'll reinforce it for you." He found three players who could help: Lansford, Dusty Baker, and Dave Kingman. The first two are no surprise: Lansford was always a player who gave everything he had to the game, as was Baker, who has since become a very successful manager with the San Francisco Giants, applying many of the lessons he learned from La Russa. But Kingman? He had a reputation in baseball as being a selfish player, interested only in how many home runs he could hit. La Russa saw an entirely different individual:

> Kingman was a very bright guy, blessed with really special talent, but he really didn't love the game of baseball. There were a lot of times the game wasn't fun for him, and it took away from his talent. I had a couple of friends who knew Dave and called him and said, "Hey, Tony's a good guy. Give him a break." So, whatever I said, Carney, Dusty, and Dave backed me up. We immediately started turning it around.

Much would go into putting together the team that would eventually win three straight American League championships. Looking back, La Russa says, "We caught our share of breaks." But La Russa and his pitching coach, Dave Duncan, were also quick to take advantage of those breaks.

The first example was Dave Stewart, whose once-promising career was in shambles: he had been 0–6 the year before. Ironically, La Russa and Duncan, when they were with the White Sox earlier in 1985, had passed on a chance to get Stewart, though they'd been advised by a Phillies scout to pick him up when he was released. Instead, he was picked up by Sandy Alderson, so he was already in an A's uniform when La Russa signed on, bringing Duncan with him.

The first game La Russa would manage for the A's was a nationally televised Monday night game against the Boston Red Sox. As he and Duncan scanned the list of possible starters, they realized they had no good choices. They decided to take a chance with Stewart. Said La Russa:

> We both remembered he had pitched well against us a couple of times when we were with the White Sox and he was in Texas. We thought we'd take a shot with him. We didn't have much to lose.

When La Russa asked Stewart if he could take the pressure of pitching in a game that would reach a big national audience, Stewart responded in what would be typical fashion: "Give me that ball." When La Russa added that, oh, by the way, you'll be pitching against Roger Clemens, Stewart only said, "That will make it even more fun." He started and beat Clemens, in what would become a familiar pattern in the years to come. Remembered Stewart:

> Roger and I had some great duels, and I usually won. Roger liked to throw at hitters but he never did in our games because he knew I'd throw at his hitters. So in a sense, I took away one of his weapons.

After that win, La Russa and Duncan decided to take a much longer look at Stewart—exactly what Stewart had hoped would happen:

> I had been with a couple of organizations that had given up on me. I hoped the A's would give me a chance to show what I could do, and they did. Dave Duncan sat down with me and talked about baseball, about what it took to win in the major leagues. That was a tremendous help to me, because he really helped me to focus.

Remembered Duncan:

At that time, Stew was strictly a power pitcher, fastball, hard curve. Well, when guys pitch like that, they don't have much margin of error. I asked him if he had another pitch, and he said he threw a fork ball but nobody wanted him to throw it in a game. I couldn't believe that because that was exactly the kind of offspeed pitch he needed.

So, I took him down to the bullpen and he threw it for me. I told him to go ahead and use it in the game. That made him a three-pitch pitcher and made all the difference to him. He didn't have to go out there and throw a 90-mile-an-hour fastball all the time and have perfect control. He had a little room for error. The rest is history.

There was more to it than that, of course. Stewart was a rare individual, an intelligent man—he has since been both an executive and a pitching coach—and extremely competitive. There are any number of talented players in the major leagues who don't want to be put in a position where what they do determines whether their team wins, whether it's a game or a championship. But, in baseball parlance, Stewart always wanted the ball:

Tony told me he wanted to have somebody he could count on to go out there every five days and give the team a good chance to win. I wanted to be that guy. I wanted to carry the team on my shoulders.

Stewart's one flaw while with the A's was his tendency to struggle at the start of games; however, he learned how to deal with that by minimizing the damage. He was willing to give up a run or even two during the first or second innings in exchange for outs that would prevent a "big inning." Once he got into the third inning, he was sailing.

Stewart was the supreme big game pitcher. He won at least 20 games four straight years, 1987–1990. He was 6–0 in American League Championship Series games for the A's. He won two games as the A's swept the San Francisco Giants in the 1989 Series. Remembered Stewart:

I changed my approach some in the postseason because I had to win that day. I couldn't think in terms of a season because if I lost the game, it might mean the end of the season for us. So, maybe my focus was just a little tighter than it was during the season. But one thing didn't change: I always wanted to win.

Already 30 when he had his first 20-win season, Stewart didn't have a long enough career to merit serious consideration for the Baseball Hall of Fame, but there are very few pitchers in the Hall you'd put ahead of him with a big game on the line.

He also had the help of a great pitching coach. La Russa, who took Duncan with him when he moved from the Chicago White Sox to the A's and then to the St. Louis Cardinals, describes him as a "complete" pitching coach:

> If a pitcher has trouble with his mechanics, Dave will straighten him out. If he has an attitude problem, lacking confidence, he can help him with that. Plus, he knows the hitters. He can tell a pitcher, "If you get the ball in this spot, you can get this guy out."

A second example of a lucky break for the A's, and one that was perhaps even more important, was Dennis Eckersley, whose career took a turn that nobody could have expected and that he at first didn't want. In so doing, he turned from an all too typical example of a player who had wasted his talents into a feel-good story about a player who turned his life around and is now headed for a first ballot election to the Hall of Fame.

Eckersley had been a starting pitcher, and a good one, since 1975, with a high-water mark season of 20–8 with the Boston Red Sox in 1978. He was a volatile, cocky individual who loved to strut around on the mound and pump his arm after striking out a hitter, which earned him the enmity of hitters throughout the league.

Early in his career, when he was pitching for Cleveland, Eckersley and fellow pitcher Pat Dobson had invented their own vocabulary: liquor was "oil," money was "iron," a big game was a "Bogart." He called fastballs "cheese," a word that is now in every baseball player's vocabulary. A curve ball was a "yakker," an inside pitch "kitchen," and "kudo" was a batter bailing out on an inside pitch.

Like a lot of players throughout baseball history, Eckersley was a heavy drinker. That was one of the reasons behind the failure of his first marriage. In 1980, he married again, to Nancy O'Neil, a model who had also earned a masters in economics at Boston College. He tried to stop drinking and would for a few months, but then he'd fall off the wagon again. It wasn't until January of 1987 that he finally admitted his problem and entered Edgehill Newport, a treatment center in Newport, Rhode Island.

The years of abuse had taken their toll and Eckersley had slipped into mediocrity. In 1986 he had been 6–11 with a 4.57 ERA for the Chicago Cubs. In 1987 he was traded with infielder Dan Rohn to the A's for outfielder Dave Wilder, infielder Brian Guinn, and pitcher Mark Leonette. The others in the trade did nothing much before or after, and nothing much was expected of Eckersley either.

Knowing nothing of Eckersley's personal history, Alderson had traded for him because the A's starting rotation was old and unreliable. La Russa and Duncan knew they couldn't get through the season without at least a couple of their starters breaking down—as it happened, every one had injury problems during the season—and they needed insurance. They didn't like what they saw when they first got Eckersley. Remembered Duncan:

> He was only throwing 83–84 miles an hour. He wasn't in shape to be a starter. At the time, we didn't know about his drinking and his rehab, but we knew he didn't look very good.

Years later, Eckersley remembered, "I was just burned out. I thought my career was over."

Knowing Eckersley couldn't start, the A's sent him to the bullpen. Said Duncan:

> He didn't like pitching relief. When we first started using him in relief, it was in mop-up roles when the game was lost, and

that was humiliating to him because he'd been a top starting pitcher. But in the end, that probably helped him. He was pissed off and he was angry, so he was going to show us. Every time we put him in, he looked good.

Eckersley's role improved with each good outing, and he was soon used as the setup man for Jay Howell. Because Howell had elbow problems and couldn't often pitch in consecutive games, Eckersley got his chance to collect saves. At the All-Star game in 1987, which was played in Oakland, Howell was booed by Oakland fans when he made an appearance. That stunned Howell, and he was increasingly ineffective as the season went on. By the end of the season, Howell and Eckersley each had 16 saves, and Eckersley was being used more often as the closer.

"But I still wanted to be a starter," remembered Eckersley. "I really felt at that point that it was giving up to go to the bullpen." After the season, he and La Russa sat down and talked. La Russa asked Eckersley what he would prefer, and Eck automatically answered: "Starting." Alderson then traded for starter Bob Welch, with Howell going to the Dodgers. Driving to his off-season home in Boston, Eckersley heard the news on the radio. When he got home, he got a call from La Russa. His manager barely had the chance to say hello when Eck said, "I know. I'm the closer." Looking back, Eckersley said:

> Even though I didn't want to do it, pitching in relief was really a good thing for me at that stage of my career. I'd always been aggressive, but if you're starting when you get older, you really have to pace yourself just to throw six, seven innings. In relief, I knew I was only going to go one or two innings, so I could just go after guys. I threw strikes, which you have to do, and I started really sinking my fastball. I had always thrown a sinker, but I worked to make it do even more. And my arm came back, that was the big thing.

There was another plus for Eckersley:

113

I was just a two-pitch pitcher, and I'd always had trouble with left-handed hitters. Especially at the end, when I was starting, teams were coming at me with almost all left-handed lineups. When I got to a right-handed hitter, I couldn't throw my breaking stuff because I was just used to throwing the backdoor stuff to left-handers. Pitching in relief gave me a chance to throw to right-handed hitters again, because they generally brought me in against right-handers.

In retrospect, Eckersley is still surprised by his success:

Being a closer is so much pressure. I don't know how guys do it for 10 years. You have to do the job every time you go out there. Then, sometimes the manager will be in trouble himself and if you have even one bad outing, he gives up on you. That was one advantage I had with Tony. I knew I didn't have to worry about him bailing on me. He'd always support me. That was a great feeling.

La Russa and Duncan had been talking for some time about the advantage of using a veteran starter as a closer because that kind of pitcher knows what it takes to close out a game. Eckersley had thrown as many as 17 complete games in a season during his career as a starter, so he knew how to deal with pressure situations. Said Eckersley:

A lot of guys today don't know what it takes to get that last out. There are guys who have like one complete game in two years. It was a lot easier adjustment for me than it would be for them.

At the same time, La Russa and Duncan were about to redefine the role of closer to get the maximum value from Eckersley. The role of relief pitchers had been changing with each decade, but it was still common for closers to pitch a couple of innings and to come in with men on base. La Russa changed Eckersley's role sharply. He would almost always bring Eckersley in at the start of an inning when the A's were ahead and only pitch him one inning. At the heart of La Russa's thinking was the fact that, by the time Eckersley became the full-time closer, the A's were in a position where each game counted: they had a good chance to win the pennant. Said La Russa:

> You can't win a game in the ninth if you give up the winning run in the eighth, so many managers would bring in their closers in the eighth. But we felt we had such a jewel in Dennis Eckersley that the fewer outs he had to get in an outing, the more available he would be for more outings. If you have a good team that's going to be ahead in a lot of games in a week, that's very important. If you have an average team, you might only have the lead in the eighth in a couple of games in a week, so you probably should use your closer to win those games, because you might not have another chance for three games. But we had a real good team, so we had four, five, six games a week we could win. Common sense told us we should be able to use Eck as much as possible.

Eckersley went on to have an incredible run with the A's, capped by the 1992 season, when he saved 51 games and won seven with a 1.91 earned run average, winning both the Cy Young and the Most Valuable Player awards. Though he figured in fewer decisions during 1990, 48 saves and four wins, he might have been even more dominant that year. In 73 innings, he gave up only 41 hits and four walks and posted a 0.61 earned run average.

The mere numbers, however, don't tell the whole story. Eckersley had simplified his style, using mostly a fastball that he could spot anywhere, pitching so quickly that hitters never got a chance to get comfortable in the batter's box. He came out of the bullpen throwing strikes, and a hitter who tried to take a couple of pitches found himself looking at an 0–2 count. Eckersley averaged more than a strikeout an inning during his five best years, and he punctuated each strikeout by punching the air. It was an almost automatic 1–2–3 and another A's win on the board. "It worked out great for us," said Duncan, "but once he got back into shape to pitch, he might have been able to be an effective starter again. You never know. He might have won 300 games." But he probably wouldn't have been as valuable to the A's as he was as the dominant closer.

$$\ominus \quad \ominus \quad \ominus$$

Given the way La Russa had set up his bullpen, it was vital that he get a setup man who was as reliable as Eckersley; it did no good to have Eck waiting to close out the game if the setup man gave up the tying or winning run in the eighth. Again, the A's had a combination of luck and design. On the advice of their scouts, the team had acquired Rick Honeycutt from the Los Angeles Dodgers for Tim Belcher in August 1987.

"We didn't know whether he'd start or relieve," remembered La Russa. What he did know was that Honeycutt could get tough left-handed hitters out; he remembered that, early in his career, Honeycutt had easily handled both Harold Baines and Don Mattingly. "If you've got a left-hander who can get left-handers out, that's a tremendous asset," he said. Honeycutt, like Eckersley, had once been a successful starter, but that time was behind him; he had gone 2–12 as a starter for the Dodgers that season. "It's good for veterans to go to relief," said La Russa. "They can use their experience, and they only have to throw 15–20 pitches."

Honeycutt could throw his breaking pitches on any count and to any spot, and he was effective against right-handers as well as left-handers. La Russa, in fact, would often bring him in against right-handed hitters when there was a dangerous baserunner on first, because Honeycutt had a great move to first:

Say Rickey Henderson's on first base. If you bring in a right-handed reliever, Rickey steals second and third. With Rick, he stays on first base and then Rick throws a sinker and you've got a double play.

When Eckersley was being rested, Honeycutt was used as a closer, and he saved 26 games in the three championship years, 1988–1990. But his chief value was as a setup man. "We knew he had the pitches," said La Russa. "What we found out was that he also had the guts of a burglar. That was part of what made him great."

With Stewart winning 20 in 1987, Honeycutt in place, and Eckersley working into the closer role, the A's made a good run, finishing four games behind the Twins in the American League West.

⊖ ⊖ ⊖

Jose Canseco had arrived in Oakland before La Russa, in September 1985. By the next spring, he was already a legend. Crowds were forming to watch him take batting practice as he sent pitches 500 feet into the Arizona desert or rocketing through the infield so fast that fielders had no time to react. He could run, he could throw, and he was movie star handsome. Just two years earlier, a movie had been made of Bernard Malamud's novel *The Natural*, and that was what everybody called Canseco that spring.

Baseball men tried to outdo themselves in superlatives. A's hitting instructor Bob Watson noted that, as a player, he had hit behind Jim Rice, Reggie Jackson, and Dale Murphy, but Canseco's bat speed was faster than any of them. When Canseco had played in Tacoma the year before, pitching coach Chuck Estrada had compared his power to that of Mickey Mantle and Frank Howard. The Tacoma manager, Keith Lieppman, said, "He's got the power of Jim Rice and the arm of Dwight Evans." A's second baseman Tony Phillips, who had played with Canseco in Tacoma, said, "One day it clouded up and he took a big swing and knocked the clouds back two days."

Canseco's reputation was such that I had been assigned to do a magazine article on him in the spring, though his total big league experience was 29 games and 96 at-bats. The article was entitled, "The Natural—Live!" and began with a paragraph from the Malamud novel.

Only 21, Canseco was not yet at ease with the media; so the A's hired Reggie Jackson to teach Canseco how to deal with all the attention, something at which Reggie himself was "The Natural." The two of them would sit on opposite sides of the dressing room, speaking in

Spanish to one another. Whether that worked or Jose simply worked it out on his own—probably the latter—Canseco eventually became very skilled at getting the media to carry his message.

That spring, the media attention was the only nettlesome factor for Canseco, who had everything else under control. His teammates masked their awe by kidding him about his muscles. Watching Canseco pull a T-shirt tight over his chest, outfielder Mike Davis commented, "You must have gotten a medium size. You've got to quit shopping in the boy's department."

None of this attention had been anticipated when Canseco was drafted in the 15th round by the A's. A third baseman in high school, he was inadequate defensively and was quickly moved to the outfield. He had three mediocre seasons in the minors, but everything changed in 1985. He had added more than 50 pounds of muscle—he was 228 in his rookie year in Oakland and as high as 245 later in his career—and the ball was jumping off his bat. He hit 25 home runs and knocked in 80 runs in just 58 games at Huntsville. Promoted to Triple-A Tacoma, he added another 11 homers in 60 games. He ended his year with Oakland and hit another 5 homers in 29 games, batting .302 in September.

Trying to hit every ball out of the park, Canseco struggled with his consistency in his first year, 1986, hitting just .240, but his 33 homers and 117 RBIs earned him Rookie of the Year honors. He improved his average to .257 his second year, with 31 homers and 113 RBIs, but the best was yet to come.

Meanwhile, he was joined during his second season by Mark McGwire, the second member of a duo that would become known as the "Bash Brothers." McGwire and Canseco were as different as hitters as they were as personalities. For all his flamboyance, Canseco was a good technician who could adjust his swing when he wanted to. He studied pitchers to see how they got him out, and he worked to correct his weaknesses. McGwire originally tried to simplify everything. "I thought there might be a ceiling on his talent because hitting is all about adjustment," said La Russa, "but he learned in time how to make those adjustments."

In 1987, La Russa hadn't even thought that McGwire would be on the major league roster, though he had a good baseball pedigree, having played on the great 1984 Olympic team that produced 13 players who eventually became major leaguers. During his two previous seasons, McGwire had had good power years but not great ones: 24 homers at Class A Modesto in 1985, 23 homers in 133 games split between Huntsville and Tacoma in 1986. The A's thought the left-handed hitting Rob Nelson would be their starting first baseman and that McGwire would start the season in Tacoma. However, in spring training, McGwire looked good enough to keep on the roster; so he came north with the A's, starting the season at third base, with Nelson on first. Said La Russa:

I thought I might use him some at first against left-handed pitchers, but he looked so good early that I knew we had to keep him in the lineup, and third base was not the right position for him.

McGwire was put at first base and he started hitting and hitting and hitting. An excellent golfer (he had played on the golf team one year in high school), he showed the same form on the diamond, going down for low fastballs, often on the first pitch in the count, and hitting towering drives over the fences. He started with 15 homers in May and ended his season with 49 home runs, setting both a major league rookie record and an Oakland A's record, surpassing Jackson's 47 in 1969.

McGwire had a chance to become the first rookie to hit 50, which was a much more important milestone than it is now, but he missed the A's last game of the season because he wanted to fly home to see the birth of his son Matthew. At the time, many baseball people thought that might be his only shot at 50, which only shows how chancy predictions can be.

The A's farm system, under the direction of Walt Jocketty, who later became the general manager for the St. Louis Cardinals, was churning out top players. McGwire was the second straight Rookie of the Year and shortstop Walt Weiss would make it three in a row the next season. The A's were on the brink.

CHAPTER 11

Records and the Road to the Pennant

The A's were developing stars, but they needed balance. Jose Canseco and Mark McGwire were providing spectacular right-handed power, but where was the left-handed power bat they needed?

General manager Sandy Alderson found him, trading young pitchers Jose Rijo and Tim Birtsas to the Cincinnati Reds for left-handed slugger Dave Parker on December 8, 1987. Parker was not the hitter he'd been in his prime, primarily because of a bad knee, but he was still dangerous enough to make opposing pitchers think twice about walking Canseco or McGwire. A day later, Alderson made a smaller but still significant move, signing free agent catcher Ron Hassey, a left-handed hitter who would split time with the right-handed hitting Terry Steinbach.

Significant improvements were being made in the starting rotation, too. During spring training before the 1987 season, Dave Stewart had shocked manager Tony La Russa and pitching coach Dave Duncan by saying he wanted to pitch 260 innings that year. When they told him that was a lot of innings, he explained that, if he pitched that much, he thought he could win 20 games. "I had won seven games in a row down the stretch," said Stewart years later, "and I thought I could do it." In fact, he accomplished both goals, pitching 261⅓ innings and winning 20 games.

But the A's still needed another big stud as a starter. Alderson had his eye on Bob Welch, who had been a solid right-handed starter for the Los Angeles Dodgers. Said Alderson years later:

> After the '87 season, I started talking to Fred Claire of the Dodgers about Welch. I remember calling him when I was down in the Dominican Republic, and later we talked while we jogged together during the winter meetings in Florida [a five-mile run]. We had Alfredo Griffin, who had some value but was tradeable because we felt Walt Weiss was ready, at least defensively, to play shortstop on the major league level. But the Dodgers felt Welch had great value, too, so we had to keep working to get enough in the deal to satisfy them.

Alderson got the New York Mets involved and brokered a deal on December 11 that brought Welch and another starter, Matt Young, to the A's. The A's gave up Griffin and their All-Star closer, Jay Howell. Welch was the key to the trade. Despite battling alcoholism early in his career, he was in double figures for wins during six seasons. Knowing that, Alderson had almost willed the trade to go through, keeping the general managers of the two other clubs at the bargaining table and making phone calls well past midnight to get it done. Significantly, in the December trades for Welch and Parker, he had used three of the four pitchers he got in the Rickey Henderson trade three years earlier. The trade produced an unexpected bonus for the A's because the loss of Howell moved Dennis Eckersley into the closer's role, and Eck would be much more effective than Howell had been.

There was one other significant off-season move, though nobody realized it at the time: on December 21, the A's signed outfielder Dave Henderson as a free agent. Henderson had bounced around baseball, starting with Seattle, going to Boston, and winding up the 1987 season in San Francisco. "He had the reputation of being a guy who liked a good time, who didn't want to work too hard," said La Russa, who nevertheless thought Henderson might be a player who could help if he changed his attitude. On La Russa's advice, Alderson signed the right-handed hitting outfielder.

When they talked the day of the signing, La Russa told Henderson:

> If you play the way you've been playing, you'll be a platoon center fielder at best—and you won't be playing much because we'll see mostly right-handers.

But, as he always did with players who were new to the club, La Russa judged Henderson by what he saw in the spring, not on what he had done with other teams.

Henderson responded to the challenge, convincing La Russa with his play in spring training that he should be an everyday player. He played a strong defensive center field and was a timely hitter with power. "He developed into a real leader," said La Russa. "He was as much the MVP as any player on the team."

Seeing the changes that were taking place, Stewart was as confident for his team as he'd been for himself:

> We had had a good run in 1987, but we'd had a bad series with the White Sox at the end that knocked us back. We knew in spring training that we were ready. It was no surprise to us.

Dennis Eckersley felt the same way:

> We had so much confidence that year, and it just flowed out to the mound to me. We were sure we would win.

Others weren't so sure. During spring training that year, many writers speculated on the problems La Russa would have in molding a collection of stars from other teams and budding stars from his own team into a cohesive unit. Former A's manager Dick Williams, now in charge in Seattle, said the A's would have power but no defense; he predicted that it would be "a circus" in Oakland. Even La Russa had his doubts:

> The year before, Minnesota had won the division but we were close. Sandy had made good trades, we had Terry Steinbach coming along at catcher, and Walt Weiss was a gem as a rookie at shortstop. Mark McGwire, Jose Canseco were there. Still, I didn't know. It was potentially a volatile mix. I couldn't tell for sure which way it was going to go.

On the first day of spring training, La Russa met with his team and emphasized professionalism:

> We've got to get to the workouts on time, we are going to put something into the practice to get ourselves ready. Before we leave spring training, we're going to meet and decide what kind of team we're going to be.
>
> Spring training is a long time. During this two months of practice, look around. The last thing you want to watch is how many balls go out of the park. Watch the line drives, watch the sacrifice flies, watch the base paths. Much later, we can try to impress each other with how cute we are, how funny we are, how much knowledge we have about the stock market or politics. Let the personal things develop slowly. Just go out there and practice your ass off and then go out there and play your ass off.

The A's listened, and they stood the American League on its ear. On April 23, they started what became a 14-game wining streak, an Oakland record, and they never looked back. Eventually, they would set another Oakland record with 104 wins, finishing 13 games ahead of Minnesota.

During one of the last series of the year, Dick Williams came up to La Russa and said, "I love to watch your team. They play the game the way it's supposed to be played." To La Russa, it was a tribute from the master.

Within the team framework, individual stars were coming out, and none was bigger than Jose Canseco. During 1988, Canseco made the most of his almost unlimited ability for the first, and sadly, last, time in his career. He finally was listening to those who told him he didn't have to knock all the air out of the park every time he swung. Studying the pitchers, looking for his pitch, and cutting down on his strike-outs—128 compared to 175 and 157 in his first two years—Canseco hit .307 while hitting what was then his personal high of 42 homers. Of those, 27 either tied the game or put the A's ahead. He led the league in home runs and RBIs and won the Most Valuable Player award unanimously, the first to do that since Reggie Jackson 15 years earlier.

Nobody had ever seen a hitter quite like Canseco, with his incredible bat speed. The ball often leapt off his bat so quickly that outfielders could take no more than a couple of steps before the ball zoomed over their heads into the stands. Some Canseco home runs were hit high into the atmosphere, but most were line drives that just kept climbing. During a midseason game in Anaheim, he hit one such liner for which the Angels shortstop jumped. As the ball went over his glove it kept climbing and climbing until it easily cleared the wall in left-center. "The shortstop could have hopped on that ball and taken a flight to New York," quipped Stewart after the game.

With the team well ahead in September, La Russa gave Canseco the green light on the bases and he ended the season with 40 steals, the first "40–40" man in history. Many in baseball discounted that mark. Mickey Mantle said, "If I'd known that was important, I'd have done it myself." In fact, Mantle could not have done it because his legs wouldn't have been able to take the pounding, but there were others who might have done it. Willie Mays, for one: Mays was an excellent base stealer early in his career, reaching 40 one year, before he was discouraged by his managers, who wanted him to stay healthy so he could hit home runs and make spectacular fielding plays.

In *The Elias Baseball Analyst*, statisticians compared the frequency of steals in the fifties and sixties to the eighties, when the stolen base again became an important offensive weapon, and concluded that

Mays and Mantle had both had seasons that were the equivalent of Canseco's. Canseco simply noted that he had the numbers and the others didn't.

Whatever anybody thought of Canseco's mark, there was no question that he had a combination of speed and power that was unmatched among his contemporaries. La Russa was also impressed by Canseco's fielding and his strong arm, which threw out 11 runners that season. In the spring, La Russa had said that he thought Canseco was capable of playing center field, the most demanding outfield position. Henderson's play eliminated that possibility, but Canseco was probably the best defensive right fielder in the league that season—incomprehensible as that may seem to those who only saw him during subsequent years, when his fielding became a bad joke.

Canseco led the league in another department: adoring female fans. Young women congregated in the right-field grandstands and bleachers at the Oakland Coliseum to get a closer look at their hero, who stretched for them and adjusted his uniform, which fit very well. His fiancée, Esther Haddad, was the reigning Miss Miami, and she insisted she wasn't worried about the female fans who were swooning over Jose—but she accompanied him on road trips, just to be sure.

Even during this glorious season, there were some signs of trouble on the horizon. Canseco bought a bright red Jaguar, and his penchant for speeding would eventually get him ticketed in four different states. In September, appearing on television, Washington columnist Thomas Boswell cited Canseco as an example of an athlete who had bulked up by taking steroids. Publicly, Canseco denied it and threatened a lawsuit, which never materialized, but he mainly laughed it off. When Fenway Park fans chanted "steroids, steroids," when he came to bat during the American League Championship Series, he stepped out of the batter's box, smiled, and flexed his muscles.

The season wasn't so cheerful for McGwire, who was trying to keep his marriage together. There were whispers in the A's clubhouse but the reticent McGwire didn't go public with the news until after the season. The breakup was shocking because, from the outside, it had appeared to be an idyllic marriage. Mark and Kathy had met at USC when she was a batgirl for the Trojan team for which McGwire had played, and they had just become parents the previous September. But the nomadic baseball life had destroyed the marriage.

McGwire had fallen off from the great numbers of his rookie year to 32 homers and 99 RBIs, but that was still a respectable performance. The assumption by those who didn't know about his personal problems was that pitchers were much more careful with him. After the breakup became official McGwire said:

Of course it was on my mind a lot, but I think I was professional enough to separate it from my playing. I think I had a pretty darned good year. Pitchers pitched me a lot tougher than they did the year before but I was still third in the league in home runs, eighth in RBIs, and second in game-winning RBIs.

"He is amazing, just a strong guy mentally," said La Russa.

The overwhelming image of the A's at that time was the Bash Brothers: Canseco and McGwire. At a time when weight lifting was still very controversial among baseball players and managers, many of whom thought it would make hitters muscle-bound, the two young A's stars were turning that theory on its head. They lifted weights constantly, going to gyms together on the road. At home games, after parking their cars behind the center-field bleachers, they'd stride in together to the A's dugout. It was an awesome sight.

But the A's pitching was at least as important to their success that year. Stewart won 21 games, Welch added 17, and Storm Davis, another of Duncan's reclamation projects, won 16. As a story, though, nobody topped Eckersley during his first season as a dominating force out of the bullpen.

Eckersley gave credit to La Russa for preserving his strength; not only did La Russa only use Eckersley for a very short period, usually only an inning and never more than two innings, he didn't tell Eckersley to warm up unless he was going into the game. Less-decisive managers often wear out relievers by having them warm up and then sit down again, without putting them in the game. Eckersley also praised Duncan for his understanding of pitchers and hitters; Duncan was amazing for his ability to tell pitchers how they could get out specific hitters.

But the main share of the credit had to go to Eckersley, who had totally rehabilitated himself. Once he quit drinking, he started a rigorous exercise program to build up his strength. At his lowest point in Chicago, he had said that his lack of speed on his fastball was "embarrassing," because he was so weak. By 1988, he was as hard as iron. Mentally, he adjusted to being a closer, though he confessed that he was driven by a fear of failure, claiming that he never took the mound without thinking this would be the time he'd finally be exposed.

In his youth, Eckersley had survived on pure physical talent. But since he had come back from the abyss, he had learned how to be a pitcher, instead of just a thrower. He didn't have quite the fastball of his youth, but he could spot it much better. In 72 innings during 1988, he walked only 11 hitters. Over the 1987–1988 seasons, he had walked only 28, and 5 of them had been intentional. With his new economical style, Eckersley recorded 45 saves and four wins, so he had a hand in nearly half of the A's wins. He would do even better during the years to come, but the A's were quite happy with his efforts that year, thank you.

CHAPTER 12

Gibson the Spoiler

The A's had won 104 games, the Red Sox only 89, but in the post-season, every team starts with a clean slate. As the American League Championship Series started, the A's were favored; they had had a lopsided 9–3 edge in the season series between the teams. But the Red Sox had baseball's dominant pitcher, Roger Clemens, and the ALCS was starting in Boston. An A's win was not a sure thing.

"When you win 100 games in a season, you don't have any real holes," manager Tony La Russa said looking back years later. That A's team did have the whole package: power, pitching, and defense. They needed all three during the first game, but it was the latter two that really made the difference.

Because the A's had clinched early, La Russa had Dave Stewart ready to go in the first game. The Red Sox had had to go down to the wire in a tight, five-team American League East race; the Detroit Tigers finished only a game behind and only 3½ games separated the Red Sox from the fifth-place New York Yankees. So, Boston manager Joe Morgan couldn't use Clemens in the first game; however left-hander Bruce Hurst, the first game starter, had actually had more success against the A's than Clemens, and he pitched another strong game in the opener. Stewart pitched a strong six innings, highlighted by his strikeout of Wade Boggs with the bases loaded in Boggs' first trip to the plate. Boggs had led the American League with a .366 average during the season.

The A's ace was also helped by an often spectacular defense. In the second, shortstop Walt Weiss made a diving stop of Rich Gedman's ground ball in shallow left field, preventing Jim Rice from scoring from second. In the sixth, after Stewart had given up a double and a walk, Weiss turned a ground ball by Todd Benzinger into an inning-ending double play.

Hurst matched the zeroes being put up by Stewart for the first three innings, but then Canseco hit a leadoff home run over the famed left-field wall, also known as The Green Monster. He admitted he hadn't hit the ball well, but he got it up into the air and it sailed out of the park.

The Red Sox tied the game in the seventh. After getting the first out, Stewart loaded the bases by walking Rice, hitting Jody Reed, and giving up a Gedman single to short center, not deep enough for Rice to score. La Russa brought in Rick Honeycutt. "Stew still had good life in his pitches," La Russa said, "but any time a pitcher has trouble getting the ball where he wants to, it is a sign he might be getting tired."

Honeycutt was thinking damage control. "I wanted to get an out," he said later. "A double play would have been nice, but I didn't want to try anything extraordinary and make a mistake." He got his out with Boggs flying to left field and the tying run scoring, then got out of the inning by getting Marty Barrett to ground out.

It took the A's only two pitches to get the lead back in the top of the eighth. Carney Lansford opened the eighth with a double and Dave Henderson singled to right to score Lansford. Then it was time for Dennis Eckersley. La Russa didn't usually use Eck before the ninth, but Eckersley was well rested now, so La Russa brought him in for the eighth—but not before pulling a stunt. Knowing that Eckersley wasn't yet fully warmed up, La Russa sent Honeycutt out to take his warm-up tosses, as if he were still pitching. When Dwight Evans, the first scheduled Red Sox hitter, came to the plate, La Russa brought in Eckersley, by that time fully warmed up.

It took Eckersley only seven pitches to get three outs in the eighth, and he got the first two Boston hitters in the ninth. But then Reed doubled and Gedman walked. It was the walk that really bothered Eckersley, because it meant he would have to face Boggs with the game on the line.

Boggs usually took the first pitch. Eckersley usually threw a strike on the first pitch. Both remained true to form, and then Boggs fouled off the next two pitches. Eckersley thought the second pitch was the best of the at-bat, a sinker that Boggs barely got his bat on. Eckersley came back with a high fastball that was probably out of the strike zone, but Boggs swung through it for one of his rare strikeouts; he had struck out only 34 times during the regular season. Hitter and pitcher were both amazed. "I looked at him as if to say, 'How did you swing and miss?'" said Eckersley later. "He looked at me as if to say, 'How did you strike me out?'" The game was over and the A's had taken a 1–0 lead.

Clemens looked ready to tie the series in the second game, retiring the first nine Oakland hitters, going on to a two-hit, eight-strikeout performance over the first six innings, including striking out the side in the sixth. When the Red Sox scored twice in the bottom of the sixth off Storm Davis, the A's looked beaten.

However, momentum shifted quickly in the seventh. Henderson led off with a single and then got Clemens trapped in a disastrous mind game. The Red Sox pitcher thought Henderson would try to steal, so he went to a slip-slide motion while pitching to Canseco. Big mistake. He didn't get his body into the pitch and his fastball, usually in the mid-90s, came in at little over 80 mph, a perfect batting practice pitch. Canseco treated it like that, hitting it into the left-field screen. Three hitters later, the other Bash Brother, Mark McGwire, singled in Carney Lansford to put the A's ahead. The Red Sox tied the score on a Gedman homer in the bottom of the inning but the A's went ahead again in the ninth on singles by Ron Hassey, Tony Phillips, and Weiss. In the bottom of the ninth it was Eckersley again, nailing down the win. The A's were going home with a 2–0 lead, knowing that the Red Sox were 0–6 in Oakland during the season and had lost 14 of their last 15 at the Coliseum.

Bob Welch had one of his rare bad outings in Game 3, giving up five runs before he came out with two outs in the second. Just like that, the A's were behind, 5–0. However, it took them only 11 batters to grab the lead back. The A's had studied videos of Red Sox starter Mike Boddicker, who was known for his big, sweeping curve ball. "He had had a lot of success against us," noted Weiss, "so we talked about staying back and waiting for his breaking ball."

Probably the A's deadliest hitter against offspeed pitches was McGwire, so it was fitting that he started the A's rally with a solo homer in the four-run second. Lansford hit a two-run shot for the final two runs of that inning and Ron Hassey hit another two-run homer in the third to put the A's ahead, 6–5, and knock out Boddicker. Henderson later added a homer as the A's cruised, 10–6. There was a surprising subplot in this game, though, as the A's showed off their pitching depth. After Welch was knocked out, Gene Nelson, Curt Young, Eric Plunk, and Honeycutt limited the Red Sox to one run until Eckersley pitched scoreless ball for the last two innings to get another save.

The big stars dominated the story line for the fourth game as the A's completed a four-game sweep, the first ever in an ALCS, with a 4–1 win. Canseco started the scoring with a home run on his first at-bat, Stewart got the win, Eckersley the save.

But the A's also showed how smartly they played the game with an eighth inning play. At the time, the outcome was still in doubt. With the A's holding a 2–1 lead and a Red Sox runner on first, they went into a strange defensive shift, Weiss moving close to second and Lansford hugging the third-base line. Honeycutt was about to throw a slider to the right-handed hitting Barrett, and their scouting reports told them Barrett would pull the pitch sharply. He did, right at Lansford, who grabbed it and threw to second to start a double play that ended the inning and the last Red Sox hope.

Eckersley was named the Most Valuable Player for the ALCS after saving all four victories. Canseco had hit three home runs. Weiss had played brilliantly at shortstop, as had Henderson in center field. Stewart had pitched two strong games as a starter. A *Sports Illustrated* article on the playoffs called the A's the best American League team since the three-time World Champions of the seventies and added, "These A's may even be better."

☻ ☻ ☻

Because of their sweep, the A's would have a full week before the World Series, as the Los Angeles Dodgers were involved in a dogfight with the New York Mets in the National League Championship Series. The Dodgers finally won the NLCS in the seventh game and had to use their ace, Orel Hershiser, who pitched a complete game. That meant that Hershiser wouldn't be able to pitch the opener in the World Series.

Everything seemed to be going the A's way. They were rested and could set their pitching rotation as they wanted. But in retrospect, La Russa thought he and his players were ill prepared because they had too much time between the ALCS and the World Series:

> When we tried to intensify our workouts, the players didn't like it. Their attitude was, we only need a little warm-up. We didn't hit very well in the Series, and I think that was the main reason.

It didn't seem that way at the start, though. The first two innings seemed classic 1988 A's. Stewart started and struggled in the first inning, and as Stew himself always said, "If you're going to get me, you'd better get me early." He even got involved in a little dust-up when he hit Steve Sax. Because Canseco had been hit by former A's pitcher Tim Belcher in the top of the inning, plate umpire Doug Harvey came out to warn Stewart; but, in fact, Stewart wasn't throwing at Sax. He was just having some control problems, and he gave up two runs before settling down.

In the top of the second, Canseco hit a grand slam home run to put the A's in the lead. Once again, they were in control of their destiny. Stewart gained his sharpness after the rocky first and gave up only one more run, in the sixth, over the next seven innings. He had a 4–3 lead going into the bottom of the ninth and expected to complete the game when La Russa came to him and said he was making a pitching change, to Eckersley.

Stewart had completed 14 games that season, and he argued with La Russa. Remembered Stewart:

I thought I was pitching well at that point and I wanted to finish. But Tony had earned our respect because he showed us he knew what he was doing. So, after our little disagreement, I said OK.

Of course, Eckersley also had everyone's respect after the great year he'd had, and he quickly retired the first two Dodger hitters. Then he walked Mike Davis. In the dressing room, where he was listening to the end of the game on the radio, Stewart thought that was an ominous sign. "Eck hardly walked anybody [11 in 72.1 innings that year] but it seemed that, every time he did, that runner scored."

An interesting drama had been playing out in the Dodger clubhouse during the game. Outfielder Kirk Gibson had been the National League's MVP that year. His statistics—.290 batting average, 25 homers, 76 RBIs—were among the least impressive for an MVP winner in history, but Gibson was honored for his ability to elevate his game in critical situations. Now, though, he could not start because of a combination of a pulled hamstring muscle and a wrenched knee. He had spent the first eight innings in the clubhouse, where the trainer applied heat to his ailing body. Though he could not even walk without difficulty, he hobbled out to the Dodger bench in the eighth inning and told manager Tommy Lasorda he could pinch-hit. So, with the game on the line in the ninth, Lasorda sent Gibson up. Eckersley went to a 3–2 count on Gibson. If Eck had thrown another fastball, he probably could have struck Gibson out to end the game; with his injuries, he was having trouble getting around on the fastball. Eckersley knew that:

> Over and over in our meetings before the game, we said, "Don't throw Gibson a breaking ball." But he kept fouling off and fouling off my fastball, way behind it, just slicing it off to the left. So, on the 3–2 count, I thought I'd fool him. Hah!

Eckersley's pitch was a good one, but it was also one Gibson could hit, and he went down to get it, golfing it and driving it over the right-field fence for a game-winning home run. "He was so strong," remembered Eckersley. "He just wristed it and hit it 420 feet. I was shocked." It was a moment that will long be remembered, and it set the tone for the whole Series. If Gibson had hit the ball anywhere in the field of play, he might not have been able to move fast enough to beat a throw to first, but he could limp around the bases into a mob of celebrating Dodgers at home plate.

After such a crushing defeat, many players will retreat to the trainer's room so they don't have to answer questions from the media. To his credit, Eckersley sat in front of his locker for 45 minutes answering questions. Unknowingly echoing Stewart's premonition, he said that what bothered him most was the walk he had given up to Davis. Over and over he said the pitch Gibson had hit was a good one, though he thought he'd throw a fastball if he had it to do over. There is no mulligan for a closer, though, as he realized.

The defeat was all the more damaging to the A's because they'd have to face Hershiser in the second game. That year, Hershiser was in a different world. He had won 23 games for a Dodger team that was very ordinary when he wasn't on the mound. He had posted a 2.26 ERA, pitched eight shutouts, and had set a major league record with 59 consecutive scoreless innings. He would win the National League's Cy Young Award easily and was named the MVP in the National League Championship Series.

La Russa had figured, going into the Series, that the A's could concede Hershiser two wins, perhaps even three, and still win by beating the other Dodger pitchers. Unfortunately, that wasn't exactly how things played out. Said La Russa:

> Hershiser didn't pitch Game 1. So, they beat us the first game with Belcher, and then they had their ace for the second game. They had a big edge psychologically. The first game was just a dramatic confrontation. It should have been Hershiser winning that first game and then us coming back to even it up in the second. But as it was, we were staring at 0–2.

Hershiser breezed through the A's lineup except for Dave Parker, who got the only three Oakland hits. Hershiser, though he looked woefully overmatched at the plate, managed three hits himself, and the first one started a five-run Dodger rally in the third. With two runners on base, A's starter Storm Davis had an 0–2 count on Mike Marshall. He threw a high fastball that he had intended to be a waste pitch, but it caught too much of the plate—and of Marshall's bat. The ball soared over the left-field fence and the Dodgers were on their way to an easy 6–0 win. Since Canseco's grand slam in the second inning of the first game, the A's had had only seven hits, six of them singles, in 16 innings. "We are fouling off balls we should be hitting and taking pitches we should be swinging at," said A's hitting coach Bob Watson.

McGwire said Hershiser should be given credit for making the A's hitters look bad:

> Hershiser doesn't overwhelm you. He doesn't have an over-powering fastball and he doesn't throw any extraordinary pitches: just fastball, curve, slider. But he knows what he's doing with every pitch. He never just throws a pitch up there; he always knows where he wants to deliver a pitch.
>
> He's frustrating to hit against because he throws to spots that make you hit it on the ground or pop it up. You come back to the bench thinking you should have hit the ball harder, but it's his pitching that makes the hitter look bad.

Though McGwire and Canseco often talked about opposing pitchers, it did no good with Hershiser. "He threw Jose a variety of pitches but threw me mostly fastballs," said McGwire. Hershiser knew McGwire's reputation for crushing any but the very best breaking balls.

The Series came back to Oakland for the third game, which La Russa thought would be an advantage for his team:

> The Coliseum was a real asset to us. The day games were beautiful, the night games were brisk, so you never lost your strength. You could play good fundamental baseball because you were never going to be out of it. With all that foul area and the fact that the ball didn't always carry very well, you weren't going to have a lot of really high-scoring games.

That was a manager's viewpoint, and a pitcher's as well. Hitters weren't so complimentary. Canseco claimed that he had lost 16 potential homers during the season when drives were blown back into the playing field. McGwire didn't put any numbers on lost homers, but he agreed with Canseco about the wind:

> Fans at the stadium don't always realize it because the wind is blowing above the stadium, but high drives get caught up in that wind and get blown back. The ball doesn't carry very well, either. A lot of drives into the alley that look like they may go out just wind up as long outs.

McGwire would hit one like that in the fourth inning of the third game, a towering drive to center that backed Dodger center fielder John Shelby up against the wall. "I thought when I hit it that it would go out," said McGwire, "but the wind caught it."

With the score tied at 1–1 in the ninth, McGwire mashed another one, this time a line drive to left field. As soon as he hit it, McGwire thought, "That's it, that's a home run," and he took a couple of steps out of the batter's box and threw up his hands. But then he remembered his fourth-inning drive and decided he'd better start running. Before he got to first base, the ball had gone into the left-field stands, so he could go into his home-run trot. The homer was his first hit of the Series and got the A's back into it, or so it seemed.

Welch had started, giving up one run in five innings, and the A's bullpen once again stood tall as Greg Cadaret, Nelson, and Honeycutt shut out the Dodgers over the last four innings, Honeycutt pitching the last two innings to get the win.

As it turned out, that was the last gasp for the A's. They were uncharacteristically sloppy in the field in the fourth game with errors by Weiss and second baseman Glenn Hubbard and a passed ball by catcher Terry Steinbach, which led to the first three Dodger runs. Former A's reliever Jay Howell had given up the game-winning home run to McGwire the night before, but he was the hero in this one, pitching the last 2⅓ innings to get the save. In the ninth, after Henderson had singled with one out, Howell had to face Canseco and Parker. Canseco took him to a 3–2 count but struck out on a fast-dropping curve and Parker fouled out to third to end the game.

The Dodgers came back with Hershiser for the fifth game and, though he said he wasn't as sharp as in the second game, he carried a 5–1 lead into the eighth. Then the A's rallied. Tony Phillips walked, advanced to second on Weiss's ground out, and scored on Stan Javier's single. When Henderson walked, the crowd sensed their team might get back in the game with Canseco and Parker coming up. Just as he had the night before, Canseco worked the count to 3–2, but then Hershiser surprised him with a fastball on his fists. "That was risky," admitted Hershiser, "because Jose can turn on a pitch like that." This time, though, Canseco popped it up to first. The overanxious Parker swung at two curves out of the strike zone, one of which bounced in the dirt, and struck out to end the threat. Though there was one more inning to play, the A's had blown their last chance. One inning later they had lost the game, 5–2, and the Series. Remarkably, they had hit only .177 for the five games.

Was it lack of preparation, as La Russa thought in hindsight? Perhaps, but then and now, it seemed the A's never recovered from the psychological blow of Gibson's game-winning homer in the first game. Said Eckersley:

> It knocked me down for a couple of weeks. Then I had time to reflect on all the good things that happened to me that year. I couldn't let that one thing spoil all of that. I wouldn't be much of a person if I did.

It was even a spur for Eckersley: "I wanted to show that the year wasn't a fluke," he said. "I wanted to show the skeptics and I wanted to prove it to myself."

When the postseason came around again, as it would in the very next season, Eckersley and the A's would be better prepared. But first they had to go through a 1989 season that was often a roller coaster.

CHAPTER 13

Rickey Returns

With the shocking results of the 1988 World Series fresh in mind, A's general manager Sandy Alderson looked for ways to improve the team. His first move was a big one, signing free agent pitcher Mike Moore. Though Moore had won just nine games with a mediocre Seattle Mariners team the year before, he was highly regarded in baseball. He would make big strides with the A's under the tutelage of pitching coach Dave Duncan, winning 19 games during 1989 and becoming the No. 2 starter behind Dave Stewart.

But even the Moore signing paled when compared to a trade that Alderson made on June 21, 1989, to bring Rickey Henderson home (and sending pitchers Greg Cadaret and Eric Plunk and outfielder Luis Polonia to the New York Yankees). As good as the A's had been during 1988, they were now much stronger, both in their regular lineup and in the starting rotation.

During his years with the Yankees, Henderson had earned a reputation as the best leadoff man in baseball history with an incomparable combination of speed and power. Pitchers couldn't win with Henderson. With his hunched-over stance he had a very small strike zone, so he earned frequent walks, and for him a walk was often the equivalent of a double because he was the most prolific base stealer in history.

With the Yankees, he didn't approach the record 130 stolen bases he had notched with the 1982 A's, but he had still led the league three times, with a high of 93 in the 1988 season. That often translated into runs, as many as 146 in a season. And if a pitcher grooved a pitch to keep from walking Henderson, he had the power to hit it out of the park; during his first two years with the Yankees, he had hit 24 and 28 home runs.

Henderson was also a fine defensive outfielder. He had played center with the Yankees but would go back to left with the A's, a more natural position for him. A relatively weak arm hampered him in making throws from center but his ability to charge balls hit to shallow left field enabled him to keep runners from taking an extra base or even scoring from second. Said La Russa:

> Rickey is blessed with an almost unbelievable body, with those strong legs. He's taken a beating over the years, because he's been a marked man for his entire career. But teams couldn't stop him. He's a very intelligent guy and very competitive. If you ever see Rickey playing a game, be careful about getting in it, because he's only going to play a game he can win.

There were occasions when Henderson and La Russa would lock horns. Said La Russa, without getting into specifics:

> What Rickey needed wasn't always what the club needed. That really only happened a few times but every time it did, it seemed to become public, so it seemed bigger than it was. Rickey was always very much influenced by those around him, but there was a lot of goodness in him. He was generally well liked in the clubhouse. He didn't carry himself like a big star there.

Henderson's mouth often got him in trouble. The way he talked was fascinating. He would jump from subject to subject, and the words came out in such a rapid jumble that they were sometimes almost incomprehensible. But not all of them. When he was traded to the Yankees before the 1985 season, his message had come through loud and clear: he was happy to go to the Yankees, he said, because he wouldn't have to carry the team. In Oakland he had been the only star. That implication didn't sit well with his former A's teammates, especially center fielder Dwayne Murphy, who had played next to Henderson in the outfield and thought they were friends.

There was no question that Henderson was a better player when he was with a better team. He often lost interest if his organization wasn't in contention. During 1982, his 130 stolen bases were only a sideshow, and he knew it. His base running was much more important with a good team, as it had been with the Yankees and would be again during his second tour with the A's, because it helped a team win.

Now it was time for Henderson to come home. Jose Canseco had been injured during spring training and, though the A's were leading their division by two games, there was concern that they could not hold on without their big slugger. Remembered Alderson:

> We needed something to pick us up. I had picked up vibes that Rickey had worn out his welcome in New York, so I called Syd Thrift. He was ready to trade Rickey but we worked for several weeks before we could come up with the right package. Those midseason deals used to be fairly minor ones, but in the free agency era, there are more and more big players being moved. I think this might have been the first real blockbuster deal. It worked out perfectly for us. Rickey was just what we needed that year.

It was a troubled season for Canseco, who would not come off the disabled list until mid-July. He was limited to 65 games, and when he was able to play, his approach to the game had changed. La Russa had felt a closeness to his young star during his first three seasons, but that was fast disappearing:

> After his 40–40 year, he got an awful lot of attention and started to make some serious money. As happens to so many young guys when they get attention, their values go sideways. You

could see it. I had conversations with Jose, telling him he was losing track of what it's all about.

La Russa jumped him after a game in which the A's had the potential winning run on third but Canseco, instead of shortening his swing and getting the single he needed, struck out taking big swings. Canseco told his manager:

I'm an entertainer. People would rather see me take three big swings, maybe hit one out of the park, maybe strike out, than just hit a single.

La Russa knew he was losing the battle because Canseco had an entourage of "friends" who were telling him, "Jose, you're really the greatest." He was listening to them instead of his manager.

Canseco was making news off the field, too, little of it good. When the A's traveled to New York, the hot rumor paired Canseco and Madonna. By this time, he had married Esther Haddad, but it was a tumultuous relationship. Once, after a verbal battle, Jose got out of the car. Esther slid behind the wheel and aimed the car at Canseco. Perhaps she had heard the Madonna rumors, too.

The car, a red Jaguar, had personalized license plates reading, "Mr. 40-40." Canseco had been arrested for speeding, reportedly going about 125 mph, in Florida before spring training. He had the car shipped to Arizona, then was cited for speeding in that state too. Back in the East Bay during baseball season, he was stopped by a highway patrolman after his speedometer had again hit three digits. "Don't you know who I am?" he demanded of the officer, who continued writing out the ticket.

Just after the start of the season, Canseco was arrested on a charge of having a concealed weapon in his car. Canseco had gone to the UC–San Francisco campus to get his injured wrist x-rayed at a medical office there. His car attracted the usual gawkers. One of them noticed a gun on the floor of the car on the driver's side, and reported the sighting to Michael Brant, UCSF assistant police chief. Brant arrested Canseco when he came outside. Canseco claimed he had a Florida license for the gun, but that was not valid in California. He later told

Alderson he was carrying the gun because he had gotten some threats in the mail and he wanted to protect his wife, who was with him at the campus. Said Alderson:

> We're upset at not being able to stem this tide of events. I'm embarrassed for the organization. This is not the message we want to send to the community.

"There are two constants in all these cases," Alderson noted, wryly: "the car and Jose." The charge was eventually reduced to a misdemeanor and Canseco got off with a fine.

In the meantime, Canseco was being barraged by unsolicited advice in the newspapers from psychologists who had him on a figurative couch. Said San Jose State sports psychologist Dr. Tom Tutko:

> One thing that happens is that young people in sports are not prepared for fame, how to handle notoriety, how to handle money. If you are in the limelight, there are a certain number of people who hate you, people who will never do anything in life and feel inadequate.

Young men who have always been surrounded by family and friends who lavish attention and affection on them are unprepared to deal with those in the stands who dislike them. In the case of Canseco, who had had an even more adoring group of fans than other players, it was coming as an even more unpleasant surprise to discover that fans were starting to turn on him.

Canseco's problems were so out in the open that he was even getting advice from former players. "All of a sudden you have so much money you don't know what to do with it," said Greg Minton, who had pitched for 16 years in the majors, most of them across the bay for the San Francisco Giants. "Not many guys get to Jose's level. He's at the top of the world. He feels invincible, but he'll learn that he's not."

"He really appears on the edge of getting into serious trouble," said Denny McLain, the last pitcher to win 30 games in a season (1968).

"You begin to believe what people write about you. When you do that, you cross the line and lose control." McLain knew about crossing that line from bitter personal experience. He had filed for bankruptcy in 1977 and was convicted in 1985 of racketeering, extortion, and drug dealing; he was sentenced to 23 years in prison, though he'd been paroled after two because an appeals court found errors in the behavior of the judge and the prosecutor in his trial.

The best advice came from former A's star pitcher Vida Blue: "He needs to sell that car and get a blue Volvo," said Blue. "It looks like a drug dealer's car."

Meanwhile, there was another pennant to be won. There would be no cakewalk this time. For much of the season, the A's and the California Angels had battled for the lead. For 21 straight days, starting on July 7, the Angels were in the lead, and they led as late as August 20. But the A's hung tough when they trailed, never falling more than 2½ games back. Most of the time, the margin was only a game, or even half a game.

Finally, on August 21, the A's would take the lead for good as Curt Young bested Frank Tanana, 6–1, in a game in Detroit. From that point, the A's steadily widened their lead. By the end, they were seven games ahead of Kansas City as the Angels faded to third, eight games back. The A's finished at 99–63, five games off of their pace of the year before but quite respectable considering the fact that their two biggest stars of the year before, Canseco and Dennis Eckersley, had been hobbled by injuries. Eckersley, who pulled a rotator cuff muscle on May 27 and missed the next 40 games, was limited to 51 appearances, with 33 saves. In case anybody doubted how important he was, the A's were a .500 club without him, 20–20. With him, they were 79–43.

It was another big year for Dave Stewart, who was 21–9, and the A's starting rotation was their strongest ever, with Moore and Storm Davis each winning 19 games and Bob Welch winning 17. In 85 games with Oakland after the trade, Henderson had hit .294, scored 72 runs, and stolen 52 bases. McGwire's averaged slipped to .231, but he hit 33 homers and knocked in 95 runs.

Their record didn't show it but this was clearly a better team than 1988's—as long as they stayed healthy. The pitching was stronger with the addition of Moore. Henderson added an element to the offense that hadn't been there before. They had been hardened by their postseason experience of the year before, especially the devastating loss in the World Series. Everybody was healthy again, and the A's had something to prove. There would be no letdown this time.

CHAPTER 14

An Earthquake Trumps the A's

Dave Stewart was always tough, but he was especially tough during the postseason, when every game counted. One other element didn't change, however: Stewart still struggled during the first couple of innings, trying to find his control. He had tried various methods to change that, including a longer warm-up, but nothing worked. He and the A's had to live with that imperfection and it showed again during the first game of the American League Championship Series at Oakland, when he gave up two runs in the top of the second inning to the Toronto Blue Jays.

But the A's were a better team than the Blue Jays in every respect, from the pitching staff to the manager's seat in the dugout, and their superiority would assert itself in what became a fairly easy 7–3 win. A three-run sixth, highlighted by a McGwire homer, vaulted them into the lead for the first time. Stewart gave up only one more run in the eight innings he pitched and Eckersley nailed down the win. Henderson stole two bases in a foreshadowing of his great series to come, and his hard slide into Toronto second baseman Nelson Liriano in the sixth thwarted a possible inning-ending double play and allowed the go-ahead run to score.

Henderson was the big story in the second game as he stole four bases, an ALCS record. It was the first two that were most crucial. With the A's trailing 1–0 in the fourth, Henderson was walked and quickly stole second and third. With the infield drawn in, Carney Lansford singled to left. Dave Parker followed with another single and then McGwire scored both to put the A's up for good. After the game, Toronto manager Cito Gaston noted sarcastically, "Maybe when Rickey's stealing second, we should throw to third and tag him out."

Starter Mike Moore gave up only a single run in the third and it should have been a breeze when the A's went into the eighth with a 6–1 lead. But reliever Rick Honeycutt had one of his rare bad outings, giving up a single to Liriano and walking Lloyd Moseby and Mookie Wilson. When he went to 2–0 on Fred McGriff, La Russa brought in Eckersley.

La Russa rarely brought in Eckersley in midinning. Nobody, including Eck, could ever remember him coming in when the batter was in midcount. Eckersley didn't like it. "You can't do much in that situation," he said. He did jam McGriff with a high fastball, but McGriff's pop fly fell in safely down the line, with one run scoring. Eckersley then got George Bell to hit into a double play. Though one run scored, it gave Eck the chance to get out of the inning with no further damage, and he breezed through the ninth as the A's won, 6–3, to push their ALCS advantage to 2–0.

The day off between the second and third game led to some verbal jousting between the teams. Toronto third baseman Kelly Gruber accused Henderson of "showboating" because he hadn't even slid in a steal of second. Gruber didn't much like Dave Parker's slow trot around the bases after a home run, either. Replied Parker: "I'm 38 years old. It takes me some time to get around the bases." Gaston, trying to calm down his troops, didn't think it was simply age: "He's been doing that ever since I've known him and I've known him for a long time. Sometimes, I've seen him take even longer."

La Russa, who always cautioned his players against taunting, had some comments of his own, no doubt to keep his own players from getting involved in this battle of words:

I don't like to see our team attacked when we don't deserve it. I've watched the Blue Jays, especially in the last two weeks, and they celebrate and demonstrate as much as anybody.

La Russa had earlier accused the Blue Jays of a double standard. "When they brush back hitters, it's pitching 'in.' When we do it, it's throwing at them."

Gaston, meanwhile, was fielding criticism because he hadn't switched catchers—from Ernie Whitt to the better-throwing Pat Borders—to at least slow down Henderson. Whitt would again catch the third game, but he'd have some help: left-hander Jimmy Key, whose pickoff motion made it difficult to steal, would be the Blue Jays starter. In the two regular-season games Key had started against the A's, Henderson had reached base four times, but had stolen only one base, in his only attempt.

Henderson didn't run wild during the third game, but he did steal a base after a leadoff double in the third and score a run. Parker also homered again, a solo shot in the fourth, and tried in vain to catch Gruber's eye as he rounded third. "I guess he realizes that's the advantage of hitting a home run, that you get to trot," Parker said.

But those were the only bright spots for the A's. They wasted two other leadoff doubles, Storm Davis was rocked for four runs in the fourth, and the Blue Jays cruised to a 7–3 win. Perhaps the worst news for the A's was that Honeycutt had his second straight bad outing. Coming on top of some bad performances down the stretch in the regular season, that worried La Russa. Honeycutt was worried, too. "I'm missing my slider," he said.

It was Henderson's bat that took the spotlight in the fourth game, as he hit two two-run homers. But it was Canseco who had everybody buzzing as he hit a towering drive where nobody ever thought one could be hit, into the upper deck at the Skydome, rattling the windows of a luxury suite. Folklore has it that Canseco's blast disturbed a couple making love. The A's power helped them build a 6–2 lead, but the Blue Jays cut the margin to 6–5 in the eighth as Honeycutt again struggled before Eckersley came in to get the last five outs and record his second save.

In the final game of the ALCS, the A's showed their complete game: hitting, fielding, and pitching. And, of course, Henderson. He led off the game with a walk, stole second (his eighth steal of the series), and scored on a Lansford single. In the third, he tripled in Walt Weiss. It was no surprise when Henderson was later unanimously selected as the MVP of the ALCS.

La Russa also surprised the Blue Jays when he used a suicide squeeze to score the A's fourth run. Mike Gallego was the hitter, the slow-footed McGwire the base runner on third. Gallego admitted that he was nervous. "I knew I had to really concentrate." He did, and McGwire lumbered home to score.

Knowing the bullpen had been stretched thin, Stewart was determined to go deep into the game as the A's previous three starters had not, and he pitched eight strong innings before turning the ball over to Eckersley. Stewart was helped by an exceptional A's defense, highlighted by a diving catch by Weiss of Whitt's fourth-inning line drive, a double play started by McGwire in the fifth, and a diving stop and throw by Gallego in the eighth to nail McGriff. Said Stewart after the game:

In the past, I have used mainly offspeed stuff against the Blue Jays, so today, I refused to throw anything offspeed early. Then, when I had the idea of the hard stuff in their minds in the middle innings, I went away from it.

The ninth was notable mainly for the mind games played by Gaston. As Eckersley was warming up, Gaston glared at him from the sidelines and eventually went over to plate umpire Rick Reed to ask that Eckersley's uniform be searched for an illegal substance, which Gaston claimed Eckersley was putting on the ball. The umpires made a half-hearted search of Eckersley's uniform. Not surprisingly, they didn't find anything; the charge had never been made of Eckersley before. Gaston was just desperately trying for an edge. With the ALCS slipping away, he needed to disrupt Eckersley's rhythm.

For a time it seemed to be working. Eckersley swore at Gaston, and he admitted later that he'd briefly lost his composure. He gave up a single to Tony Fernandez, who stole second, went to third on Whitt's ground out, and scored on Gruber's fly to left. But Eckersley struck out Junior Felix to end the game. The A's would be back in the World Series.

For Eckersley, that meant more questions about the Gibson homer. The questions weren't necessary to remind him, though:

> I'll never forget that. I think it will always be there in my mind. It was there in the playoffs. Of course I'd like a chance to redeem myself. So would the rest of the team. We all have something to prove. We know we were better than the Dodgers, but we didn't win.

Their opponent this time would be the San Francisco Giants, who had won a dramatic victory in the National League Championship Series when Will Clark singled in the winning run off Mitch "Wild Thing" Williams of the Chicago Cubs in the fifth game. It would be the first-ever "Bay Bridge Series."

To objective observers, it was clear that the A's were the better team. The Giants were really a two-man show—Clark and Kevin Mitchell, who had been the National League MVP with 47 homers and 125 RBIs—and their veteran pitching staff was held together by medical tape. But the A's had been the better team the year before and had lost to the Dodgers.

This time, they would be better prepared and better motivated. Remembered La Russa:

> The quality of our workouts was 180 degrees different that year than it had been in '88. We really turned it up. We talked about it. We had intense workouts.

So intense, in fact, that when Eckersley though Canseco was digging in a little too much at the plate during an intrasquad workout, he drilled him in the back.

"This club was fired up," said La Russa, who was further encouraged when he heard Giants manager Roger Craig saying in a radio interview that his team had had a brief workout because that was all the players needed. "They were doing the same thing we had done the year before. The Giants weren't as good as we were, but they also didn't have the same edge we had."

The players were as confident and determined as their manager. Remembered Stewart years later:

> There was no doubt in our minds that we were going to win because we'd beaten the Giants regularly in spring training, and we'd beaten them bad in some of the games. And we played this whole Series with a chip on our shoulders. We were really angry because we'd let the Dodgers beat us the year before.

For Stewart, an Oakland native, there was an additional incentive:

> There was a lot of stuff in the papers at the time about the San Francisco mayor [Art Agnos] talking about San Francisco being a glamorous city and Oakland being like the ugly stepsister, and we resented that. We were really fired up going into that Series.

Stewart put his money where his mouth was during the first game, at the Oakland Coliseum, as he pitched perhaps his finest game of the year, a five-hit shutout, walking only one and striking out six in the 5–0 A's victory. Not until the ninth inning did the Giants get a runner as far as third base. Only one of the Giants' five hits was for extra bases, a double by Clark. Each of the Giants' big hitters, Clark and Mitchell, got two hits, but Stewart shut down the rest of the lineup, so those hits didn't hurt him. Meanwhile, Weiss and Parker each homered and McGwire got 3 of the A's 11 hits in a game that was never in doubt after the A's scored three times in the second inning.

Mike Moore was almost as dominant as Stewart in the second game, pitching four-hit, one-run ball for seven innings as the A's won, 5–1, and took a 2–0 lead in the Series. Moore had been a pleasant surprise for the A's after he was signed as a free agent pitcher in the off-season. Originally brought in as the No. 3 or possibly No. 4 starter, he had vaulted past Bob Welch to the second spot in the rotation and had been only a shade less effective than Stewart all season.

The improvement was due to a pitch that he had learned from A's pitching coach Dave Duncan. Called the forkball in the American League and the split-finger in the National, it was a pitch thrown like a fastball but with the index and third fingers widely split in the pitcher's grip. That grip caused the ball to sink sharply as it went over the plate. Because it looked like a fastball coming in, hitters weren't prepared for the break and usually swung over the ball, either missing it entirely or topping the ball for an easy ground out. Not every pitcher could master it but it was a very effective pitch for those who could. Giants manager Craig was famous for teaching it to his pitchers, first as a pitching coach in Detroit and then with the Giants. Craig tried to get all of his pitchers to use it, while Duncan was more selective. The pitch had turned Stewart's career around and greatly enhanced Moore's. Craig himself noticed what a difference it had made for Moore:

I saw Mike Moore in Seattle, and he didn't have the split-finger then. He's a much better pitcher now. Of course, he also has a much better team behind him.

For the Giants, 40-year-old Rick Reuschel was trying to become the oldest pitcher to win a World Series game. That dream ended in the fourth as the A's broke a 1–1 tie with a four-run outburst to make the score 5–1. Catcher Terry Steinbach hit a three-run homer to end any suspense.

The best news for the A's, though, may have been the fact that Honeycutt pitched a scoreless 1⅓ innings before Eckersley got the final two outs. "I finally got my slider back," said a relieved Honeycutt after the game. Welch was scheduled to be the A's starter for the third game, and there was an ironic touch to that because he lived in San Francisco. He had developed a fondness for the city when he was with the Dodgers and he and his wife, Mary Ellen, had bought a home in the Marina neighborhood the previous fall. Though the Giants were returning to their home park and making brave statements about how they'd get back in the Series with the games at Candlestick, they weren't eager to face Welch, who'd had the reputation of being a Giant-killer during his Dodger days. Overall, he'd been 19–4 against the Giants, and he had a perfect 6–0 record at Candlestick.

Welch would never get the chance to show whether he still had that mastery. About 45 minutes before game time, an earthquake that was later measured at 7.0 hit the ballpark. Temblors are no surprise in the Bay Area, but the usual ones just rattle houses and break a few dishes. Everybody at the park realized this was much more severe. On the field, players rushed from the dugout to the center of the field and called for their wives and children, sitting in the stands, to join them. On the television monitors mounted in the press box and the auxiliary areas in the upper deck, images of the Bay Bridge soon started to appear. It had buckled and broken on the eastern span, whose support was in landfill. There would be no game that night.

It would be several hours before the park could be cleared but, to everyone's credit, there was no panic. It took hours for people to get home because freeways and roads around the area had been so damaged that they could not be used. The power was off downtown, which meant there were no traffic lights, but drivers displayed a courtesy they seldom had during less trying times, taking turns going through intersections.

The earthquake had been centered near Santa Cruz, about 70 miles south of Candlestick, and that city had suffered the most damage; but the television cameras were in San Francisco, so that's what viewers around the country saw. To those viewers, it seemed that the city had been devastated but in fact, most of the damage was confined to the part of the Marina neighborhood that had been built on landfill.

In one sense, the earthquake had come at a good time. In addition to the more than 60,000 people actually at the park, many thousands more had already driven home to watch the game on television; the freeways and bridges were far less crowded than they would have been during a normal rush hour.

One of the worst catastrophes was the destruction of the Cypress Freeway, a double-decked structure in Oakland leading to the Bay

Bridge. The entire structure collapsed, burying cars and people and injuring thousands. As rescue crews attempted to dig out those who might still be alive during the next few days, Stewart went there to see what he could do to help:

> I didn't do much. I was just doing what everybody else was doing, bringing in food and supplies. It's a helpless feeling to see all that damage and to be able to do so little.

It would be several years before the Cypress was finally replaced with a single-deck freeway about a mile west of the old structure.

During the next few days, baseball commissioner Fay Vincent met with other baseball officials and San Francisco Mayor Agnos to decide when the Series could continue, or even whether it should. Engineering consultants were checking Candlestick Park to see if it could be used; the San Francisco 49ers, who had been scheduled to play a football game at Candlestick on what would have been a time at least three days after the last Series game there, played the game at Stanford instead. Meanwhile, Agnos and his staff, who had been campaigning for a proposition to build a new park for the Giants, shifted all their efforts to earthquake relief. In November the new park proposition would be narrowly defeated; the Giants wouldn't get a new park until they built Pacific Bell Park, which opened in April 2000.

At one point, Vincent and Agnos discussed the possibility of shifting the remaining games back to the Coliseum. In typical fashion, they didn't think of asking Oakland Mayor Lionel Wilson to join those discussions. When Wilson and George Vukasin, president of the Coliseum board, heard about this possibility, they pointed out that a rock concert sponsored by Bill Graham Productions had been scheduled for those dates, and Graham had not even been asked if he would reschedule his concert. When he learned of the possibility of the remaining games being played at the Coliseum (when this writer called him), Graham said he'd be willing to reschedule. However, it never came to that. The inspections of Candlestick discovered only minor damage. The park might be a dump, but it was structurally sound.

While the debate went on about when and where the rest of the Series would be played, the A's went back to their Arizona spring training camp to work out. When the Series finally resumed after a 12-day break, the question was whether the A's had lost their momentum. Looking back years later, Stewart said, "We still had the same intensity," and they proved it with a 13–7 win in the third game. Only a four-run rally in the bottom of the ninth made the score look even reasonably respectable for the Giants.

Craig felt that the break had helped the A's:

They were able to just use Stewart and Moore. Not that Bob Welch is a day at the beach, but those guys were definitely their best that year.

Stewart pitched seven innings, giving up three runs, and got the win.

The A's put the game away in the fifth with a four-run inning that again displayed their varied offensive talents. Canseco came to bat with two runners on base, one of whom was Henderson on second. Concerned about Henderson stealing third, Giants reliever Kelly Downs lost his focus and grooved a fastball for Canseco, who hit a three-run homer to put the game away.

The A's seemed on their way to an easy sweep in Game 4 after six innings, with Moore holding an 8–2 lead. But when he left, relievers Gene Nelson and Honeycutt struggled. The Giants actually closed the gap to 8–6 and had a chance to tie the game in the seventh when Mitchell, against Todd Burns, hit a deep drive to left with a runner on. His drive fell just short of the fence, and that was the last gasp for the Giants. Eckersley closed out a 9–6 win.

The sweep was the first in the World Series since 1976 and the first ever for the Oakland A's, and the A's had been dominant throughout, outscoring the Giants 32–14. The Giants were out of every game but the last one after the fourth inning. It was a monumental accomplishment, but the A's celebrated very quietly because they knew their achievements paled in the shadow of the human devastation around them. Remembered Eckersley:

We knew going in that we were the better team, but after the quake, when we won, it was like, so what, because it no longer really meant anything.

He was right, of course. Nothing they had done would be long remembered. The 1989 Series would be forever known as the Earthquake Series.

CHAPTER 15

Success and Failure

Sustaining success is one of the most difficult tasks in sports, and cracks were already showing in the A's foundation when they opened the 1990 season in defense of their world championship. Most of the cracks emanated outward from Jose Canseco's locker. Remembered Dave Stewart:

> We had bad chemistry all that year. It all centered on Jose. It was always about Jose.

Some of Canseco's problems were physical. He missed 31 games because of a bad back, which would continue to bother him for the rest of his career. But most of the problems were emotional. Jose had turned a corner in his life during 1988. The once shy rookie had become an ego-driven star, ignoring advice from his manager and setting himself apart from his fellow players, even those who had contributed as much to the A's success as he had. The all-around player of 1988 had become a one-dimensional power hitter by 1990. He was not concentrating in the out-field, and balls were dropping in that he would have caught easily two years earlier. He was no longer throwing out runners either.

Those watching Canseco during 1988 thought he would continue to hit .300, and with big power numbers, if he simply tried to make solid contact in each at-bat. Line drives leaped off his bat and shot through the infield; if they were not hit directly at a fielder, they could not be caught. Third basemen had to play deep for fear of being decapitated by a Canseco rocket if they didn't, which meant that Jose could beat out infield hits if he topped the ball; a few of those in the season meant the difference between .300 and .270.

But by 1990, Canseco didn't care. It was all or nothing. He hit 37 homers and knocked in 101 runs—the only numbers that still concerned him—while his batting average slipped from the .307 of 1988 to .274. His strikeouts shot up to 158 in just 481 at-bats, a much worse strikeout/at-bat ratio than when he was a rookie. Even his base running suffered. Though he stole 19 bases, he was also caught stealing 10 times. Anything less than 70 percent success is unsatisfactory for a base stealer; the success rate for the best approaches (and sometimes surpasses) 80 percent. Rickey Henderson was also caught stealing 10 times that year, but he stole 65 bases.

Henderson had his best year, hitting .325 with 28 homers and 119 runs scored. He scored in the first inning in 33 games that season, and the A's were 26–7 in those games. After the season, he would be voted the league's Most Valuable Player for the first time, getting 14 of 28 possible first-place votes.

With Henderson leading the way, the A's won their third pennant convincingly. There was no spectacular wining streak, as there had been during 1988—in fact, the longest streak was just seven games—but the A's kept winning steadily. They were out of first place for only nine days all season, the last time on July 7. Starting on September 2, they won 9 of 10 games and shoved their lead to 11 games. They clinched on September 25 in Kansas City as Stewart pitched a shutout, 5–0. Their final margin was 9 games, and they approached their record 1988 pace with a 103–59 mark.

Stewart had a 22–11 record with a 2.56 ERA, his best yet, but this time he was overshadowed by Welch, who shot to 27–6, earning the Cy Young Award. It was the most wins by a major league pitcher since Steve Carlton had also won 27 during 1972, and the most by an American League pitcher since 1968, when Denny McLain had won 31. The combined 49 wins by Welch and Stewart was the most by two teammates

The "Bash Brothers"—Jose Canseco and Mark McGwire—pose in a takeoff of the Blues Brothers during the 1988 season.

Catcher Terry Steinbach confers with Dave Stewart on the mound during the third game of the 1989 World Series, won by the A's.

In a characteristic pose, Dennis Eckersley points his finger after striking out a batter during a July 1990 game against the Milwaukee Brewers at Oakland.

A's general manager Sandy Alderson, who built a championship team with astute trades and free-agent signings, during the 1990 season.

A's owner Walter Haas, the last of his kind, during the 1990 season.

Rickey Henderson ties the career stolen-base record during a game in Oakland against the Cleveland Indians on May 26, 1990.

A's manager Tony La Russa and general manager Sandy Alderson chat with slugger Jose Canseco before a 1990 game against Cleveland.

A mighty swing produces another mammoth Jose Canseco home run during a May 24, 1991, game at Oakland against the Milwaukee Brewers.

Mark McGwire hits the ball on the sweet spot for another towering home run during a May 5, 1991, game in Oakland against the Cleveland Indians.

The A's celebrate after winning their third straight American League pennant, sweeping the Red Sox in the 1990 ALCS.

since Sandy Koufax and Don Drysdale had combined for the same number with the 1965 Los Angeles Dodgers.

Though Dennis Eckersley finished fifth in the Cy Young voting (he also got one first-place vote for Most Valuable Player and finished sixth in that contest), he had as astounding a year in relief as Welch did as a starter, saving 48 games and allowing just 41 hits and four walks in 73⅓ innings. He allowed only five earned runs all season and had an ERA of 0.61, one of those numbers that make you blink and rub your eyes to make sure you're seeing right.

These gaudy numbers helped the A's to post a Bay Area attendance record of 2,900,217. The combined Oakland attendance for the three World Series winners, 1972–1974, had been only 2,767,779. The comparison is a vivid reminder of the way Charlie Finley's operation had undermined A's attendance.

Aside from the change in Canseco's game, there was only one unsettling element in the A's play that season: the continued slide in Mark McGwire's batting average. He had hit .289 during his rookie season, and had been as proud of that as he was of his 49 home runs. But he had slid to .260 the following season, to .231 during 1989, and .235 in 1990. His power production remained high—his 39 home runs and 108 RBIs both led the team—but he had become a "mistakes" hitter. If pitchers got their pitches where they wanted them, they'd get McGwire out.

The A's defense, always stressed by manager Tony La Russa, was a largely unnoticed but very important part of their success. They were especially solid up the middle. Terry Steinbach was developing into the best catcher in the league. Walt Weiss was a far-ranging shortstop and, whether teamed with Opening Day starter Mike Gallego or with Willie Randolph (who was acquired in May), was part of a strong double-play duo. Gallego, who had trouble holding a starting job because of his weak hitting, was a superb fielder who filled in nicely for 17 games when Weiss went down with an injury in August. Center fielder Dave Henderson ran down everything, helping to compensate for Canseco's fielding lapses in right. Rickey Henderson was the best left fielder in the game. He had a weak but accurate arm, and charged balls so aggressively that runners could not take an extra base on him. Carney Lansford was an excellent third baseman and McGwire, who had quick reactions though he was a slow runner, was above average at first base, as well as being a great target at 6'5".

The first game of the American League Championship Series, held in Boston, again matched up Stewart and Roger Clemens. The two were locked in a great duel for the first six innings, with a solo home run by Wade Boggs in the fourth the only score. But a tiring Clemens was relieved in the seventh, having apparently told Red Sox manager Joe Morgan that he couldn't go any further, and the A's tied it with a single run. They added another in the eighth and then made it a laugher with a seven-run ninth. Eckersley came on in the ninth to nail down the 9–1 win.

The second game looked like a replay of the first most of the way. Again, the A's got a strong effort from a starter, Welch this time, and took a 2–1 lead into the bottom of the eighth. Then it got interesting. Welch came out after consecutive one-out singles by Boggs and Ellis Burks, and Rick Honeycutt got Mike Greenwell on a comebacker to the mound. La Russa brought in Eckersley to face Dwight Evans. When both were playing for the Red Sox, Evans had been a close friend, but friendship was not a factor for Eckersley when he was on the mound. "I'm really psyched by situations like that," said Eckersley, who was fully into the emotional role of closer, which he had resisted for so long. "I just threw hard cheese ["Eck-talk" for fastballs]." Evans knew what was coming, so he didn't look at any pitches. Three times he swung and missed. The A's were out of the inning and, after scoring twice in the top of the ninth, Eck went 1–2–3 in the bottom of the inning.

The A's were coming home with a 2–0 lead, having beaten the Red Sox in their last six ALCS games. The sweep in 1988 had surprised La Russa, but he wouldn't be surprised by the sweep this time:

The Red Sox were a very good team in '88, but they'd slipped. They weren't a very good team in '90.

The only question was the A's starter: Mike Moore had been maddeningly inconsistent during the season with a 13–15 record and a 4.65 ERA. Said pitching coach Dave Duncan:

At times, his fastball has been in the 90–91 mph range. Other games, it's only been 83–84. And I have no idea why.

The A's third most effective starter during the season had been Scott Sanderson, who had won 17 games. But La Russa decided to start Moore. "He has pitched better in the more important games," said La Russa, remembering Moore's two World Series wins the previous year. "I think he can rise to the occasion."

Moore did, along with the A's bullpen, giving up only one run in the six innings he pitched. Morgan, who had been betrayed by his bullpen in the first two games, let his starter, Mike Boddicker, pitch a complete game, though Boddicker yielded four runs. Gene Nelson, Honeycutt, and Eckersley each pitched an inning in relief, Eckersley closing out the game by again striking out Evans on high fastballs.

It would be Stewart and Clemens again in the fourth game, but not for long. In the second inning, with one run in and McGwire on first, Clemens walked Randolph, then started a heated argument with plate umpire Terry Cooney. The umpires for the series were not happy with Clemens because he had been on plate umpire John Hirschbeck from the Boston dugout during the second game, in which Clemens was a nonparticipant. Crew chief Jim Evans had gone over to the dugout to tell Clemens to shut up, but the combative right-hander had also been on umpires during the third game.

This time, Cooney tossed him.

After the game, Clemens claimed that it had been Cooney who had instigated the argument. His position was that he had only replied to the umpire and had not used profanity. Unfortunately for his argument, lip readers looking at the television monitor could see that Clemens was indeed cursing Cooney. "He said a couple of the magic words," said Stewart, referring to the specific profanities that merit automatic ejection. Said Cooney:

I was fully aware of the magnitude of the game, but what he said was audible to all the players in the Oakland dugout. I just felt I had to do my job, and I don't think Roger did his.

Clemens was looking down when Cooney made the gesture that ejected him, so he did not realize at first that he was out of the game. When he did, he charged the umpire and had to be restrained.

Eventually, the game went on. Gallego hit a two-run double off Boston reliever Tom Bolton, and that was all Stewart needed. Though he didn't have a good fastball, he held the Red Sox scoreless for eight innings. The Red Sox finally broke through for a run in the ninth but Honeycutt came in to shut them down as the A's completed the sweep, 3–1.

Stewart was named MVP of the series after winning two games, allowing only two runs in 16 innings. Said an admiring Duncan:

> Dave Stewart manufactures pitches when he has to, and that's what pitching is all about. Look at all those ground balls today. He didn't have his good fastball, so he turned his curve over to get them to hit the ball into the ground.

The playoff games had been impressive, but the World Series against the Cincinnati Reds would be quite different. In retrospect, La Russa knows why:

> That season, we had won 103 games but I thought we won some of those games on reputation. There were some slippages. When we got to our third postseason, we had lost our edge. It wasn't new any more, and we were strutting around. Cincinnati just beat us to the punch in every way. To this day, I think of the '88 Series as a lost opportunity, but '90 is the one that bothers me the most. I don't think you ever take it lightly when you get to the World Series. But I blame myself. When we had a meeting before the Series, I could tell they weren't listening. I probably should have yelled and screamed, but I didn't. When we went out there, we were totally flat.

Despite Welch's spectacular season, Stewart was still considered the A's ace, so when there was a six-day gap between the end of the ALCS and the start of the World Series, there was no question that Stewart would start the opening game. Sadly, this time, he didn't have much to give. The Reds got off to a 2–0 lead in the first inning (after a walk to Billy Hatcher and a homer by Eric Davis), knocked out Stewart after four innings, and cruised to a 7–0 win behind Jose Rijo, which was an especially bitter pill for the A's. They had given up on Rijo, convinced he'd never turn his potential into performance, and had traded him to the Reds, where he had blossomed. He had won 14 games for the Reds that season, the second of what would become five seasons during which he posted win totals in double figures.

But it was the second game that really hurt, because it was a game the A's thought they should have won. They had taken a 4–2 lead with a three-run third, started by Canseco's first home run of the postseason. But they could make no more headway against the Cincinnati bullpen, and everything started to come unraveled in the eighth. The A's were still leading, 4–3, when Hatcher led off the Cincinnati eighth with a long fly to right. Canseco was late starting for the ball and never could catch up. Near the wall he got close enough to touch the ball with his glove but not catch it. The ball fell in for a triple.

Canseco later claimed the ball carried more in the Cincinnati park than he had expected. La Russa's comment: "If you want to win the game, you have got to make that play." The A's manager was usually careful not to publicly criticize his players, but he was losing patience with his temperamental star.

Eckersley seldom came into a tie game, but when the game went into the tenth inning, 4–4, La Russa brought in his ace closer, who quickly learned that all the breaks were going Cincinnati's way. He got a fastball in on the fists to the first batter, Billy Bates, but the weak grounder was so close to the plate that Lansford, coming in from third, couldn't reach it in time to throw Bates out. Playing close to the line for the next batter, Lansford couldn't reach a ground ball through the hole by Chris Sabo that he probably would have handled had he been playing in a normal defensive position. Then Eckersley left a breaking ball out over the plate and Joe Oliver slapped it into left field for a single that scored Bates with the winning run.

The Series came to Oakland for the third game, but the A's looked like a beaten team. Moore was once again the inconsistent pitcher he'd been during the season and was knocked out in a seven-run Reds third. Cincinnati cruised, 8–3.

La Russa benched Canseco, whose only Series hit was his second-game homer, for the fourth game, but that didn't waken the slumbering Oakland offense. They got only a first-inning run off Rijo, who pitched eight innings before giving up the ball to Randy Myers in the ninth.

It seemed for a time that that might be enough for the gutsy Stewart, who carried a 1–0 lead into the eighth. But in the eighth the Reds parlayed two hits (one of which was a bunt), a fielding error by Stewart, and a ground ball into the two runs they needed to win and sweep the Series. Rijo got his second win of the Series, which Eckersley thought made the difference:

> He was as good as Hershiser was in the '88 Series. Any time you have a starter who can win two games in the Series, you've got a tremendous advantage.

Canseco's wife, Esther, called La Russa a "punk" for benching her husband while, publicly at least, Canseco accepted it as part of the game. La Russa said of Esther's criticism, "Its importance to the club is the slightest shade above zero."

What was important was the fact that the A's loss would forever taint their reputation in baseball history. "We were better than the Dodgers in '88 and we were better than Cincinnati in '90," said Eckersley, "but we didn't prove it." La Russa feels that his team was the equal of the three World Series teams of the seventies, but he would never make that claim because his teams won only one World Series:

> We had a special group, but it wasn't as special as those teams in the seventies because they won the big dance three times.

🥎 🥎 🥎

Following his MVP year, Rickey Henderson signed a new, four-year contract for $12 million. At the time, it was the biggest contract in baseball. A beaming Henderson said he wanted to spend the rest of his career with the A's. He couldn't have known that a cycle of new contracts, each bigger than the last, was beginning. Within a few weeks, his contract had been surpassed by several others. Athletes are insecure people, and they sometimes measure their worth by the size of their contract compared to those of their peers. Henderson saw his contract being surpassed almost daily, and he didn't like it one bit.

It would get worse. Just short of the halfway point in the 1991 season, on June 27, Canseco was signed to a five-year, $23.5 million contract. Now Jose was the highest paid player in baseball. There was justification for that contract because Canseco, healthier than he'd been since 1988, was on his way to another great power year, ending with 44 homers and 122 RBIs, a team record. But in Henderson's mind, the A's were telling him that, even coming off an MVP year, he wasn't as important to them as Canseco. Said La Russa:

> We had a kind of ceiling: all our great stars were at $3 million or less. When Jose signed that contract, it really hurt Rickey because the ceiling wasn't the ceiling any more. Sandy [Alderson] said he'd take a look at the contract, but Rickey and his agent didn't like the changes Sandy said he'd make, and that caused a lot of problems.

While not disputing that Canseco's contract caused problems, Alderson thought those disputes were inevitable:

> Rickey was unhappy with his contract a week after he signed it. At the time, we had the attitude that we wanted to keep all our stars. It was almost like a family feeling. So, we went ahead and signed Jose to his contract. That probably contributed to the bad feeling with Rickey, but I think that would have happened, anyway.

Rickey's unhappiness was only part of a general malaise that attacked the A's that season, and not the most important part. Canseco was the only star who had a good year. Henderson broke a record that had once seemed totally out of reach—Ty Cobb's career stolen base mark of 938—finishing the season at 994, but he pulled a left calf muscle early in the year, spent 15 days on the disabled list, and suffered through a subpar season with a .268 batting average, though he did score 105 runs. McGwire looked lost at the plate, falling to a .201 average with just 22 homers; La Russa kept him out of the final game for fear his average would fall below .200, which would have been humiliating.

The A's pitchers suffered correspondingly. Stewart pulled a muscle in his left side in May and had to go on the disabled list; when he came back, he was not himself and finished at 11–11, with a 5.18 ERA. Welch fell off to 12–13. Mike Moore bounced back for a 17–8 year but that was hardly enough to compensate for Stewart and Welch. Eckersley saved 43 games, though he wasn't quite as otherworldly as he'd been the year before.

Even with all their problems, the A's stayed in the race for the first 2½ months; they were in first place in their division as late as June 15. In the first week of September, they were in second place, but it was a distant second, nine games behind Minnesota. At the end, they'd fallen to fourth at 84–78, 11 games back. It was a startling reminder of how quickly a great team can lose its edge.

There would be one more divisional championship the following year, but it was overshadowed by a much more dramatic event: the trade of Canseco to the Texas Rangers for outfielder Ruben Sierra, relief pitcher Jeff Russell, and starter Bobby Witt on August 31. It was all the more dramatic because Canseco had been in the on-deck circle in the first inning when he was pulled back by La Russa, who'd been told a trade was imminent. Remembered Alderson:

> We'd been working on this trade for some time. We were struggling at the time and thought we needed something to get us going again. We liked the closer we got in the deal, although as it turned out, he didn't help us much that year. Ruben Sierra actually played pretty well for us that year and the next year. We lost 5–6 games right after that trade and then Bobby Witt came in and won a game for us.

Jose played that out pretty well, making himself the victim, but when you're on the West Coast, with the time difference [two hours earlier than Texas], trades are often completed just before a game or during it. The trade hadn't actually been made at the moment Canseco was pulled back but we were very close. I didn't think it would be fair to the Rangers if Jose had played and gotten hurt.

Canseco was not having anything like the year he'd had in 1991, with just 22 homers at the time he was traded. Nobody can know whether the A's would have won that year with him. What we do know is that they won without him, eventually winning by six games with a 96–66 record, not as gaudy as their previous championship year marks but a 12-game improvement over 1991.

La Russa has always said that he was proudest of the 1992 team because they won with a much lower talent level than the 1988–1990 teams. Of the big stars from the earlier teams, only McGwire was much of a factor. Resurrecting his career, he hit 42 homers and knocked in 104 runs. With injuries limiting him to 117 games, Rickey Henderson scored only 77 runs. Dave Henderson played only 20 games. Lansford hit just .262. Stewart won just 12 games, Welch 11. Moore and Ron Darling were the top starters, with 17 and 15 wins, and Eckersley had another great year as a closer, with 51 saves. Mike Bordick stepped in at shortstop for the often-injured Weiss and hit an improbable .300 while fielding impeccably. La Russa juggled a number of role players, even including career minor leaguer Eric Fox, and somehow got the team home in front.

McGwire hit a two-run homer to give the A's an early lead in the opener of the American League Championship Series against the Blue Jays, and Stewart pitched well enough to win as the starter, with a 3–2 lead with two outs in the eighth. But when he gave up a double to Dave Winfield, La Russa brought in Russell, who allowed a game-tying single by John Olerud. In the ninth, Harold Baines hit a solo homer to give the A's the lead and Eckersley recorded his 10th ALCS save by retiring three of the four batters he faced in the ninth. Russell got a win he didn't deserve because he was the pitcher of record when Baines homered.

David Cone pitched four-hit shutout ball for eight innings, allowing only three A's to get as far as third base, as the Blue Jays evened the series with a 3–1 win the next day. A Sierra triple and a Baines single in the ninth scored the only A's run.

The Blue Jays won a slugfest in the third game, this one in Oakland, 7–5. Though they got 13 hits, the A's never led and trailed from the fifth inning to the end of the game. Baines had two hits, his third multihit game of the series.

The ALCS turned on the fourth game, a heartbreaking loss for the A's. They had taken a 6–1 lead early, and had a 6–2 lead with two outs and two on base in the eighth. In their successful seasons, La Russa had always had great setup men in relief: Rick Honeycutt and Gene Nelson. Now, however, he no longer had that depth and had to rely more on Eckersley. He brought in his great closer, but this time Eck didn't have it. He gave up two runs in that inning and yielded a two-run homer to Roberto Alomar in the ninth. Said Eckersley:

> That one hurt even more than the Gibson homer because we should have won that game. If we had, we'd have been in the World Series again, I'm sure of that.

In the eleventh, Pat Borders hit a sacrifice fly off Kelly Downs to score Derek Bell with the winning run.

Reaching back into his past, Stewart pitched a complete game seven-hitter to beat the Blue Jays, 6–2, in the fifth game and send the series back to Toronto. There Sierra knocked in three runs, two of them on a first-inning homer. But there would be no Cinderella story this time. Toronto scored twice in the first inning and four times in the third off A's starter Mike Moore in the sixth game, and the Blue Jays coasted to a 9–2 win to clinch the ALCS. It left a bad taste in everyone's mouth, none more so than Eckersley:

> All the awards I won that year meant nothing. All I could think about all winter was that home run I gave up to Alomar.

That was the last gasp for the A's. There would be nothing but bad news ahead for several years. Instead of turning over the team and bringing in younger players, a constant necessity in pro sports, the A's had hung on to veterans who were, in many cases, long past their prime. In part, that was because of owner Walter Haas, who admitted, "I fell in love with my players." But there was also the reality of playing in the Bay Area, where fans can quickly lose interest when the team doesn't win. Said Billy Beane, then a scout who later became the team's general manager:

> We knew there was nothing left in the gas tank, but in the Bay Area, it's very hard to strip a team down when you're still winning. It's like the 49ers: until they went 4–12, nobody really believed that they needed to rebuild. So, we went out and signed some veteran free agents, and that probably set us back a couple of years.

There were some bad moves with their own roster, too, as Alderson admitted in looking back. Ruben Sierra was the main example. As it turned out, the A's had traded one temperamental player, Canseco, for another one with less talent. Sierra played when he wanted to, hustled when he wanted to. His statistics looked better than they really were because he often got hits and home runs in games that were already hopelessly lost. Yet the A's re-signed him when his contract was up. Said Alderson:

> That's where I'd fault myself. Sometimes you get in the position where you think you have to sign the player you traded for to justify the contract. What you have to realize is that, in this free-agent era, you're really trading money, and that money is fungible. You can use it to re-sign the player, or you can use it to go out and get another one. That decision led to some other bad ones, as we tried to hang on to veteran players and it went downhill in a hurry.

171

At one point, Sierra referred to Alderson as "the village idiot." An angry La Russa, already disenchanted with the outfielder, defended Alderson and criticized Sierra, who was soon traded.

$$\ominus \quad \ominus \quad \ominus$$

Sadly, as his team was going downhill, Walter A. Haas was dying. He put the team on the market, eventually selling it to Steve Schott and Ken Hofmann for $70 million, probably $30 million below market price, to ensure that the team would be kept in Oakland.

Haas was truly the last of the gentleman owners. He had taken huge losses in the last years of his ownership to try to keep the team together, he had never interfered with the baseball operations, and he had treated everyone, from players to newspapermen, with respect. His like will never be seen again.

CHAPTER 16

Changing of the Guard

The A's new owners, Steve Schott and Ken Hofmann, were greeted by a hailstorm of criticism shortly after they took over and started trading and releasing veteran players to reduce their payroll. Noted announcer Bill King:

> They really had no chance, following Walter Haas. Anybody would have looked bad in that circumstance.

Schott was designated as the managing partner because Hofmann preferred to stay in the background, as he had in a previous ownership position with the Seattle Seahawks. Though Hofmann was influential enough in NFL circles to be on some important committees, he was so determined to stay out of the spotlight that his picture never appeared in media guides.

Schott had made his money in real estate, beginning his career with the late Wayne Valley (one of the original owners of the Oakland Raiders), and he was a tough businessman. He had negotiated for a protracted period before concluding the deal on the A's, asking and getting additional concessions. "You never saw such a reluctant buyer," said Wally Haas. His father, who was selling because he didn't want to burden his heirs with estate tax problems, almost pulled out because he was so annoyed by Schott's bargaining. He didn't, and the deal was finally made for about $70 million, $10 million below Haas's original asking price, which had already been at least $30 million below market value.

A's fans feared that Schott was a replica of Haas's predecessor. Said Schott:

> I'm getting letters saying, "Don't Finley us." That's not me. Nobody wants to win more than I do, but we couldn't do it with the club we had. We have to rebuild.

In fact, that was the strategy that had been proposed by general manager Sandy Alderson:

> I advised Steve to cut the payroll and put that money into scouting and development. He and Ken have put more money into those programs than we've ever had. We have more scouts than ever.

It wasn't the first time Alderson had thought of rebuilding. In 1990, even as the A's were in the process of winning their third straight American League pennant, Alderson had drafted four pitchers in the first round or as supplemental picks in between the first and second round, the extra picks coming because of trades or free-agent losses by the A's. The four pitchers—Todd Van Poppel, Kirk Dressendorfer, David Zancanaro, and Don Peters—were called "The Four Aces." Alderson and his scouts thought these young pitchers would be the starting rotation in 3–4 years, allowing the A's to make a nearly seamless transition from the Dave Stewart/Bob Welch/Mike Moore years.

In fact, none of these pitchers ever helped the A's. Dressendorfer had arm problems from the start; he had pitched too many innings in college ball. Zancanaro and Peters also had arm problems on and off.

But Van Poppel, whose arm was sound, was the biggest disappointment. The A's had fallen in love with the radar gun. Van Poppel's fastball had been timed at 95 mph when he was a high school pitcher, overwhelming hitters at that level. He had been projected as possibly the very first pick in the draft, but other teams backed off when he insisted he was going to college. The A's drafted him in the middle of the round and convinced him he should take their offer and forego college. When he did, everybody thought the A's had stolen a pitcher who would be the best of his generation.

It didn't happen that way. Van Poppel's fastball had no movement. That made no difference in high school because the overmatched hitters couldn't get around on it. To major league hitters, though, a 95-mph fastball with no movement is simply an invitation to hit a home run. Van Poppel's curve was barely adequate, and he made no attempt to learn another pitch. The A's tried to move him to the bullpen, where he might have been able to survive, but he resisted. When they put him on waivers in August of 1996—he was claimed by the Detroit Tigers—he had compiled an 18–29 mark in 3½ major league seasons. Other clubs continued to be mesmerized by his fastball, though, and Van Poppel was still on a major league roster, that of the Chicago Cubs, going into spring training for the 2001 season, at which time he had a 26–42 career mark with a 5.88 ERA.

With the youth movement faltering and the veterans fading, the A's were in free fall, finishing 68–94 in 1993, a whopping 26 games back of AL West division leader Chicago. They were somewhat better in the next two years, both of which were abbreviated because of a players strike that started at the end of 1994 and continued into 1995, as they finished 51–63 and 67–77.

There was no hope for the future and, with the new ownership taking over, Alderson advised his friend, Tony La Russa, to leave and take a managerial offer made by the St. Louis Cardinals. Said Alderson in the spring of 2001:

Tony is very competitive. He wants to know that he has a chance to win every day, as well as cumulatively. It was obvious at that point that we were going to have to tear everything down and rebuild, and it would be some time before we could be competitive again. He was much better off going to St. Louis, where he had a chance to win.

Shortly after that, Dennis Eckersley was traded to the Cardinals, at his request, to be with his favorite manager. Another chapter in A's history was closed.

To replace La Russa, Alderson hired Art Howe, who was as different from La Russa as it was possible to be. La Russa drove players hard, and he was not patient with young players who didn't produce. Howe was much more laid-back, much more patient. "I thought he would be the right manager for the kind of club we would have for the next few years," said Alderson. Howe had previously managed for five years in Houston after a 10-year major league playing career, and he was dead-center for those five years: two winning seasons, two losing seasons, and one at an even 81–81. His teams had won as many as 86 games and lost as many as 97 in a season. After the big losing season, when the Astros were rebuilding, he had brought the team back to 85–77 two seasons later, but it wasn't enough to save his job.

Howe understood what he was facing in Oakland:

When I was hired I knew there was a great tradition of championship teams here, but that it was time to rebuild. I thought maybe we could hold things together for awhile because we still had some good veteran players, guys like Mark McGwire, Terry Steinbach, and Mike Bordick. But we didn't have the pitching we needed. You can't tell your fans that, though, especially when they've been used to winning teams. They expect you to keep winning, no matter what.

Howe was understating the case when he said the A's didn't have enough pitching. In fact, the talent level on the pitching staff was lower than it had been since 1979, when the A's lost 108 games. Nothing was working for the A's. The young pitchers they drafted failed. They selected Cuban pitcher Ariel Prieto as their top pick in the 1995 draft (fifth pick overall), because at 27, Prieto seemed ready to help immediately. But despite his success in Cuba, Prieto did little for the A's. When they traded for young pitchers Steve Karsay and Jimmy Haynes, both of whom seemed to have bright futures, they failed too, Karsay because of arm problems, Haynes because he seemed to have no comprehension of what it took to win. Eventually, the A's got rid of both.

Said Howe:

> When I went to spring training that first year, I didn't know the team, and I especially didn't know the pitching staff. I told the guys before we started that I'd be going on spring results to determine the staff. That's a terrible way to do it, but I had no choice. Billy Taylor, who was a guy I wanted on my staff, looked terrible that spring. I didn't want to cut him but I had to stick with my word. Billy wanted to quit, but I told him to stick with it, he'd be back, and he ended up being my closer for three years.

Howe also had to learn a new league, and a new philosophy.

> I was a National League guy. I'd been a player in the National League, a coach, a manager. There's definitely a different style of play in the two leagues. You really see it now in the inter-league games. You see the hit-and-run, the bunt much more from National League teams.
>
> There are still times when I'd like to use the bunt more. I believe in the bunt. But players today can't bunt. You have to want to lay down a bunt to do it. You can see it in the body language with a lot of these guys. They'll miss the ball the first time, then take a strike, so you've got to take off the bunt sign. They never wanted to bunt in the first place.

The management of his new team didn't believe in the bunt, either. Alderson's theory was, as he said later, "a walk and a dong [home run]." While others talked of batting average and the running game, Alderson talked about on-base percentage, which measures both hits and walks. Said Alderson:

There's very little correlation between a team's batting average and the number of runs scored. There is a great correlation between a team's on-base percentage and the number of runs scored.

Alderson didn't rule out the stolen base as a weapon—this was, after all, the team that had employed Rickey Henderson off and on during his Hall of Fame career. But he made it plain that he didn't believe in some of the hoariest adages of baseball. For instance, he didn't accept the belief that a hitter is doing his job if he advances a runner from second to third by grounding out to the right side. The A's had gotten into the computer age ahead of most teams in the eighties, and Alderson had statistics to back up his contentions.

The A's were hardly the first team to use this style. In the sixties, Baltimore Orioles manager Earl Weaver had preached the virtues of the three-run homer (with the home run often preceded by at least one walk), over the running game, the stolen base, and the hit-and-run. But the A's had been teaching that style of play throughout their minor league system—even to their Latino players, who are not, traditionally, patient at the plate. The players from the Dominican Republic even had a saying—"you don't walk off the island"—meaning you had to be a strong hitter to get the attention of the American scouts.

Howe was a reluctant convert to the A's station-to-station game, but Alderson and his successor, Billy Beane, kept reminding him that the game was different in the American League, and he gradually began to understand that.

In Howe's first season the A's finished 78–84, even though the pitching staff didn't have a starter who won more than the eight wins posted by John Wasdin (and Wasdin's ERA was a sky-high 5.96). As Howe had promised, Taylor was promoted from the minors early and, with 17 saves, was perhaps the only bright spot on the pitching staff. Hitting powered the A's and compensated for some of the pitching shortcomings; Mark McGwire hit 52 homers, free-agent pickup Geronimo Berroa added 36, Terry Steinbach hit 35, and the A's set a franchise record with 243 home runs. The usually clear-thinking

Alderson was encouraged enough with that showing, and with Jose Canseco coming back to the team as a free agent, to predict that the A's could win 10 more games the following season. Instead the team fell back, to 65–97.

It was a disastrous year in many respects, and nothing demonstrated that more than the forced trade of McGwire, whose career had gone through some amazing twists and turns. Constant foot problems had limited him to only 74 games combined in the 1993–1994 seasons, and critics said his work with weights had built up his upper body so much that it put impossible strain on his feet and legs. In 1995, McGwire was able to play 104 games, and he hit 39 home runs. In 1996, he played 130 games and his 52 homers, a personal best, led the league. In 1997, he was on the way to an even bigger season.

But the A's couldn't afford him. He was making $5 million a year, roughly 25 percent of the A's total payroll. Alderson estimated that the average customer meant a profit of $10, counting admission and the club's share of parking and commissions, so McGwire would have to bring in an additional 500,000 customers to pay his salary. The A's total attendance was less than 1.2 million in 1996 and only up about 100,000 the next year, so McGwire's home runs weren't doing much for the gate. And, with or without McGwire, the A's were a losing team. Said Alderson:

> There was no way we were going to keep McGwire. He didn't want to stay, either. He was a 10/5 guy [10 years in the majors, at least 5 of which were with one team, which gave him the right to veto a trade], but he waived his rights so he could be traded. We wanted to trade him during the season because we didn't want to be dealing with that story all year, and we felt it would be better to go into the next season with that well behind us instead of being still fresh in everybody's mind.
>
> There wasn't much of a market for him, surprisingly. The Angels were the only other club at all interested, and they didn't want to give up players in a trade because they thought they had a chance to pick up McGwire as a free agent after the season.

When it comes to midseason trades, teams are usually looking for pitchers, not position players, and as it happened, Mark didn't make a difference for the Cardinals that year.

The A's had no leverage, so Alderson knew he couldn't get full value for McGwire. He made the best trade he could under the circumstances, getting reliever T. J. Mathews and minor league pitchers Eric Ludwick and Blake Stein. Mathews was still with the club in 2001 (he's since been released), but the other two were long gone. Meanwhile, McGwire was setting major league home-run records in St. Louis.

However, trading McGwire was by no means a total loss for the A's; it made room for Jason Giambi at first base. Said Howe:

> We didn't really know what to do with Jason at that point. We knew he could hit, but we couldn't find a position for him. We tried him at third base when Scott Brosius was injured, but then Scott came back so we put Jason in the outfield, but he can't run very well so he was never going to be good there. Then his mentor and close friend gets traded, so that gave him an opening at his natural position. Since then, he's improved his statistics every year.

By 2000, Giambi was the American League's Most Valuable Player.

Even though the A's had added another free-agent find in Matt Stairs, who hit 27 homers, McGwire's departure left a serious void. Canseco battled injuries all season and hit a disappointing 23 homers. Overall, the A's hit 197 homers, still an impressive total but not good enough to compensate for the dreadful pitching staff. Once again, the A's had no starter in double figures and once again Taylor, with 23 saves, was virtually the only bright spot.

After the season the A's would also lose Steinbach and Bordick to free agency, but it was the McGwire trade that really demonstrated how far the A's had fallen. Said Howe:

> We were just trying to avoid losing 100 games. I'd been in that situation before in Houston, and it's ugly.

The A's did manage to fall three games short of that negative standard.

Alderson would be moving on in a couple of years to work as an assistant to Commissioner Bud Selig, but first he wanted to get the A's house in order. His first move was to bump assistant general manager Beane, a former A's player and scout who was only 35 years old, to the role of general manager. That would turn out to be a critical change for the next great stage in Oakland A's history.

Though the move didn't come until after the season, Beane knew it was coming:

I remember when we were walking out to the parking lot the night we'd traded McGwire. It had been a very long day for Sandy. He was close to Mac personally, and he knew what trading him meant for the image of the franchise. But he said to me, "That's one thing you won't have to worry about." That was the first sign of what was coming for me.

The Beane promotion was a no-brainer for Alderson. Certainly Beane's youth didn't matter; Alderson had also been 35 when he'd been put in charge of baseball operations for the A's. Said Alderson:

After the '97 season, everything seemed in disarray. There was pressure to fire the manager, to fire the coaches, to fire everybody. Instead, I promoted Billy. He had been in on all of the decisions, anyway, and I was getting more involved with other [business] parts of the operation. I knew he was ready, and that he'd do a good job. And this took the emphasis away from making other changes.

We were in better shape than everybody realized. If you win on the major league level, everybody thinks that you're doing everything right in the organization, that you're scouting better, you're doing a better job of evaluating talent, you're even better at taking out the trash. If you're losing at the major league level, everybody assumes the organization is doing a bad job everywhere.

Just the opposite can be true. Winning at the major league level can cover up for mistakes, and you can be doing the right things at the minor league level and not yet winning at the major league level. That's what was happening with us at the time. We were building a good foundation but the players that would win for us hadn't yet made it to the major leagues.

Soon those players would be arriving in Oakland and, with the help of judicious moves by Beane, would sweep away the ugly memories of the 1997 season.

CHAPTER 17

Enter Billy Beane

Billy Beane is the architect of the success of the current A's; he's also an example of how the role of general manager has changed. The model general manager for most of the 20th century was the schmoozer who knew everybody in baseball and who spent his day in the office making phone calls. When he made a trade, he relied on the evaluations of scouts, almost never getting out in the field himself.

The Oakland A's had never had that kind of general manager. Charlie Finley was his own general manager and Sandy Alderson had been an attorney who learned about baseball and the art of the deal on the job.

Beane was still another type: a young man who had been a major league player, starting his six-year career with the New York Mets and ending it with the A's, and who went into scouting with the A's when his playing career ended. His strength was in evaluating talent, and he would never be deskbound.

At Alderson's urging, Beane would add another facet to his job. Said Beane:

Sandy told me when I became his assistant that he wanted me negotiating contracts. A lot of general managers leave that for somebody else, but Sandy said with a small-market team, you always have to know how a contract will affect your team. You always have to be conscious of your payroll. So, I've always negotiated contracts.

Throughout their history, Beane noted, the A's have often been a team with limited revenues. The original owner and manager, Connie Mack, was a former player whose lack of money forced him to break up two dynasty teams: the 1910–1914 squad, which won four pennants and three World Series, and the 1929–1931 teams, which won three straight pennants and two World Series. Finley's operation had always been run with a tight control on spending. Only during the Walter Haas years of ownership had the A's been big spenders and now, with Steve Schott and Ken Hofmann, they had returned to a tight payroll. Said Beane:

. . . that has encouraged creativity. Sandy brought in young guys who were bright and had varied backgrounds and then gave us all the chance to show what we could do.

Now it was Beane's turn. At the end of his first year he would hire 26-year-old Paul DePodesta, who had worked three years for the Cleveland Indians. Said Beane:

Here's a guy who graduated cum laude from Harvard with an economics degree who wanted to work in baseball. He's terrifically bright, and he's doing a great job for us.

Beane was part of a legacy that had started with Roy Eisenhardt, who had looked for intelligent people to work in the operation, disregarding factors like relative youth or lack of experience. Now, with the A's budget lowered again, the franchise needed the enthusiasm and energy of young men in charge. But Beane also relied on Grady Fuson, who had been in the organization since 1982 and was named scouting director in 1995, and Keith Lieppman, who had been named director of player personnel in 1992, after both managing and playing in the A's minor league system. Said Beane:

The fact that we've had that kind of continuity in our organization has been a tremendous help. We're all on the same page.

With limited resources, Beane knew he had to lay out ground rules. The A's couldn't compete with the big-market teams for star players from other countries (who do not go into the major league draft), such as the top Japanese players. They would spend time and money in the Mexican and Caribbean areas (where so many players are now emerging), but they would go after the younger players that they could sign for small bonuses (or none at all) before they had developed enough to attract attention from other teams.

They would also look for specific types of players. Said Beane:

We know, with our financial limits, that we can't get players who have everything, so the one thing we sacrifice is speed. We'll never be able to sign the "five-tools" player [who is above average in running, fielding, throwing, hitting for average, and hitting for power]. But hitters who are not fast are undervalued, and this has become a hitter's game. We know we can win with that kind of player.

A's scouts concentrated on finding players who hit for high averages. Again, Beane:

I don't want to hear about a player who has good power but doesn't hit for average. A player who hits for average when he's young will develop power as he adds weight and strength and learns what pitches he can drive for home runs. But a kid who can only hit for power will never be able to hit for average, and major league pitchers will take away much of his power when they learn his weaknesses.

Although Beane wanted good defensive players, he also thought the change in the game in the nineties—to one with much more offense—meant that a team couldn't afford to sacrifice offense, even at the prime defensive positions like shortstop and catcher:

You can't afford to sacrifice a spot in your batting order. And I've told my scouts never to push a high school catcher who can "catch and throw." You and I could catch a high school pitcher who's only throwing 75 miles an hour. If a catcher is a good hitter, we can find a position for him if he isn't good enough defensively. But if all he's got is defense, we can't play him.

Beane has also changed the way the A's scouts look at pitchers:

In 1990, Todd Van Poppel was clearly the top pitching prospect in the draft, and Steve Karsay was in that draft, too. Three years later, Karsay was much more advanced, so I took out the video tapes from '90 to see what the scouts were looking at when they made their evaluations. You could see that Van Poppel had a big fastball but even in those tapes, you could see that Karsay was a much better athlete. He was quicker moving around the mound, he was quicker throwing.

From that point, we started looking more at athletic ability when we evaluated young pitchers. Tim Hudson was an All-American as a designated hitter in college, and he also played center field. Mark Mulder played some first base in college. And we had the example of Kenny Rogers [acquired for Scott Brosius in a November 1997 trade], who is a great athlete. He's the best fielding pitcher I've ever seen, almost a fifth infielder, and he really helped himself with that ability.

In evaluating prospects in the minor league system, Beane looks closely at the age of the players; he knows that the age at which a young player proves he can play in the major leagues is a great predictor of both the player's longevity and the type of career he will have. Almost without exception, major league position players are at their best when they're in the 27–32 age group, although pitchers can sometimes extend that period because the smart ones use their knowledge to compensate for declining physical skills in their thirties.

Since it usually takes a player a couple of years to really learn how to cope with major league pitching, a player who first arrives at age 25 will be in his peak in two years; so, it's reasonable to expect that he can be an effective player for the next five years and perhaps for another two after that. By 35, he'll probably be out of the major leagues. A player who doesn't arrive until he's 27 is already at his peak, so he'll probably be on the downside of his career when he hits 30–31. But a player who can make it when he's 20–22 quite likely has Hall of Fame potential. Willie Mays, Mickey Mantle, and Hank Aaron were 20 when they arrived. Ken Griffey Jr. was only 19.

So, the emphasis in the A's scouting has been to sign players who have a good chance to reach the majors at an early age. But there was another important component in building the A's: the lower tier of major league free agents. Beane wasn't concerned about age with these players. He wanted the nucleus of the team to be homegrown young players, but he also planned to fill in some gaps with older role players. To do that, he had to separate the wheat from the chaff. There are many players who bounce around, get in a few major league games, and then go back to the minors. The trick is to find ones who can stick and help the team, even though it won't be for a long period.

One such player was Geronimo Berroa, who was already 29 when he signed with the A's in 1994, having played just 115 major league games. But in the equivalent of just over three full seasons, he hit 87 homers for the A's.

A more important example (because he played at a time when the A's were building a contending team) was Matt Stairs, who had seemed to be a career minor leaguer when, already 28, he joined the A's in 1996. Stairs flourished with the A's, hitting 26 homers and knocking in 104 runs as they returned to respectability in 1998. He was also very popular with fans, media, and teammates, an always cheerful man whose build made him look more like a bowler on a beer distributor's team than a baseball player. He had a sweeping swing that was almost as much vertical as it was horizontal, and he never gave less than his best.

Beane would sign another such player, Olmedo Saenz, after the 1998 season. Saenz was a perfect role player, so happy at finally getting a chance to stick in the big leagues at 28 that he would play third, first, or designated hitter—or stay on the bench until he was needed. When he was in the lineup, he gave the A's a solid right-handed bat, and manager Art Howe was confident enough of his ability that he would use Saenz as a cleanup hitter in the 2000 playoffs.

Billy Taylor, who had been signed when Alderson was the general manager and Beane the assistant, was another example of the kind of steals the A's were getting, although he was a pitcher, not a position player. Taylor was perhaps the most amazing story of all. At 32, he had not pitched an inning of major league ball when the A's signed him in 1994, and then he was injured and missed all of the 1995 season. Yet he persevered and was a very effective closer for the A's until he was traded in midseason 1999. He had his best season in 1998, saving 33 games.

While the team was still in spring training in 1998, Beane showed that he wasn't fearful of making big moves when he fired pitching coach Bob Cluck and replaced him with Rick Peterson, who had just been hired in the off-season as the roving minor league pitching instructor. Said Beane:

> The timing maybe wasn't the best, and it was hard because Bob was a good friend, but Rick had already shown that he had some special qualities.

Peterson worked on the mental game with his pitchers as much as the physical mechanics. His philosophy:

> There are four elements to pitching: velocity, motion, changing speeds, and location. Of those, location is the most important on the major league level because it does no good to have motion if you can't get the ball over the plate. Changing speeds is the second most important because you have to keep hitters off balance; motion is the third and velocity is the least important. But when pitchers are starting out, it's just the reverse: velocity is the most important because high school and even

minor league hitters can't catch up to a really good fastball. But major league hitters can, if they know it's coming and where it's going to be. The pitchers who can change their approach are the ones who are successful. The ones who can't, who keep thinking velocity is the most important, are the ones people look at and wonder why they aren't winning.

Perhaps the best example of a pitcher succeeding because he listened to Peterson's message is Gil Heredia, who had bounced back and forth between the major and minor leagues when he arrived in Oakland in 1998. He improved enough under Peterson's tutelage to warrant the starting assignment for the 1999 opener against the Yankees and Roger Clemens. It seemed that Heredia was being thrown to the wolves, but the A's won the game, 5–3 (though Heredia did not get the win); and he went on to win 13 games.

Heredia followed Peterson's instructions on location and changing speeds, compensating for a mediocre fastball. He also listened to what seemed like a heretical notion from his pitching coach: that his control was sometimes too good. Heredia had prided himself on seldom walking hitters but Peterson pointed out that a walk could be preferable to giving a good hitter a pitch he could drive for extra bases or even a home run.

Because baseball is such a random game, Peterson monitors his pitchers for pitch count and strikes but doesn't pay much attention to individual games. Instead, he watches their season-long performance. Pitchers can throw good pitches that are hit and bad pitches that are not, but over the course of a season, those who throw more good pitches will be more successful.

Peterson is also a strong advocate of pitching ahead in the count. He explains:

That doesn't necessarily mean throwing a strike on the first pitch, but it does mean throwing two strikes in the first three pitches. The pitch that's thrown on a 1–1 count is the most important because hitters facing a 1–2 count average .220 hitting the next pitch. If the count is 2–1, they hit .280 and if it goes to 3–1, the league-wide average for hitters is .460. There are some guys who hit better than .500 on a 3–1 count.

Peterson would have more to work with than Cluck, who had been hired by the A's because he was Howe's friend (he had been Howe's pitching coach in Houston, too). In 1998, the A's would finally have a true staff leader. Just before turning over the reins to Beane, Alderson traded for Rogers, who won 16 games for the A's in 1998. Before much longer, the young pitchers would be arriving—Hudson, Mulder, and Barry Zito—and they would give the A's the framework for a contending team. In 1998, the A's were just beginning the building, but it was clear that better things were coming.

$$\ominus \quad \ominus \quad \ominus$$

"We knew as far back as '92, when I was still a scout, that we'd have to retool," remembered Beane:

> The first really big step for our organization was when we signed Ben Grieve in the '94 draft. That was a little different move for us because he was a high school player, but everybody knew he'd be a big hitter in the majors in time. The Haas family still owned the team, and I can remember Wally saying, "This isn't going to do me any good. I'll be gone before he comes up." He was kidding, of course, and he gave his approval to sign Ben.

Grieve had a great baseball pedigree. His dad, Tom, had been the general manager for the Texas Rangers, and Ben remembered picking up towels in the dressing room when he was a kid. In high school, with a left-handed swing that reminded everybody of Ted Williams, he had scouts drooling. Nobody doubted that he'd hit both for average and power in the big leagues, and that he'd have a long career. The A's took him with the second pick in the first round.

Grieve struggled with minor league pitching for a good part of his first 2½ seasons, but he hit his stride in a big way in 1997, the year he turned 21. Starting at Huntsville in Double A, he hit .328 with 24 homers and 108 RBIs in just 100 games. Advanced to Tacoma in Triple A, he hit .426 with seven homers and 28 RBIs in 27 games. In 127 minor league games, he had hit .350 with 31 homers and 136 RBIs, totals that won him the minor league Player of the Year award from both *Baseball America* and *The Sporting News*.

The A's brought him up in September and he hit .312 with three homers and 24 RBIs in 24 games. In a full season in Oakland in 1998, he hit a respectable .288 with 18 homers, 89 RBIs, and 94 runs scored. He was the American League Rookie of the Year, and it was obvious that he was just beginning.

Another significant arrival in 1998 was shortstop Miguel Tejada, who was brought up in late May, just after his 22nd birthday. Tejada would probably have made it even sooner but an injured finger had forced him onto the disabled list for a time. That first season, Tejada was alternately awesome and awful. He committed 26 errors, the most by an A's shortstop since Alfredo Griffin had made 30 in 1985, though he played only 105 games. At other times, though, he made breathtaking plays, often going deep into the hole to throw a batter out. Still, his decision-making was poor, with many of his errors coming when he rushed throws, and he sometimes lost concentration, making errors on what should have been routine plays. He was just as inconsistent as a hitter. He showed signs of power, with 11 home runs, but he was more likely to swing at a ball over his head than wait for a good strike. He hit only .233. The A's were willing to live with Tejada's inconsistency for the moment because of his youth and potential. With much hard work, and some excellent coaching by Ron Washington, Tejada would smooth out his game in the next two seasons. By 2001, his manager considered him to be the team's most indispensable player.

There was one last significant arrival in September: third baseman Eric Chavez, who came with a minor league season comparable to Grieve's the year before. Chavez had hit .328 with 22 homers and 86 RBIs in just 88 games at Huntsville. Promoted to Tacoma, he hit 11 homers with 40 RBIs in 47 games. His minor league numbers (a combined .327, 33 homers, and 126 RBIs) had earned him Player of the Year honors. When the A's brought him up in September, he hit .311 in 16 games—and he would not be 21 until December. Mindful of his age, Beane thought Chavez had the best chance for a great career of any of the A's young players.

This was a better balanced A's team, with improved pitching. Jason Giambi, at 27 a senior citizen compared to the youngest A's, had his best year, with 27 homers and 110 RBIs. The A's were never in serious contention but their 74–88 record was a significant improvement over the bleak 1997 season. With the pipeline still full of good prospects, the future was bright.

CHAPTER 18

A Glimpse of Hope

By 1999, more of the A's future was arriving. When he took over as general manager the year before, Billy Beane identified four position players as key to the A's future: outfielder Ben Grieve, shortstop Miguel Tejada, third baseman Eric Chavez, and catcher Ramon Hernandez. Grieve was American League Rookie of the Year in 1998, Tejada had come up in May, and Chavez joined the A's in September. Only Hernandez was still in the minors, but he would be brought up in June. Beane, a very competitive man whose ideal as a manager was Tony La Russa (for whom he had played briefly), knew that a team that had only young players had no chance to win; so, he filled in around the edges with veteran free agents with low price tags, including Olmedo Saenz, Tony Phillips, and Tim Raines.

But none of those three would be as important as John Jaha, whose contribution came as a surprise to virtually everybody but Beane. Jaha was a powerful right-handed hitter who had hit .300 with 34 homers and 118 RBIs in 1996, but it seemed as if he could not stay healthy. Because of his constant problems with his feet, he had only twice played more than 100 major league games in a season since he had first come up in 1992. The previous two years, he had played in 119 games combined for Milwaukee. He was a free agent in the winter of 1999 and the consensus in baseball was that, at 32, his career was virtually over.

Beane didn't think so. In private conversations for two months he had talked enthusiastically about how much Jaha could mean to the club, but he had to wait and hope that Jaha wouldn't get a better offer than the minimal one the A's could make. Finally, the process ended when Jaha signed with the A's on February 17, just before the opening of spring training.

Used primarily as a designated hitter, Jaha would be everything Beane expected and more in 1999, hitting a career-high 35 home runs and knocking in 111 runs. He won the Comeback Player of the Year award and was named to the All-Star team in July.

Jaha's contribution was especially important early in the season because Grieve was locked in a fearsome slump, hitting only .131 in May, and Chavez was also struggling in his first full season. Manager Art Howe benched Grieve for a time against left-handers. He eventually got back in the groove and, though his season average would slip to .265, he increased his home runs from 18 to 28. Chavez was also platooned for a time, with Saenz, because of his problems against left-handers. In September he would also be sidelined by a foot injury. Though nobody close to the club doubted his potential, Chavez hit an unremarkable .247 in 115 games. Surprisingly, the strongest part of his game as a rookie was his defense. In the minors, he had the reputation of being a poor fielder, but he worked very hard in spring training that year and played very well during the season, despite an occasional flub of what should have been a routine play.

The other veterans weren't much help. Raines was diagnosed with lupus in midseason, after hitting just .215 in 58 games. Phillips was a versatile player who could play in the infield or outfield, but at 39, there wasn't much left in his tank; he hit .244 in 106 games. The A's were at least solid in right field with Stairs, who hit 38 homers and was especially deadly in the clutch. Three of his home runs won the game in the ninth and 22 of them either tied the game or put the A's ahead. Grieve, when he emerged from his slump, was a productive hitter, though an uncertain fielder in left field.

The A's never did solve their center field problem. Ryan Christenson was their best outfielder but a weak hitter and Jason McDonald was mediocre in both departments. In August the A's would trade for veteran Rich Becker, but he gave them only marginal improvement.

There was one position the A's could improve: catcher. A. J. Hinch, a steady defensive catcher with a mediocre throwing arm, was supposed to at least keep the position warm while Hernandez was improving his catching skills in the minors. But with Hinch hitting only .197 in late June, Beane ran out of patience with him and brought up Hernandez, who would have to learn on the job. Hernandez improved greatly when he got his chance, both defensively and as a hitter.

Beane had a similarly pragmatic approach to the A's pitching staff. The A's were emphasizing pitching in the draft; they would take Mark Mulder in the first round in June and Barry Zito in the first round the following year, and they drafted several other pitchers in lower rounds. But in the meantime, they had to have some veterans to keep the team afloat while the young pitchers were developing. Gil Heredia had been an unexpected boon, but Tom Candiotti was the most interesting story because of his age—he would be 42 in August—and the fact that he threw the knuckleball, a very rare pitch.

Candiotti had started his career in 1979 and spent most of his first seven seasons in the minors. At the time he threw the same pitches as every other pitcher, none of them very well. He would fool around on the sidelines at times with the knuckleball and, with the encouragement of a teammate, decided to try it in a game. The pitch had kept him in the big leagues ever since.

The knuckleball is usually thrown with the knuckles of a pitcher's two first fingers against the ball, though it can also be thrown with the tips of the two fingers against the ball. Thrown with the same motion as a fastball, its speed is considerably lower, and the ball will behave unpredictably as it approaches the plate. It is very difficult for the catcher to catch, which makes it almost impossible to prevent base runners from stealing, and it is often a difficult pitch to control. For those reasons, most managers discourage pitchers from throwing it. But it is also a very difficult pitch to hit, and it puts much less strain on the arm, so a pitcher who masters it can pitch more innings. For instance, in a four-year span (1971–1975), knuckleball pitcher Wilbur

Wood of the Chicago White Sox won 90 games while pitching 334, 376, 359, and 320 innings.

Candiotti wasn't that effective but he did win 16 games for Cleveland the first season he threw the knuckler, and he helped hold the A's staff together in 1998, winning 11 games and giving advice and encouragement to the young pitchers. A native of nearby Walnut Creek, he was active in charity work and was closely associated with the A's; he even supplied the voice message for the A's telephone answering system. But he struggled early in the 1999 season with a bad knee and a torn fingernail, going 1–3 with a 7.53 ERA in his last five starts.

Candiotti was about to give way to the future. On June 7, the A's brought up Tim Hudson and released the veteran Candiotti. "Tim's performance really forced this move," Beane said. "Tim has earned this right." In college, Hudson had been known as much for his hitting as his pitching. As a senior at Auburn in 1997, he had been the Southeastern Conference Player of the Year as he hit .396 with 18 homers as an outfielder and designated hitter while posting a 15–2 record with a 2.97 ERA as a pitcher. Despite those spectacular feats, he lasted until the sixth round of the draft, when the A's picked him. He did not look like an athlete, with just 165 pounds on a frame that is generously listed at 6'1" in the A's media guide, though most observers think he's less than 6'0". Nor was his fastball overwhelming, usually in the high 80s, low 90s. He was not overly impressive when he started minor league ball, going 3–1 in a rookie league in 1997, then 4–0 at Modesto (Class A) and 10–9 at Huntsville (Class AA) the next season.

In the spring of 1999, however, everything came together for Hudson. His pitches had so much movement that hitters rarely got a good swing off him. San Francisco Giants broadcaster Mike Krukow, a former pitcher, said Hudson was the most impressive pitcher he had seen in Arizona.

The A's had switched their Double A affiliation to Midland, Texas. Hudson pitched three times there, giving up nine hits and one earned run in 18 innings, and won all three games. Promoted to the Triple A Pacific Coast League in Vancouver, he went 4–0, gave up 38 hits in 49 innings, and struck out 61. "The kid is unbelievable," said Vancouver pitching coach Pete Richert, a former major league pitcher. "He keeps the ball down and everything moves."

"I think mainly I've just learned how to pitch," said Hudson, when he arrived in Oakland:

> Last year, I just tried to overdo it. Now I'm trying to hit my spots, have guys put the ball in play. If they don't put it in play early in the count, I try to finish it out with two strikes, get them to swing and miss.

Hudson became an even better pitcher after he joined the A's and learned a changeup from pitching coach Rick Peterson. "I showed him the five basic grips," said Peterson. "He decided on one, and he threw it." After he threw one, Hudson turned to Peterson and said, "Is that what you're talking about?" Peterson said, "It doesn't get much better than that." Teaching Hudson was so easy according to Peterson that, "The guy making the popcorn could be the pitching coach for Tim Hudson."

Meanwhile, another interesting pitching story was playing out with the unquestioned ace of the staff, Kenny Rogers. He would be a free agent at the end of the season and had made it clear that he didn't want to stay in Oakland. His home was in Tampa, Florida, and he wanted to play for a team closer to that location.

Beane said frequently that he wouldn't trade Rogers if the team were in contention at midseason. He was prepared to have Rogers walk away at the end of the season because the A's would get a first-round draft pick and a "sandwich" pick between the first and second rounds in 2000 as compensation. Given their recent history, Beane was confident that they could draft players who would help in the future.

Two factors changed Beane's mind. One was that the New York Mets dangled minor league outfielder Terrence Long in front of him. Long had been rated just behind Grieve as a high school hitter in 1994. He had taken longer to develop as a hitter but was a much better all-around player, an excellent defensive center fielder who could run and throw. Beane was convinced he would develop power and hit for average, too. "We don't often get a chance at a player with his athleticism," he said.

Rogers' attitude, though, was the more important factor. The pitcher had hoped that he'd be traded to an East Coast team before the start of the season, and his attitude was dragging everybody in the clubhouse down. The final straw came when Rogers tried to beg off from a start because he didn't feel completely healthy. Beane lit into him in the clubhouse, telling Rogers he was hurting his own cause. "What kind of message does this send to other teams?" he said. "Who's going to trade for you if you don't go out there?" Rogers pitched and won, and on July 23, Beane traded him to the Mets for Long and pitcher Leoner Vasquez.

Long was sent to Vancouver without playing an inning for the A's that season, though he might have been ready. "I don't want him to come here right away and have the pressure of people looking at him as the guy we got for Kenny Rogers," said Beane. "It's not fair to put him in that position."

Beane took some criticism in the immediate aftermath of the Rogers deal because of his earlier promise not to trade the left-hander; at 49–47 the day of the trade, seven games back of Texas in the AL West, the A's were still in the divisional race, at least theoretically. Since they had lost their best veteran starter without getting a player who could help them immediately, it seemed inevitable that the A's would fall out of contention. Before the end of the month, however, Beane would put together a couple of mind-boggling trades that would make everybody forget Rogers.

In the first trade, Beane acquired pitcher Omar Olivares and second baseman Randy Velarde from the Anaheim Angels in exchange for three minor league players: outfielders Nathan Haynes and Jeff DaVanon and right-handed pitcher Elvin Nina. Haynes was the most highly regarded of the three, a 19-year-old who was hitting .313 with 12 steals at Class A Visalia.

One of Beane's strengths as a general manager has been his ability to balance moves to finish with a stronger hand. Even as he had arranged the Rogers trade, he had been working on the deal with the Angels. After the two trades were concluded, he pointed out that Olivares (8–9, 4.05 ERA) had a better record than Rogers (5–3, 4.30 ERA). He hadn't wanted to trade Haynes, but once he had Long, the same kind of player, he could afford to give up Haynes. Long was probably two years ahead in his development. As a bonus, Beane got Velarde, who was hitting .306 and playing outstanding defense. He would be a huge upgrade from Scott Spiezio, a once-promising young player who had never developed, and the over-the-hill Phillips.

While announcing his latest trade, Beane said he might not be through. He pulled off yet another dramatic swap at the July 31 inter-league-trading deadline, involving Kansas City and the New York Mets. This trade was even more complicated because Beane had to stay within the A's $22 million budget. He had agreed to a trade with Kansas City for veteran starter Kevin Appier but to stay within the budget, he had to send his closer, Billy Taylor, to New York. Remembering what went on behind the scenes, Beane said:

> Kansas City had agreed to the trade earlier but then started to back off. I was pushing them, saying, "Hey, you already agreed, so let's make the deal," but they were still hesitating.
>
> Meanwhile, on the other phone, I'm talking to Steve Phillips of the Mets about Taylor. I said I had to wait on Kansas City and Steve said, "Well, I've got a press conference on another trade, so maybe I'll do that and then get back to you."
>
> But then Kansas City said they'd go ahead with the Appier deal, so I jumped back on the other phone and told Steve he had Taylor.

The A's gave up pitchers Brad Rigby, Blake Stein, and Jeff D'Amico, none of whom figured prominently in their future. The one loss that seemed to be big was Taylor, but those who had been following the A's closely knew that he was losing it. The ninth inning had become far too exciting when Taylor took the mound, mostly because of his control problems. The A's would do just as well dividing up the closer activities for the rest of the season.

Beane also knew that he would lose Taylor at the end of the season, for economic reasons. "He's 37 and would have gotten $5 million in arbitration next year, which we wouldn't have paid," Beane said. As a little-noted side issue, Beane had also gotten Jason Isringhausen, once a highly touted Mets prospect who had had arm problems. Recovered from those problems, Isringhausen still had a lively fastball and a good breaking ball, and Beane thought he would eventually become a closer for the A's, though not that season.

The A's starting rotation had been greatly strengthened by the trades for Appier and Olivares, who would each win seven games for the A's in their two months in Oakland uniforms; but the rookie Hudson had already taken over the role of No. 1 starter, even before the departure of Rogers. He put an exclamation point on that by out-dueling Pedro Martinez, who had won the Cy Young Award in both leagues, in a memorable August 19 game in Boston.

Martinez had come into the game angry because of a dispute with Red Sox manager Jimy Williams, who had kept Martinez out of a previous start because he had arrived at the park late. Martinez seemed to be taking out his anger on the A's, as he stuck out the side on 10 pitches in the first inning. His first 12 pitches were strikes. "I didn't think he was ever going to throw a ball," said Chavez. In seven innings, Martinez had 11 strikeouts.

Hudson, though not as spectacular, was more effective, giving up only one earned run while striking out seven in eight innings. Miguel Tejada homered and drove in two runs, and the A's won, 6–2. Hudson had earlier beaten Randy Johnson in an interleague game, so his 8–1 record included wins over the best pitchers in both leagues. He would finish at 11–2 (18–2 overall, counting his minor league record).

Hudson was one of the few who stayed strong for the A's in September. The A's were never really in the pennant race but they had a good shot at the American League wild card slot, trailing the wild card leader, the Boston Red Sox, by only a game after a 2–1 win over the Detroit Tigers behind, of course, Hudson on September 4. But the young A's had never been in contention for the postseason in September and it soon showed.

In September, baseball changes for the teams in the race for a postseason spot. The marathon becomes a sprint. Every game, every play, every pitch is crucial. Players are already worn down physically, and the added mental pressure is almost too much for those who have not experienced it before.

Probably nobody felt it more than Tejada, who had been perhaps the most important player in the A's rise to the top, starting 159 of the 162 games that season because the A's had no other shortstop on the roster. Tejada had become defensively consistent, with frequent highlight-film plays. In August, he had put on a hitting surge that led many to compare him to the top rank of American League shortstops: Derek Jeter, Nomar Garciaparra, and Alex Rodriguez.

But September would be different—for him and for all of the A's. After the Hudson win over Detroit, the A's had two more games left against the Tigers and then two crucial games against the Red Sox in Oakland. They were obviously looking ahead to the games against the Red Sox during the weekend games against the Tigers. They lost the Saturday game, 5–4, when Jimmy Haynes couldn't hold an early lead. Haynes had tantalized the A's with flashes of brilliance sandwiched between blowups, but Beane had lost patience with him. "Haynes is going to be a good pitcher someday," he said, "but it won't be with us."

The next day, the A's lost again, 9–7, while the Red Sox won again to take a three-game lead in the wild card race. The pressure was on the A's to win both of their games against the Red Sox.

Their chances of doing that disappeared in the first inning of the first game. Boston leadoff hitter Jose Offerman lofted a pop fly to short, which Tejada dropped. The Red Sox went on to a five-run inning. Tejada also dropped a throw from second baseman Velarde on a potential double play later in the inning, and he was helpless at the plate against knuckleballer Tim Wakefield. He wasn't alone. Though Wakefield had started only three games and had a 4.99 ERA going into the game, he totally baffled the A's, striking out five consecutive batters in the second and third.

The A's couldn't do anything right. Starter Gil Heredia gave up four hits, walked one batter, and hit another in that disastrous first inning, and Tejada wasn't the only fielder to have problems. Right fielder Stairs twice overthrew the cutoff man, allowing Red Sox hitters to take two bases on singles. Third baseman Saenz was slow coming in on weakly hit balls twice, though he was only charged with an error on one of the plays.

The A's won the second game of the series but they had lost their opportunity to really close ground. Only once, when they were two games behind the Red Sox on September 11, would they be closer than three games. They would finish seven games back in the wild card race, eight behind Texas in the AL West.

Meanwhile, there was even a question of who would own the A's after the season. After the 1998 season, owners Steve Schott and Ken Hofmann had exercised an option to go on a year-to-year lease; to do that, they had to allow the club to be put up for sale to buyers who would agree to keep the team in Oakland. Two groups had made offers for the team. The group that emerged was bankrolled by supermarket owner Robert Puccinini (who had also owned and operated the A's California League team in Modesto for a time) and headed by former A's vice president and marketing director Andy Dolich. It seemed a natural because of Dolich's earlier connection with the A's. He and Beane were good friends, which was also important, because Beane's contract contained a clause that would allow him to leave if the ownership changed. The A's needed his creative hand at the wheel, and he was likely to stay if Dolich were in charge.

Dolich was cautiously optimistic that his group would get the approval it needed, a three-quarters approval by American League owners and a simple majority of National League owners, at a meeting in Cooperstown, New York, home of the Baseball Hall of Fame, on September 16, 1999. Said Dolich the day before the meeting:

> We've talked to people in the commissioner's office and to owners on the ownership committee, and there have been no red flags raised. We've given them budgets going out several years, so they know exactly what we're going to do.

But Commissioner Bud Selig hinted that there were questions about the financial resources of the proposed new owners. "When we've had trouble with new owners," he said, "it's always because we haven't done our due diligence on the financial reports." There were rumblings from other clubs that the budget estimates hadn't been detailed enough for them to know what to expect.

The day of the vote, owners voted to table the proposed sales of both the A's and the Kansas City Royals. The Royals deal eventually went through, but the Dolich/Puccinini group dropped out of the bidding for the A's, who would continue under the Schott/Hofmann ownership.

While the major league team was falling short in its bid for the postseason, there was good news from the minors: the A's farm system produced its third straight Player of the Year in Adam Piatt, the 23-year-old third baseman at Midland. Piatt became the first player in 72 years to win the Texas League triple crown as he led the league with a .345 batting average, 39 homers, and 135 RBIs in 129 games before being promoted to Triple-A Vancouver.

It was a measure of the A's improvement on the major league level that there wasn't an opening for Piatt. The two previous winners of minor league Player of the Year honors, Grieve and Chavez, had been immediately written into the starting lineup. But Chavez, though he'd had a disappointing rookie season, was having a solid second season and was firmly established as the A's third baseman. Piatt would have to move to platoon duty in the outfield and an occasional stint as the designated hitter in the 2000 season.

Meanwhile, the 1999 version of the A's had made a remarkable 13-game improvement, to 87–75. Grieve, Stairs, Jaha, and Jason Giambi all had good offensive years, Giambi continuing his yearly improvement by hitting .315 with 33 homers and 123 RBIs, all personal career highs. They had fallen short, but next season the A's would set their sights on returning to the postseason for the first time since 1992.

CHAPTER 19

One Inning Away

Because of the team's youth, the A's clubhouse often resembled a college frat house more than a major league baseball facility. The clubhouse leader was Jason Giambi, who was only 29 and as exuberant as he'd been when he first came up. Giambi had never met a double cheeseburger with a side of fries that he didn't like, and he was addicted to wild rides on his motorcycle. Giambi was even happier, and perhaps wilder, now that his younger brother, Jeremy, was around, having been obtained through a trade with Kansas City.

The loose A's roared through spring training in 2000, winning 20 and losing only 11. Because managers tend to pay attention to player development more than wins and losses during spring training, there's little correlation between spring results and what happens in the regular season. But after their improvement in 1999, the A's felt they were looking for better things in 2000.

Still, there were some areas of concern. Jason Isringhausen had seemingly been a steal in a midseason trade, especially when he was 8-for-8 in save opportunities as a closer in September. But nobody who knew about his history could feel terribly confident that he was for real. Isringhausen, who had a 95-mph fastball and a variety of breaking pitches, had been a bright prospect for the New York Mets in the early nineties, and that promise seemed ready for fulfillment when he came up in midseason during the 1995 season and went 9–2 with a 2.81 earned run average in 14 starts. Then his career started taking some bizarre, and sometimes frightening, twists and turns.

In 1996, hit by a sore arm, he went just 6–14. It would get worse, much worse. On April 11, 1997, he broke his right wrist. Shortly after that, he began feeling sick and went back to the hospital for X rays. What those X rays revealed was startling. He told *San Francisco Chronicle* beat writer Susan Slusser:

> They could see a big lump that had eaten its way through my esophagus. My right lung was filled with a growth, and for two weeks everyone thought I had cancer. That was the scariest time. They also tested me for AIDS.

The eventual diagnosis was tuberculosis. Isinghausen took 13 pills a day for nine months and recovered completely. There was also a side benefit: during treatment, Isringhausen, who admitted he had been "a real bad drinker," had to stop boozing. Doctors told him that combining alcohol with the tuberculosis treatment would kill him.

While Isringhausen was recovering from his illness, Mets public relations man Jay Horwitz arranged a conference call between the sick player and several beat writers. At the end of the mass interview, Isringhausen said to Horwitz, "Thanks, Jewboy." When that was reported, the pitcher was vilified in the New York press. "I didn't mean it in an insulting way," said Isringhausen, who said he had many Jewish friends. "Jay even calls himself that sometimes, and I was just joking around."

Later that year, Isringhausen was in his car attempting to open a package containing an anti-theft device for his steering wheel. When he couldn't get the box open, he went into his house for a large knife. As he attempted to cut the package open, the knife slipped and he stabbed himself in the thigh. He applied pressure to the wound with paper towels and drove to the hospital. Teammate Todd Hundley was also in the hospital. Told that Isringhausen had stabbed himself, Hundley said, "I'm not surprised."

Isringhausen's bad luck had continued in 1998, when he missed the entire season after having reconstructive elbow surgery. When Billy Beane asked about him in July of 1999, the Mets were only too happy to send him away. Shifted to the bullpen in Oakland under the patient tutelage of pitching coach Rick Peterson, Isringhausen flourished, and would go on to have the best season of his career in 2000.

The other serious question for the A's was center field, where there were four candidates: Ryan Christenson, who had come up through the A's system and was regarded as being the best man defensively; Rich Becker, a slap hitter and adequate defensive outfielder whom Beane had traded for in August of 1999; Bo Porter, picked up when the Chicago Cubs decided not to keep him on their 40-man roster; and Terrence Long, obtained in the Kenny Rogers trade the previous July. Long was definitely the center fielder of the near future, but Beane thought he might need some additional time in the minors.

The decision was made to start the season with a platoon of Christenson, a right-handed hitter, and Becker, a left-handed hitter. But Long quickly changed that thinking, hitting .400 with three homers and 15 RBIs in 15 games at Sacramento. He was called up on April 24 and went on to finish second in the American League Rookie of the Year race. Christenson was relegated to late-inning defense and pinch-running and Becker, at his own request, was eventually traded away.

Even before Long came up, Mark Mulder, who had been the A's first pick in the 1998 draft, was brought up. Mulder would make 27 starts before being knocked out by a herniated disc in his back in mid-September, by which time he had a 9–10 record. It was a respectable showing for a pitcher who had only one minor league season behind him, but everyone around the A's was convinced he'd do much better in the future.

Piece by piece, the young A's were being built, winning as they took shape. When Barry Zito, a very important piece, was brought up on July 24, the A's were in the middle of a streak that would take them to 14 games over .500, at 61–47.

Zito, the A's first pick in the 1999 draft, had made it to the majors even faster than the other two A's prodigies, Mulder and Tim Hudson; just 13 months earlier, he had been pitching for USC. He was another validation of Beane's plan to go for the best athlete, not the best fastball. Zito's fastball seldom exceeded 89 mph. "Left-handers throwing that speed can win in our league," said Beane. "I liked everything about Zito, the way he moves, his attitude."

Ah, yes, the attitude. After his senior year in high school in San Diego, the Seattle Mariners drafted Zito in the 59th round. Craig Weissman, then a Seattle scout, had worked with Zito on his mechanics, improving his fastball by about five miles an hour, and he convinced his bosses to offer Zito a $90,000 bonus. But Zito turned it down, saying, "I should be a 1st-round pick." He then went on to UC Santa Barbara and transferred to Pierce Junior College so he could turn pro after his sophomore year. This time he was drafted in the 3rd round by the Texas Rangers, who offered him $300,000. Still not enough. He transferred to USC, where he went 12–3 with a 3.28 ERA and 154 strikeouts in 112 innings. The A's then offered him $1.59 million. Finally, an offer he could live with.

If his confidence is unusual, well, that's because Zito is a very unusual young man. His family background is different; both his parents worked with the Nat King Cole Trio, father Joe as conductor/ arranger, mother Roberta as a member of the backup vocal group. As a young boy, he was very independent; his mother remembers that he bought clothes he liked, not clothes his peers wore. Other athletes hunt, fish, and golf; Zito spends his winters surfing in southern California.

On the mound, he's admitted, Zito sometimes talks to his arm. After he did an ESPN interview in which he talked about his collection of stuffed animals, teammate Matt Stairs made him carry a three-foot teddy bear on all the road trips. On a road trip to Baltimore, all the A's rookies were required to wear costumes in the hotel lobby; since Zito had once jokingly told a reporter that he wouldn't mind "dressing like a girl," he had to dress in a white wedding gown, which embarrassed even him.

None of this would matter if Zito couldn't pitch, but he and Hudson formed an unreal combination down the stretch for the A's in 2000. Said Peterson:

Usually, pitchers have to make a mistake and then correct it after you've told them what they've done wrong. With Timmy and Barry, you don't have to go through that step. They only have to watch. You just point out to them what another pitcher is doing wrong and tell them how to do it right, and they'll go out and do it. It's amazing.

Meanwhile, another question had been resolved: the relationship between Beane and manager Art Howe. Beane had long had his doubts about Howe. He was not particularly happy about inheriting Alderson's manager, and at various times he had debated with himself about whether to fire Howe at the end of a season. Still, before the 2000 season, Beane extended the manager's contract for another year. He feared that if he didn't, there would be constant questions from the beat writers, who loved Howe because he was so cooperative. That would be disruptive to the team. But before Beane did that, he talked with Steve Schott to explain to the A's owner why he thought it was best to extend Howe's contract despite his earlier doubts about the manager.

There were reasons for this lack of accord. Beane had played under Tony La Russa, who was his idea of what a manager should be. Howe was totally different, much more patient when a player screwed up, and that bothered Beane. The two also had a serious disagreement on strategy: Howe still preferred the traditional baseball strategies of the bunt and the hit-and-run, while Beane constantly argued that a team could not afford to give up an out with a bunt (except perhaps in the ninth inning of a tie game) because that took away the chance of an inning in which a team could score multiple runs. Yet as late as spring training 2000, Howe went to the bunt in the eighth inning of a game against the Anaheim Angels, and the A's went scoreless in the inning. "He took us right out of a big inning," Beane fumed after the game.

Slowly, however, the two philosophies were beginning to merge, especially since Howe realized his team wasn't the type to play the traditional style he'd been accustomed to as a National League player and manager. In the 2000 season, he would use the bunt and the hit-and-run only as surprise moves, effective because the A's usually played station-to-station baseball, going for walks, hits, and three-run homers.

Howe's willingness to change his strategy—the result of many postgame conversations with Beane during the previous three seasons—

helped smooth over the glitches in their relationship. And Beane had come to appreciate the fact that Howe didn't try to interfere in personnel decisions; though Beane consulted with his manager, his trades were his own doing, and the draft selections and free-agent signings were also decisions made in the front office. "If we had a strong manager like Tony, he'd insist on having a voice in all this, which would complicate matters," said Beane, who remembered that La Russa had squelched an attempt to trade Dennis Eckersley for outfielder Manny Ramirez in 1993. La Russa's recollection is different. He said he wanted Ramirez, at that time still a minor-league outfielder, but the Cleveland Indians were not interested in trading him.

$$\ominus \quad \ominus \quad \ominus$$

The first sign that the 2000 A's might be something special came at the end of May in a three-game series in New York against the two-time defending world champions. The A's had been the definition of average in the first two months of the season and slipped to 25–26 when Andy Pettitte beat them, 4–1, in the opening game of the series. But they rebounded to win the next two games of the series; Isringhausen saved the wins for starters Kevin Appier and Gil Heredia, and that started a string of eight straight series victories. Included in those wins was a nine-game streak in June, which would be the longest of the season; the A's stretched out to 45–30 in early July, a superb 20–4 run. They held the AL West lead for most of June, but when they fell back to 48–38, they also fell three games behind Seattle at the All-Star break.

The A's were a classic case of a glass that could be either half full or half empty. There certainly were plenty of encouraging signs. Hudson had bounced back from a miserable start and was on his way to 20 wins in his first full season in the majors, and Zito would soon bolster the starting rotation. Isringhausen was solid as a closer. Jason Giambi was having a monster year, which would bring him the AL Most Valuable Player award. Ben Grieve, Miguel Tejada, and Eric Chavez were all improving at the plate; Tejada would set an Oakland record for shortstops with 30 homers. Long was the team's best center fielder since Dave Henderson in his prime.

But there were some dark clouds too. Middle-inning relief was shaky. In too many games, Isringhausen couldn't come in for the ninth because the A's had fallen behind in the middle innings. Stairs, who had been such a great story with his dramatic late home runs during the previous season, had seemingly grown old in the months between seasons. He seemed absolutely hopeless against left-handers, and he wasn't much better against right-handed pitchers. He would finish the year at .227, the lowest average for any American League player with at least 450 at-bats. Stairs was perhaps the most popular player in the clubhouse, and his problems weighed heavily on the others.

John Jaha was an even more serious problem. His right-handed power had been a perfect balance for the otherwise predominantly left-handed A's lineup. Jaha was especially good protection for Giambi because pitchers couldn't pitch around Jason if Jaha was waiting. But the season would be a lost one for Jaha. It was obvious in the spring that he was having an injury problem; he couldn't get around on the fastball, hitting late. In his first 12 games, he hit .129 with no home runs and one RBI before going on the disabled list with a sprain in his left shoulder. He missed 36 games before returning on June 3, but he was no better. He played 21 more games, hitting only .197 with one homer and four RBIs. In those combined 33 games he had had 97 at-bats and had struck out an astounding 38 times. On July 9, he went on the disabled list again for tendinitis in his left shoulder. He was operated on 10 days later after doctors found extensive damage to the shoulder.

Howe would try several different players in the cleanup spot behind Giambi, with Olmedo Saenz the most frequent hitter in that spot, but none of them frightened pitchers the way Jaha had. Giambi had by far his best season, with a .333 average, 43 homers, and an Oakland-record 137 RBIs, but he might have done even better if Jaha had stayed healthy. Without a credible cleanup man behind him, Giambi walked a major league–leading 137 times; he also led the majors with a .476 on-base percentage, the highest in franchise history, including both the Philadelphia and Kansas City years as well as those in Oakland. With Jaha behind him the year before, Giambi had walked 105 times. It was praiseworthy that he had developed the plate discipline necessary to keep from swinging at bad pitches, but if he'd had 31 more at-bats when he had a chance to hit a good pitch, he could have done more damage.

Beane made a move to plug one of the holes when he traded for Tampa Bay right-hander Jim Mecir on July 28. Mecir, a right-hander, had a fastball that moved away from left-handers; for the season, left-handers would hit only .204 against him in 152 at-bats while right-handers would hit .245 in 159 at-bats. Significantly, the pitcher Beane gave up was the highly touted Jesus Colome, who had perhaps the best fastball in the A's organization. He was expendable in part because the A's had other good pitching prospects but mostly because Beane felt the A's were good enough to reach the postseason.

The future was now.

In fact, Beane was willing to make an even bigger gamble that he thought would give the A's a better chance to win. Manny Ramirez—the same outfielder that Sandy Alderson had wanted to get five years before—was on the last year of his contract with Cleveland and had said he would leave as a free agent. Beane was willing to trade second base-man Randy Velarde to get Ramirez, even though he knew he'd be "renting" Ramirez for only half a season. The A's would have then brought up Jose Ortiz from Sacramento to play second. Beane reasoned that Ramirez's potent right-handed bat would more than compensate for the defense and veteran leadership he'd lose if Velarde left. Luckily, Beane never said publicly that he was trying to make the deal; in the end, it never happened. Cleveland wasn't interested. Ortiz's debut with the A's wouldn't come until September, when the rosters were expanded.

As the season turned into the last two months, it seemed that no team really wanted to win the AL West; from the All-Star break until September 1, no team in the division won even half its games. A five-game losing streak at the start of August put the A's seven games behind Seattle on August 11; but they started regaining ground as the Mariners lost more frequently. The margin was down to 2½ by the end of the month.

Then came September. Said the cerebral Peterson:

A pennant race is like a long ocean voyage. You start out and everybody is celebrating, smashing champagne bottles. Then, after about three weeks at sea, you can't see anything but open water and you feel lost. When you get to this part of the season, you see land again.

As September arrived both the A's and the Mariners realized that they had a chance to win, and both turned up the pressure. The AL West race would go down to the final day, and the A's would have to battle a hurricane and subsequent schedule problems to win.

What turned out to be the critical series was a four-game set in Seattle, September 21–24. With just 12 games left in the regular season, the Mariners led by three games; a split in that series in their new park, Safeco Field, would have virtually clinched the divisional title. But they couldn't do it.

Winning the first game was vital for the A's, especially since they had their No. 1 starter, Hudson, going for his 18th win. Hudson delivered, allowing just one earned run in six innings, though his own error on a squibbler down the first base line by John Olerud led to an unearned run and a 2–0 Mariners lead.

The A's had been only 17–24 against left-handed starters going into the game, and Jamie Moyer seemed ready to extend that negative streak as he went 12 batters without giving up a hit. Tejada was hitting in the cleanup slot for the first time, a decision made at the last minute by Howe, and he justified the decision in the top of the fourth when, with two outs on the board, he lined a home run into the right-field stands, ending Moyer's streak and halving the Mariners' lead.

Howe had also made another lineup switch, giving Ortiz just his second career start at second in place of the slumping Velarde. That paid off too, as Ortiz singled to start a sixth-inning rally. Giambi doubled, with Ortiz stopping at third. Tejada was intentionally walked and rookie Adam Piatt, originally scheduled for the cleanup slot before the switch with Tejada, also walked, forcing in a run to tie the game.

The next two hitters were the worst in the American League against left-handers, but they both got hits. Stairs, hitting just .189 against lefties, hit one off the end of his bat that dropped into center, with two runs scoring. "One of the best cue shots I've ever hit in my life," he said. Chavez, hitting .190 against left-handers, lined a single to right to score Piatt with the A's fifth run. "It's always tough because I've been sitting so much against left-handers when I could have been learning to hit them," said Chavez, who had chafed at being platooned earlier in the year.

The A's 5–2 win set the tone for the rest of the series. They won the next two games, 8–2 behind Omar Olivares and 8–3 behind Kevin Appier to move into a tie for the division lead. For Olivares, who had spent much of the season on the disabled list, it was his first victory since May 7. More and more, it seemed momentum was swinging the A's way. Because Mulder was out for the season with a herniated disc, Howe had to go to Ariel Prieto as his starter for the fourth game, and the Mariners won, 3–2, to move back into a one-game lead. Howe had tried to get the Mariners to close the roof on their stadium but it remained open and hard-throwing left-hander Arthur Rhodes, pitching in the sunlight-to-shadows light, shut down the A's in relief.

Still, the series win had given the A's a confidence boost as they battled to get into the postseason. "There's no secret we showed who has the better team," said Long. Pointing to the seven-game homestand still left to play, Isringhausen said, "We can win all seven of them."

There were two races going: the one for the divisional title and the one for the wild card spot. The second race seemed to change daily, involving the A's, the Boston Red Sox, and the Cleveland Indians, all in second place in their divisions. But the A's still had a chance to win the AL West and, amazingly, the Red Sox were back in the race in the AL East due to the Yankees' surprising free fall.

As if the race weren't complicated enough, it was confused further by Hurricane Gordon, which knocked out the A's September 17 game in Tampa Bay. At one point, it was conceivable that the A's would have to go to St. Petersburg the day after their last scheduled game for a Monday game and then start a divisional playoff series the next day.

Thankfully, it didn't come down to that. The A's nearly fulfilled Isringhausen's prophecy, winning six of their last seven. First they took three out of four from the Anaheim Angels, then swept a three-game series against the Texas Rangers; meanwhile the Mariners were taking two out of three from the Angels, with their loss in the first game of the series dropping them to second. The A's had held first place for only three days during the last three months, but they were the last three days of the season. They finished just half a game ahead of Seattle, but they had a 9–4 edge in their season series, which was crucial. The A's didn't have to make up their game in St. Petersburg because a loss in that game would have meant a tie for the divisional title—and the A's/Mariners season series would have been the tie-breaker. After winning 22 of 27 games in September, the A's were division champs. The Mariners settled for the wild card.

The A's certainly played like champions in that last weekend, walloping the Rangers on Saturday, 23–2, behind Zito, and then winning a beautifully played game on Sunday, 3–0, as Hudson became the A's first 20-game winner since Bob Welch (27) and Dave Stewart (22) in 1990, the year in which the A's had won their third straight American League pennant.

But the fact that the A's had had to use their best pitchers to nail down the divisional title would be a problem. Beane saw one immediately: Hudson couldn't start the divisional series against the Yankees. "For a young team, being able to start your ace in the first game is so important," he said. "You really want to be able to win that first game if you've never been in the postseason before."

Despite Beane's worries, the bigger problem—and the fatal one—would be that Hudson and Zito could pitch only once each in the five-game series.

The Yankees had slumped badly in the final weeks of the season, losing 13 of their last 15 and the last 7 as their 9-game lead over the Red Sox shrunk to 2½ by the end of the season. Their slump cost them home-field advantage for the divisional playoff. That was significant. Visiting teams playing in Yankee Stadium in the postseason were often overwhelmed by history: the many pennants, the monuments to stars of the past in center field. The Yankees wouldn't have that advantage for the start of this series and announcer Joe Morgan, who had been a Hall of Fame second baseman in his playing days, thought that could be the difference:

215

You can't overestimate the importance of a champion's heart, but I think the Yankees really hurt themselves by not getting home-field advantage. If this series had started in New York, the A's would have been "playing the monuments" in the first game. But now, by the time they get there, the A's will already have played two games, and they might be 2–0. Right now, they have no fear of the Yankees.

That was true, even though the Yankees started Roger Clemens against Gil Heredia. Perhaps the A's realized that Clemens had not built a Hall of Fame career on his postseason performances, where he had been ordinary. Clemens blew through the A's lineup for the first four innings, allowing only an infield hit, but the A's broke through for three runs in the fifth. The key hit was a two-run double to right by Ramon Hernandez. The Yankees tied the score with a run in the top of the sixth, but the A's scored single runs in the sixth and eighth to come away with a 5–3 win.

Unfortunately, they would have to contend with Andy Pettitte the next night. The left-handed Pettitte, the kind of smart pitcher who always gave the A's fits, had an 8–3 lifetime record against Oakland and had been especially tough in the 2000 season, yielding only two earned runs in the two games he pitched against the A's, one of them a two-hitter.

Pettitte continued his mastery by scattering five hits over 7⅔ innings as the Yankees evened the series with a 4–0 win. The series would go to New York, where the Yankees had a chance to close it out with weekend wins. If they didn't, they'd have Pettitte ready to go for the fifth game.

The young A's were admittedly nervous in their first playoff game in storied Yankee Stadium, and it showed, especially on the field. Hudson pitched well but hurt himself at times. In the second, with the swift Bernie Williams on third, Hudson threw home on a slow grounder to the mound instead of getting the automatic out at first. Williams easily beat his throw. Later in the inning, Hudson walked the No. 9 hitter, Scott Brosius, on four pitches. Derek Jeter followed with an infield single that scored Paul O'Neill for the second run of the inning. Although

Orlando "El Duque" Hernandez didn't seem sharp, the A's couldn't capitalize on their chances and went down, 4–2.

All season long, the A's had been most dangerous when it seemed that they didn't have a chance; now, facing elimination and playing in an unfriendly environment, they rallied behind Zito in Game 4 to trounce the Yankees, 11–1, and even the series. Once again Clemens fell on his face in a postseason game. Zito, who had given the A's a great boost by going 7–4 with a 2.72 ERA after being brought up in July, gave up the Yankees' only run in the 5⅔ innings he pitched. Incredibly, in the last two games he pitched in the 2000 season, the A's had scored 34 runs. Now they'd be coming back to Oakland.

But the A's had used their best starters in New York, and Heredia had nothing when he took the mound for the fifth game. He gave up a single to Yankee, leadoff hitter Chuck Knoblauch on the first pitch of the game, walked Derek Jeter, and loaded the bases on an infield single by Paul O'Neill. Bernie Williams brought in one run with a line drive to right, the only out Heredia would record. David Justice walked and then Tino Martinez lofted a fly to deep center. Bothered by the sun, Terrence Long couldn't catch up with the ball as it bounced once before hitting the center-field wall. All three runners scored as Martinez went to second. When Jorge Posada slammed a ball off the back of Heredia's right leg for an infield single, Howe brought in Jeff Tam in relief.

Tam had been an important part of the A's success, particularly in the early season, as a setup man. His sinker often induced batters to ground into double plays. Sadly, this time he just didn't have it. Luis Sojo hit a sacrifice fly to center, Brosius singled, and Knoblauch got his second hit of the inning, an RBI single to right. The Yankees had scored six times in the inning, and that would be enough to win.

Not without a fight, though. The A's broke through against their nemesis, Pettitte, knocking him out in the fourth inning, by which time they had collected 10 hits and scored five times to get back in the game, or so it seemed. The first big hit came in the second, when Velarde singled with the bases loaded to drive in two runs. In the third, Tejada singled and Chavez blasted a double to left center to cut the lead to 6–3. Justice pushed it to 7–3 with a fourth-inning home run, and the A's scored two more runs in the bottom of the inning. With the bases loaded, Giambi and Saenz hit consecutive sacrifice flies for the RBIs.

But the Yankees got outstanding relief the rest of the way, first from Mike Stanton, then from Hernandez making a rare relief appearance, and finally from their superb closer, Mariano Rivera. In the eighth, after a one-out, pinch-hit double by Stairs in what would be his last at-bat with the A's, Rivera came in to strike out Long and got Velarde to fly out. In the ninth, he gave up a two-out single to Tejada but got Chavez to foul out. The series was over.

The season had ended, but the A's were still confident. "We had a great season," said Long, whose sentiments were echoed by his team-mates. "We played like a championship team. We'll be back."

CHAPTER 20

A Bright Future

The good news came early in 2001 for the A's as general manager Billy Beane swung a nine-player, three-team trade that brought outfielder Johnny Damon to the team on January 9. The Kansas City Royals had been shopping Damon for months because the speedy outfielder would become a free agent after the 2001 season, and he had no desire to stay in Kansas City, even if the Royals made a competitive offer.

The Royals were frank about what they wanted in a trade: a top-notch closer. Beane was not going to trade Jason Isringhausen but, in talking with Tampa Bay, he learned that the Devil Rays were willing to part with Roberto Hernandez. So he brokered a deal that brought Damon and pitcher Cory Lidle, who would become the No. 5 starter with his work in the spring, to the A's, sent outfielder Ben Grieve to Tampa Bay, and dispatched catcher A. J. Hinch and minor league short-stop Angel Berroa to Kansas City.

Damon was an intriguing player for the A's because he gave them a dimension they'd lacked: speed on the base paths. In the 2000 season, the A's had stolen just 40 bases as a team. Damon had 46 steals, and had scored 136 runs. He was an improving hitter who had hit .307 in 1999 and .327 in 2000. He was the leadoff hitter the A's had lacked since Rickey Henderson left and, like Henderson, he had surprising power, with 42 doubles, 10 triples, and 16 home runs in 2000. Beane pointed out that Damon's slugging percentage, .495, was actually higher than Grieve's; he had hit 27 homers with a .487 percentage.

Earlier, Beane had sent Randy Velarde to the Texas Rangers for minor league pitchers Ryan Cullen and Aaron Harang as well as shipping Matt Stairs to the Chicago Cubs for pitcher Eric Ireland. Both moves were addition by subtraction. Stairs' contract was up and Beane didn't want to re-sign him because it had become obvious during the previous season that the popular outfielder was on the downside of his career. Velarde was still an excellent second baseman but he was 38; 2000 had been the last season of a contract paying him $3 million a year. Beane always had to be aware of costs, and he also wanted to make room for Jose Ortiz, a 23 year old who had been the Pacific Coast League's Most Valuable Player the previous season after hitting .351 with 108 RBIs, 107 runs scored, 24 homers, and 22 stolen bases in 131 games. Ortiz, who had had only one year at second after playing shortstop in previous seasons, was still a work in progress defensively; but Beane felt he would contribute more over a full season than Velarde, whose hitting had declined sharply during the previous September. "We'll be even younger than we were last season," said the A's general manager.

Damon was definitely an upgrade and Ortiz might have been by midseason; but the A's still faced some serious questions as they headed into training camp. The first question was: how long would they have Jason Giambi? The reigning American League MVP was in the final year of his contract, which would pay him $4 million in 2001—chump change for a player of his accomplishments. The benchmark for power-hitting first basemen in the American League was the $17 million a year contract for Toronto's Carlos Delgado. Under owners Steve Schott and Ken Hofmann, the A's had trimmed their payroll and, though it had risen above the $30 million mark, they had not yet had to sign a player to a really big contract. With Giambi they would. Jason wasn't asking for as much as Delgado because he wanted to stay in Oakland, but he wasn't going to settle for much below that figure either. The A's first serious offer was for six years, $91 million—but about a third of that would be deferred until Giambi was 55. "I might be dead by then," said Giambi.

Beane was optimistic because he was close to Giambi and his agent, Arn Tellem. "Everybody wants to make this deal," he said. "I've never known of a deal not to get done when everybody wants to do it." Beane regarded Giambi as a friend, not just another player, often talking and joking with him by the cage during batting practice. "Other players are talking about changing their contracts [most notably, Frank Thomas of the White Sox and Gary Sheffield of the Dodgers]," he noted. "All Jason has said about his contract was 'thank you' when he signed it."

Beane and Tellem met or talked on the telephone several times during spring training, though both were trying to stay away from media scrutiny, often leaving reporters with the impression that they were trying to arrange a meeting but their schedules wouldn't allow it. They were making progress, mainly because the A's were gradually moving away from their deferred money proposal. Eventually they dropped it completely, which seemed to be the last roadblock. "Our ownership has stepped up to the plate on this one," said Beane.

But then Giambi decided he wanted a no-trade clause in his contract. He cited the example of his good friend, Mark McGwire, who had been traded to the St. Louis Cardinals in midseason in 1997. "If they can trade Mark, they can trade anybody," said Giambi. Somehow, he had lost sight of the fact that McGwire *wanted* to be traded. As a 10/5 player (10 years in the majors, at least 5 with one team) he could have vetoed any trade, but he waived that right because he wanted no part of the rebuilding project that lay ahead.

The A's tried to accommodate Giambi, offering him a limited no-trade clause until he became a 10/5 player himself in the 2004 season. But that wasn't enough. He wanted a guarantee that he would stay in Oakland, though the effect of his demand might mean that he would end up leaving after the 2001 season. Said a frustrated Beane:

> Every time they've asked for something, we've given it to them. Then they ask for something else. That's not negotiating, that's blackmail.

With the Giambi negotiations at a seeming impasse, Beane started looking at his other options:

You have to do that. The mark of a good organization is that you always have another way to go if something doesn't work out. We've been looking at this since last fall, looking at what we could do if we couldn't re-sign Jason.

One possibility was using the money to re-sign Johnny Damon. In one sense it would be easier for the A's to replace Giambi than Damon, because they had so little speed among their top prospects. They did, however, have power hitters in their system, and they were especially high on Jason Hart, a 23-year-old right-handed-hitting first baseman who had hit .326 with 30 home runs and 121 RBIs at Midland (Class AA) during the previous season. Hart, who was regarded as a much better first baseman than Giambi, was scheduled to play in Sacramento for the 2001 season, and it was expected that he'd be ready for the majors by the 2002 season. Some thought he might be ready now.

But Beane pointed out the danger of expecting Hart to replace Giambi's production immediately:

The bar is set very high for first basemen in the American League. Thirty-five home runs is really just about the average. We certainly wouldn't get that out of Hart in his first year, and probably not his second, either. A representative year for him as a rookie would probably be about 20 home runs, 80 RBIs. So, we'd have to get more from other parts of the lineup.

Beane thought Miguel Tejada might move up from his already impressive 30 homers from the previous year (a record for an A's shortstop), and that Ortiz might be a 20-homer hitter in another year.

The other option would be to put more money into long-term contracts for Tejada and third baseman Eric Chavez. Said Beane:

In another five years, Tejada will be 30 and Chavez 28, and Jason will be 35. Miggy and Chavvy are the future.

Beane had always looked closely at age with his players, knowing that players go downhill after 30, sometimes sharply. His concern about a six-year contract for Giambi was that he wouldn't be anywhere near the same kind of player in the second half of that contract that he had been in the first.

If he didn't sign? "People forget that I'll still have the Most Valuable Player for maybe the best year of his career."

⊖ ⊖ ⊖

Meanwhile, the question arose again: how long will the A's be in Oakland?

There had been concern that Schott and Hofmann would eventually move the A's out of Oakland, though still in the Bay Area, ever since they bought the team. One idea, to build a new park on land owned by Schott near the junction of freeways 580 and 680 in Contra Costa County, roughly 15 miles southeast of the Oakland Coliseum, had surfaced early. But that would have to be done with private financing, since there was no city big enough to help fund it, and Schott's preference was for a park to be built with public money.

Privately, Schott said the Giants had been crazy to build a park— Pacific Bell Park—in San Francisco with their own money. The Giants had pulled it off, but with the help of corporate financing that wouldn't be available in either Oakland or Contra Costa County.

Schott had been unhappy with the Oakland Coliseum since it was remodeled for the Raiders on their return to the Bay Area. There had been some improvements that helped the A's, the biggest one of which was a club for season ticket holders, but the stadium had a strange look to it. On its east side, one grandstand was built so high, looming behind center and right field, that it had been dubbed "Mount Davis" (a reference to Raiders owner Al Davis). Only a handful of those seats were ever occupied for baseball games. While changes were being made to the stadium in early 1997, the A's claimed it was unsafe and actually held their home opener in Las Vegas. Schott renegotiated his contract to get better terms and the A's made money despite one of the lowest attendance rates in the majors, but Schott knew his revenue streams were limited at the aging Coliseum, built in 1966. A resident of Santa Clara and a graduate of Santa Clara University, Schott looked longingly at the burgeoning Silicon Valley area around that city.

The A's and Giants both drew fans from the Santa Clara area but Schott feared the increasing congestion on the 880 corridor would discourage fans from coming to the Coliseum. By exercising the option in their contract to go to a year-to-year lease, Schott and Hofmann were free to look at other sites; Schott started talking actively to those in the San Jose/Santa Clara area who wanted to bring a major league team there. At first the focus was on San Jose, but it shifted to Santa Clara when that city's council voted in March of 2001 to hold off approval of a proposal to build an additional parking lot for the Great America theme park there, indicating that the land could be donated for a baseball park.

There were two problems for Schott. One was that it seemed unlikely that public financing could be provided. Santa Clara County assessor Larry Stone, head of the county's stadium authority group (which was trying to get the A's) said it was unlikely that the county would contribute any money. San Jose and Santa Clara County voters had turned down proposals to build a park for the Giants years before and, if anything, there was less enthusiasm for using public money for a sports stadium than there had been then.

The second problem was that the Giants claimed territorial rights in that area. The A's could market the team and sell tickets there, but the agreement the Giants owners had made to buy the team from Bob Lurie in 1992 included a clause that forbid other teams to move into the area. The new owners had insisted on exactly that language because Horace Stoneham had *not* insisted on territorial rights when he moved to San Francisco—leaving Oakland as open territory for Charlie Finley to move the A's there in 1968. The Giants' attendance, which had ranged from more than 1.2 million to just under 1.8 million a season in the team's first decade in San Francisco, fell by a third the first year the A's were in town, and inched over 1 million only once in the second decade. Many East Bay fans who had followed the Giants switched over to the team in their own backyard. The Giants, who drew well from the South Bay, feared the same thing would happen to their fan base there if another team moved in.

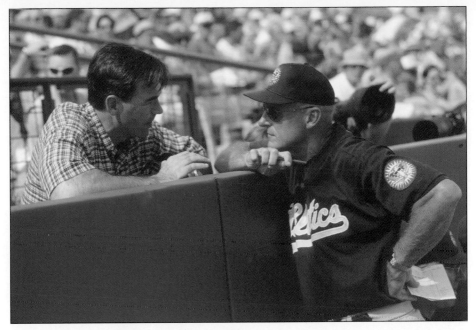

General manager Billy Beane and manager Art Howe confer at the edge of the stands during spring training, 2000.

Miguel Tejada prepares to throw out a Seattle Mariners base runner during a July 20, 2000, game at Oakland.

Tim Hudson throws to the plate as he beats the Tigers in Detroit on June 19, 1999, less than two weeks after making his major league debut.

Jason Giambi watches his home run as the A's beat the Yankees, 7–4, in New York on May 30, 2000.

Third baseman Eric Chavez, who surprised everybody with his good defense, waits in a crouch during a May 31, 2000, game in Yankee Stadium.

Jason Isringhausen throws his 95-mph fastball as he saves a win for the A's in New York on May 30, 2000.

Ramon Hernandez prepares to catch a foul pop-up as the A's win their second straight in New York, May 31, 2000.

Terrence Long connects for a base hit during a June 29, 2000, game against Texas; the Rangers went on to win the game, 3–1, in Oakland.

Barry Zito, who won seven games in just half of the 2000 season, is shown in one of his wins, on July 22 against the Angels in Oakland.

That feeling intensified when the Giants built their own new park. Roughly a third of their nearly 14,000 "charter seat" holders, who had paid extra money to reserve their seats for any event at the park, came from the Silicon Valley. Debts had been secured with the promise of advertising and sponsorships from Silicon Valley firms, which would probably transfer their business to the A's if a park were to be built in Santa Clara.

A month before the action by the Santa Clara city council, baseball commissioner Bud Selig spoke at a Fox Sports Bay Area baseball luncheon on Treasure Island. He was peppered with questions from reporters about the Giants' territorial rights. He insisted that "baseball must have its rules" and that territorial rights were among them. He had taken the same position regarding proposals to build a park in either northern Virginia or Washington, D.C., for a transferred franchise because both areas were within the Baltimore Orioles' territory. After the Santa Clara city council's action, Selig was asked again about the possibility of an A's park there. His position hadn't changed:

Once a club has a territory, it has a territory. We don't have anarchy. We have rules and we have guidelines that have been in existence for many years.

Major League Baseball owners have the power to control franchise moves because, unlike the situation in other professional sports leagues, baseball has an exemption from anti-trust laws. That exemption was established in a 1922 case argued before the Supreme Court, and has never been overturned. This is a major reason why no baseball franchise has been moved since the Washington Senators became the Texas Rangers in 1972.

Because of Selig's opposition, Schott had two choices: (1) challenge the anti-trust exemption in court, which would be a long and torturous campaign (Schott rejected that idea immediately); or (2) convince two-thirds of baseball's owners that Selig should be overruled and the Giants' exemption dropped, allowing the A's to move to Santa Clara. Said Schott:

I'm not trying to play hardball with the Giants or with the commissioner. I'm not threatening legal action or anything like that. I just want a fair hearing.

There had been speculation that Schott would pay the Giants to drop their territorial claim, but Giants executives said privately that they would not do that. Any money they got wouldn't compensate for the loss in franchise value. Schott wasn't planning that, anyway. "We barely have enough money to pay the players," he said. Schott had continually poor-mouthed his financial status, though a person who was involved in the negotiations to sell the club in 1995 said that Schott and Hofmann's combined worth actually exceeded that of Walter Haas.

Schott told the Santa Clara people that he could get the owners' vote, but there was little objective evidence to support that. Selig had been a cautious commissioner, making certain that he had a consensus, preferably an overwhelming one, before he made a move. It was unlikely that he would take such a strong stand if he didn't think he had the support of the owners.

Schott himself is not particularly popular among his fellow owners. The A's have benefited from the limited revenue sharing begun in 1995, which transfers money from teams at the top of the economic ladder to those at the bottom. The original idea was that the money would be used to better the poorer teams; but the A's have simply pocketed it, as have the other organizations that receive such funds. This irritates the owners who are paying money; even midrange owners, who are not getting any extra money but are putting as much as they can into their teams, are irritated.

If Schott could get a stadium built in Santa Clara, the franchise value would probably be $100 million higher. Would other owners make a move to give Schott and Hofmann windfall profits at the expense of the Giants owners, who had risked their own money to build a park? It didn't seem likely.

Meanwhile there was a plan to build a park in Oakland on Laney College land, which is next to the downtown area and accessible by two freeways and the Bay Area Rapid Transit (BART) system and city buses. The plan was drawn up by a private citizen, Larry Jackson, who grew up in Oakland and didn't want to see the A's leave.

As always, the question was financing. Some thought it might be possible to tap into urban redevelopment money. That had been done to build an arena in downtown San Jose, adding $100 million to the arena budget. The Sharks, a National Hockey League team, had put in another $50 million to add the luxurious touches they felt were necessary.

San Jose's goal was to build up a dormant downtown area, and city officials were satisfied that the scheme had worked, with new hotels and restaurants revitalizing the neighborhood. Oakland's downtown area, which was a ghost town at night and on weekends, could also use that help. But although Oakland mayor Jerry Brown and city manager Robert Bobb both liked the idea of an economic boost for the city, nobody seemed prepared to move.

As the 2001 season started, the A's were still stuck with their 35-year-old ballpark.

⊖ ⊖ ⊖

The A's once again mopped up in the Cactus League, finishing with the best spring training record at 22–11, and they were the team du jour for baseball writers, who were virtually unanimous in predicting that the A's would at least repeat as American League West champions and quite possibly would replace the Yankees in the World Series. Before they started their first home stand against the Anaheim Angels, however, and after losing two out of three in their opening series in Seattle, manager Art Howe talked about his concerns:

> In a way, this is the sophomore year for these young players because last year was their first year in the playoffs. This time around, they'll have a little better understanding of what it takes.
>
> But I just hope they don't get carried away with what people are saying this year. Everybody remembers our September when we looked great, but in August, we looked like one of the

227

worst teams in baseball. We were seven games back at one point, but we didn't panic. I told them just to keep playing and we'd be all right, and then, it all seemed to come together in September.

The thing I worry about this year is that we're so young. Our oldest regular is Jason Giambi, and he's only 30. Last year, we had guys like Matt Stairs and Randy Velarde. When you've got some veterans and you get off to a slow start, they've been through it before and they'll calm everybody down. But young players tend to get too excited. I'm trying to tell them to just do their jobs.

Howe's concerns were soon manifested as the A's went in the tank in the first two weeks, a 1–8 home stand leading to a 2–10 record. Nothing seemed to be going right. The A's weren't hitting and they weren't pitching. The two young pitching stars, Tim Hudson and Barry Zito, were getting bombed. Gil Heredia, who had been steady during the previous season (with the exception of his self-destruction in the fifth game of the divisional playoffs), was throwing everything high in the strike zone, and he was getting bombed, too.

One player who might have helped, John Jaha, was still with the A's farm club in Sacramento, trying to regain the strength in his surgically repaired shoulder. Just as he had the previous March, Jaha had been swinging late all during spring training; in the next to last game of the spring, in San Francisco, he could not even get around on the pitches of Giants left-hander Kirk Rueter, who seldom threw anything faster than the mid-80s. Doctors had told Jaha it might be a year before he fully recovered, so the A's couldn't be sure that he'd be back to help them until July. In the meantime, some writers suggested the A's might consider signing Jose Canseco, who was playing in a an independent professional league in the East after being released by the Angels. But Beane said he wasn't interested.

The A's seemed to be coming out of their funk a bit on the road, winning two of three in Anaheim, splitting four games in Texas, and then winning two of three in Chicago against the White Sox, who had finished with the best record in the American League the previous year. One of the wins was a 16–6 rout in which Eric Chavez hit two home runs, the second a near 500-foot blast that was the longest in the 10-year history of the White Sox's new Comiskey Park.

Beane was preaching patience and dismissing the thought that dramatic changes were needed:

> The worst thing we could do is panic. I still believe in this team. It's a young team and so much of the players, feeling about themselves is tied up in their hitting, so the fact that they're hitting again is a good sign.

But others were not so patient. A writer for *USA Today* claimed that Howe was on thin ice; Beane met the team in Chicago and told writers the story was "ridiculous." The writer had not talked to Beane, who was the one who would make any decision on Howe.

Then the A's went on to New York and lost three straight to the Yankees, once again falling into a hitting slump. They finished April with an 8–17 record, their worst start in seven years.

To compound the A's problems, the Seattle Mariners were red-hot, setting a major league record for most wins in April by winning 20 of their first 24. They lost a fifth time in their last game in April but still ended the month with a 12-game lead over the A's, who were in last place in the division. Nobody in the division was closer than 9 games to the streaking Mariners.

Privately, Beane was saying he didn't think that the Mariners were anywhere near that good. They would certainly start coming back to the pack, and there was a huge chunk of games remaining. But the question was whether the A's had lost their confidence. If they could regain the swagger they'd had the previous September, they could make up that ground. There was no sign of that as they began May by blowing a lead against the Toronto Blue Jays at home and losing in extra innings.

Those moves seemed to be a catalyst for the A's, who finally started playing as everybody had expected them to—and then some. They streaked throughout much of the rest of the summer, winning 33 of 43, the last 11 in a row. They then swept into the lead in the wild card race in August. Even a report that the A's would be sold and moved to Las Vegas, which eventually turned out to be bogus, didn't slow the flow of victories.

The most impressive part of the 11-game winning streak was the fact that seven of those wins came against three of the top teams in the league. The streak started with a win over the Indians in Cleveland, giving the A's a 2–1 break in that series. It concluded with back-to-back sweeps of the Boston Red Sox and the New York Yankees in Oakland. At that point, the A's record, 68–50, was better than that of the Indians (who were leading the AL Central), and better than the three division leaders in the National League.

The final game of the streak was the best. Yankee Mike Mussina pitched almost flawlessly for eight innings, walking nobody and allowing only two hits—but those hits were back-to-back homers by Miguel Tejada and Eric Chavez in the fifth inning. The A's Mark Mulder pitched shutout ball into the eighth. He then made one bad pitch, a change-up, which was hammered into the left-field stands by Clay Bellinger for a two-run homer that tied the score. Mulder shut the Yankees down through nine innings but fully expected to get a no-decision for his efforts.

Then, with two outs in the bottom of the ninth and Damon on first via a walk, Yankee reliever Mike Stanton dueled with Giambi, who worked the count to 3–and–2. Stanton thought Giambi would be looking for a fastball, so instead he threw a breaking ball, low in the strike zone. However, Giambi was guessing curve ball; he caught up with the pitch, driving it deep into the right-field stands to give the A's a 4–2 win and sending the crowd of 47,725 into a frenzy. For the six-game homestand, the A's had drawn exactly 238,000 fans, a record for an Oakland homestand of at least five games.

Around that same time, A's owners Steve Schott and Ken Hofmann quietly signed a lease for the A's to play in the Coliseum for the 2002 season.

The A's renaissance had started with Damon, who had suffered through an early season slump. He was like a fish out of water in left field, but there were other problems as well. His wife, Angie, and two-year-old twins, Madlyn and Jackson, had stayed behind in Kansas City while he looked for a temporary home in the Oakland area. Damon and his wife started going steady when Damon was a freshman in high school; the couple married as soon as he signed his first pro contract, immediately after his high school graduation. Being separated from Angie and his children caused Damon considerable emotional distress before his family joined him in June.

Damon had been moved to left field in the spring because Howe wanted to give Terrence Long a chance to learn center, knowing that Damon might be gone the next year. Long played well in center but Damon was much better; he was able to play shallow to come in for balls hit in front of him and yet could still race all the way back to the fences—and sometimes over them—to catch the longest drives.

Because of his strong arm, Long was better in right field, but he didn't get much of a chance to show it. On July 25, less than a week before the end of the time during which teams can make inter-league trades without getting waivers on players, Beane pulled off another big one: he traded Jose Ortiz, outfielder Mario Encarnacion, and reliever Todd Belitz to Kansas City, receiving right fielder Jermaine Dye in exchange. The Royals then sent the three A's prospects to Colorado for shortstop Neifi Perez.

Beane still thought Ortiz and Encarnacion might become stars someday. But Frank Menenchino had taken charge at second base and the A's general manager was looking at 2001, not the future. Dye was the last piece of the puzzle, a Gold Glove winner in right field and a strong right-handed hitter who could hit behind Giambi.

Dye showed the fans how he won that Gold Glove during the A's third win of their Red Sox sweep. Dante Bichette got the first hit off Barry Zito, a blooper down the right-field line that went into foul territory. Thinking he could get a double, Bichette went roaring into second base. But he was an easy out when Tejada took Dye's bullet throw at the bag. Three innings later, Bichette hit another ball down the right-field line. This time, he didn't even take a step toward second.

But the biggest factor in the A's turnaround was their starting pitching, which had become the best in the league. Hudson had dominated since April, lowering his ERA to 2.99, second in the league. Mulder had been almost as good, matching Hudson win-for-win.

They both seemed on their way to 20-win seasons. Zito had some struggles but he also had a three-game stretch in August in which he yielded only eight hits and limited opposing batters to an .082 average. Lidle was pitching almost as well, although it wasn't reflected in his record because he had left games with a lead eight times only to see the bullpen lose that lead. Lidle had seemed like a throw-in to the Damon deal but Beane insisted he wouldn't have made the trade without the pitcher's inclusion:

> I had been trying to get him in a trade for a year. He had four pitches, he was always around the plate. I thought he could be a good starter for us.

Sometimes, when a team makes a big run, it will fall back a bit at the end of the run. Not these A's. They continued at the same pace, winning ¾ of their games, into September. By the first week of that month, they had made a mockery of the wild card race, with a commanding lead over the Boston Red Sox and the Minnesota Twins. It was only a question of when they would clinch, and it seemed that would be within a couple of weeks.

Then, on September 11, terrorist attacks hit New York City and Washington, D.C., destroying the twin towers of the World Trade Center. There would be no baseball again until the week of September 17.

The A's were as traumatized by the events as the rest of America, but they regained their focus when play resumed with a series against the Rangers in Texas. They won the first game of that series, stretching their latest winning streak to nine, before the Rangers snapped it the next night. They won the next night to win the series and then returned home to sweep the Seattle Mariners. When the Twins lost both weekend games, the A's had clinched the wild card.

Fittingly, Mulder won his 20th game on that Sunday against the Mariners, beating Freddy Garcia, who was leading the league in ERAs. It had been a great year for Mulder, who had missed the last month of his rookie season in 2000 because of a bad back. His hard work on rehabilitation had paid off; he was stronger and had a much better fastball when he returned.

232

The one disappointment for the A's was that Hudson had faltered in September, eliminating his chance of having back-to-back 20-win seasons. Otherwise, the A's were having great individual years that matched their collective success. Jason Giambi was having as good a year as 2000, when he had been the league's Most Valuable Player. The shortstop–third base duo of Miguel Tejada and Eric Chavez had joined Giambi in the 100-plus RBI column, and both were closing in on 30 homers. Dye had been the American League Player of the Month in July.

After their playoff-clinching win over Seattle, the A's had won 57 and lost only 18 of their last 75 games. The Mariners, who had been on a record pace since the opening bell, were 50–25 in that stretch. The A's terrible 8–18 start had taken them out of the division race immediately, but their magnificent comeback had given them the second-best record in the majors when they clinched the wild card.

And they were confident that the best was yet to come. "Our goal last year was to get to the playoffs," said closer Jason Isringhausen. "Our goal this year is to go further. We have more purpose going into the playoffs."

CHAPTER 21

A Final Disappointment

The A's finished the season on a roll with 102 victories, third in Oakland history only to the 104- and 103-win seasons of the 1988 and 1990 teams, and with a record of 58–17 since the All-Star break. In baseball history, only the 1954 Cleveland Indians, en route to the then American League record of 111 wins in a season, had had a better second half, 55–16.

Even with that fabulous record, the A's finished 14 games behind the Seattle Mariners, who tied the all-time record of 116 wins, set by the 1906 Chicago Cubs, while also setting an American League record. Thank God for the wild card! Because of it, the A's were again in the post-season, matched against the three-time defending World Champion New York Yankees in the divisional playoff.

The season yielded many individual high points for the A's, too. Jason Giambi made a strong bid for a repeat Most Valuable Player award with a .342 average (second in the league), 38 homers, and 120 RBIs. Eric Chavez hit 32 homers and knocked in 114 runs, both records for an Oakland third baseman. Miguel Tejada was just a step behind with 31 homers and 113 RBIs; it was the first time a shortstop and third baseman had hit 30 homers in the same year. Jermaine Dye ended with 59 RBIs in the 61 games he played for the A's. Mark Mulder won 21 games, Tim Hudson 18, and Barry Zito 17, and Zito finished the season with a nine-game winning streak during which his ERA was 1.37.

Because the Yankees had won the AL East, they would host the first two games of the series, and the last one if need be; still, the A's were very confident going into New York. Even their manager, Art Howe, made an uncharacteristically bold statement, saying the Yankees would "have to play great baseball to have a shot at beating us." The *New York Daily News* ran the statement across the back page of the paper, which amused Howe and his players. "I've been telling our young players not to say anything the Yankees can put up on their bulletin board," said Giambi, mindful of Chavez's boasts before the playoff series the year before, "and now our manager says this!" Giambi was joking, of course, as were his teammates when they put a picture of Howe with tape across his mouth on the bulletin board in their dressing room.

The A's justified their confidence with a 5–3 win in the opening game. The final score should have been more lopsided; the A's had runners on base in each of the first eight innings, but squandered several opportunities, going 0-for-11 with runners in scoring position. The long ball saved them, as Terrence Long homered twice and Giambi once, and they never trailed in the game. Johnny Damon was a perfect 4-for-4 and walked in a fifth appearance. Mulder yielded only one run before coming out with two gone in the seventh. Jim Mecir got out of that jam but yielded a two-run homer to Tino Martinez in the eighth which brought the score to the final 5–3.

The fear going into the series had been that the A's closer, Jason Isringhausen, who had a league-high nine blown saves, would be vulnerable; but Isringhausen, who had converted his last nine save opportunities in the regular season, was overpowering in the ninth in a 1-2-3, two-strikeout inning. He ended the game by blowing a 97-mph fastball past Yankee second baseman Alfonso Soriano.

Hudson was even more effective in the second game, putting up zeroes for his eight innings. Knowing the Yankees were going to try to run up his pitch count, Hudson threw first-pitch strikes to 11 of the first 13 hitters, going to 0–2 on 8 of them. His only anxious moments came in the sixth and seventh. The Yankees had two on with two out in both innings, but Hudson got Paul O'Neill to fly to center in the sixth and Scott Brosius to ground out in the seventh.

Andy Pettitte, an A's killer in the past, was almost as effective, but he gave up a leadoff home run to Ron Gant in the fourth and that was the difference until the ninth. Then Damon tripled off the Yankees great closer, Mariano Rivera, and came in when a hard smash by Tejada went through the legs of Yankee third baseman Brosius.

Isringhausen made it exciting in the ninth when he gave up a lead-off double to Bernie Williams and walked Martinez; still, Howe showed his confidence in his closer—there was nobody warming up in the bullpen. Izzy struck out Jorge Posada and, when Giambi came to the mound to encourage him, said, "I can't feel my legs." The two laughed at Izzy's joke, breaking the tension, and Isringhausen got David Justice and Brosius to pop up to end the game. The A's would be coming back to Oakland with a 2–0 lead.

The largest crowd in Oakland baseball history, 55,861, came to the first game in Oakland. This was actually more than 12,000 people over the official baseball capacity; the remaining fans sat in the stands that are normally used only for football games. Sadly, their hopes for an A's sweep evaporated in the closest game yet of the series, a 1–0 Yankee victory. Zito pitched a nearly perfect game, yielding only two hits and one walk in eight innings. However one of the hits was a home run by Jorge Posada leading off the fifth, which was both the first hit and the first run of the game for the Yankees. Posada's drive didn't seem to be going out, so left fielder Terrence Long positioned himself to get an expected rebound off the wall in left-center; but the ball hit the ledge just above the fence and below the out-of-town scoreboard. It was the first time the Yankees had had a lead during the series.

The A's should have tied it during the seventh. With Jeremy Giambi on first, Long doubled into the right-field corner. As Giambi rounded third, right fielder Shane Spencer overthrew both cutoff men (second baseman Soriano and first baseman Martinez). Then short-stop Derek Jeter came out of nowhere to glove the ball and pitch it

237

backhanded to Posada, who tagged Giambi out as he barreled into the plate.

Why didn't Giambi slide? After the game he said that he thought the throw would get there earlier, so he was going to try to knock the ball out of Posada's glove. But on-deck hitter Ramon Hernandez was signaling wildly for Giambi to slide. Third-base coach Ron Washington said flatly that Giambi should have slid. Even Howe, who rarely criticized a player, said that with Hernandez signaling, Giambi should have slid. "The on-deck batter is the 'eyes' for the runner," said Howe.

So the A's had to play another game, and it was a nasty one, with the Yankees winning, 9–2. Everything went wrong for the A's; they even lost a key player when Dye fouled a pitch off his leg and broke three bones, ending his season. Cory Lidle was ineffective and didn't get much help in the field as F. P. Santangelo, a replacement for Frank Menenchino at second base, made an error on a potential double-play ball that allowed the Yankees to score two second-inning runs. That gave them a lead they never lost. A half inning before, Damon and Tejada had singled to lead off the bottom of the first, with Damon going to third, but now the A's couldn't even get the ball out of the infield. Jason Giambi and Dye popped up and, after Long walked to load the bases, Jeremy Giambi fouled out. To make matters even worse, the game, played in 90° heat, seemed to last forever. The first three innings took almost two hours and the game finally went four hours and 13 minutes.

The A's headed back to New York without Dye, who had been a key to their second-half success, to face Roger Clemens, whose 20–2 season was expected to win him his sixth Cy Young Award. Nobody gave them much of a chance, but the A's weren't ready to concede, as they showed by striking for a run in the top of the first as Damon doubled and Jason Giambi singled. In the second, they added another run with the same combination, this time a double by Long and a single by Jeremy Giambi.

In the first four games, the team that scored first had won the game; so the A's had hope. But it was quickly doused in the bottom of the second when the Yankees tied the game. With one out, Posada and Spencer singled and Brosius was hit by a pitch. Soriano singled to knock in two runs. By that time, it was obvious that Mulder, who had pitched so brilliantly in the series opener, was not on his game, having yielded five hits in the first two innings. He escaped a first-inning jam with a double play, but that would be the last time the A's defense would help him.

In the third, with one out, Mulder struck out Bernie Williams, but Williams reached base when catcher Greg Myers could not handle the pitch and then threw wildly to first. Martinez was hit by a pitch and Williams reached third on Posada's fly. Spencer walked to load the bases. Mulder got Brosius to ground to Chavez, which should have ended the inning, but the A's third baseman booted the ball, allowing the Yankees to score the go-ahead run.

In the fourth, Chuck Knoblauch singled to lead off the inning. Mulder picked him off but Knoblauch headed to second and Jason Giambi's throw was off-target for the third A's error. Randy Velarde sacrificed Knoblauch to third and Jeter hit a sacrifice fly to left to score him.

Whether it was the pressure of playing in Yankee Stadium or just overall mental fatigue, the A's were not playing their game. That showed again in the fifth when they should have tied the score. Frank Menenchino walked and, with one out, moved to second on Clemens' wild pitch. Tejada was hit by a pitch, and Yankee manager Joe Torre replaced Clemens with left-hander Mike Stanton. Jason Giambi singled to right on Stanton's first pitch to score Menenchino; but as the throw came home, Tejada failed to advance to third, as he should have. An angry Giambi screamed at Tejada for failing to advance—Tejada later said he didn't want to be too aggressive and get thrown out at third. Chavez followed with a fly ball to right that would have scored Tejada; instead, the A's shortstop could only advance to third, and he got no further as Long flied out to end the inning.

That was the last gasp for the A's. Pinch-hitter Justice hit a solo homer for the Yankees in the sixth off Tim Hudson, who had come on in relief of Mulder in the fifth. The New York bullpen shut down the A's. Rivera pitched the final two innings for the save in the 5–3 win.

"I'm only sorry we didn't play our A game," said Howe afterward, fully aware that the A's should have won the series. There would be more bad news soon as Jason Giambi made his expected bolt to the Yankees as a free agent. Even without Giambi, the A's nucleus of great young starters and position players would enable them to remain in contention; however, once again they'd have to regroup to have another chance to snatch a championship ring, as their predecessors in the seventies and eighties had.

Index